TARGETED

TARGETED

One Mom's fight for life, liberty and the pursuit of happiness.

Lindsey Graham, The Patriot Barbie

CONTENTS

"Our struggle is not against flesh and blood, but against the rulers, against the authorities, against the powers of this dark world and against the spiritual forces of evil in the heavenly realms. Therefore, put on the full armor of God, so that when the day of evil comes, you may be able to stand your ground."

(Ephesians 6:11)

INTRODUCTION

Hello, my name is Lindsey Graham.

No, not the senator.

Yes, that's my real legal name.

I was called to write the story of what my family and I endured in the year of 2020, during government-imposed lockdowns. What happened was that as I began writing, God started redirecting my words. It became clear to me that what I endured this last year was something that God knew, anticipated, and prepared me for. I discovered through this journey that God has been using my life, and my decisions, to build me, mold me and use me for His glory.

As I began writing, I continually tried to skip the hard parts of my life. There are so many things that I did not want the world to know about me. However, those are the times in my life that God was using to refine me for His purpose. As the book took form, I found myself telling the brutal stories. The hard ones. The ones that bring up pain and angst even as I tell them, as if I am telling someone else's story. I found myself committed to telling the reader what I have been through, in order to become the person God wanted me to be. God has directed that the most secret, and painful parts of my life be revealed so that you, the reader can understand how God really does work all things for good.

As you read, I imagine you will be shocked and disgusted at the person I have been capable of being, especially when I was younger. My life has not been beautiful, as hard as my parents worked to raise me right. I made my own choices, and I suffered for them. And, as good as God is, He has made me stronger having endured them, and although I have so many regrets, I know God does not. He used these trials to strengthen me and build my character, as well as direct my path back to Him. As you read this, have mercy on me for the person I haven't always been. Pray for empathy as you unravel the nightmare life I lived by my own free will. Have grace that I was once a weak minded, selfish girl. Remember that as you read each horrifying experience although they are ugly, God was with me, using those moments to mold me and form me into someone new. Remember that because of what I endured, I have an even stronger faith, more resolve, and belief, even harder in the things I do, because I've experienced them. I have convictions not because I can imagine what they must be like, but because I have endured them.

> *"And we know that in all things God works for the good of those who love Him, who have been called according to His purpose." (Romans 8:28)*

After reading my life's journey, you can, without a doubt, see that God has always been hard at work in my life, preparing me for what He knew would come. In this process of writing and revealing my life, He has made it clear to me. I have found that throughout my writing, God has revealed to me that I have been made for such a time as this. There has been no moment in my life that God was not already ready for, and He allowed my burdens to be my blessings, so that I could be free from my own shackles and accept His purpose for me. It has been beautiful!

My hope as you read this book is that is becomes undeniable to you how incredible God is in my life and that you yourself find it crucial to recommit your heart to the Lord. My hope is that as you read just a small portion of some of my endurances, you find yourself shocked and in awe of how God could make so much good from my bad. I pray that your heart is open, and you see more clearly how much we all need our savior! What I reveal in this book, I do so with conviction and pride. I say what I believe needs to be said and there's nothing I hesitate to speak out about. I have already endured the woke mob. I have lost everything in this journey. I have been cancelled and persecuted, and it's been the greatest journey of my life.

CHAPTER ONE

THE BEGINNING

LET'S START AT the beginning of my career. I think it's important to understand where this journey started, how it became, and the foundation of my business.

I was never handed my salon or given money to open it. My daddy didn't fund my dreams. I built my business with my money, my hard work, my dedication, and my brain. God gave me drive and passion for a reason, and I used it to build a successful business from the ground up. My parents instilled in me at a young age to work hard for what you want. If you want something, you must save for it, sacrifice for it, and earn it yourself. We were never gifted cars or other luxurious items. We were told to earn them. Because of this reason, we did.

Our dad encouraged us to get paper routes at a young age. I started delivering papers at 4 o'clock in the morning when I was 13 years old. I had to deliver the entire route on foot, in the dark, carrying the weight of my papers, before I needed to get ready for school. It was motivating after some time for me to get my route done and try to sneak in another precious hour of sleep before school. I learned to be motivated. I learned to work harder and earn my sleep. With this hard work, I bought my first car at 14 with cash! I couldn't even drive it!! I bought it with the money I earned on my paper route and waited patiently for one year until I could get my license. How amazing to see what I could get with the money I had worked so hard for. It was now in my blood to strive for the things I wanted, to manifest them, pray for them, and go out and get them the honest way. That is all I have done my entire career. This type of dedication and discipline instilled in me at a young age, played a major role in my drive to succeed and my desire to work hard for my income. So, thanks dad. I hated you every single time that darn alarm went off at 3:30 am, but that job really solidified my work ethic and the basis for how I conducted business the rest of my life. I took this discipline with me throughout my younger years, excelling at school and applying that dedication to more after-school jobs, our church drama group, church choir, worship team and a girl's chorus choir.

In high school, I was involved in Fellowship for Christian Athletes, Young Life, drama, choir and sometimes a sport or two. I was, as everyone would later call this, a "social butterfly". I didn't look down on any younger students, I never teased or tormented anyone. In fact, if anything, I was the most likely to get made fun of. I was late to puberty and held onto my baby fat all the way until the end of my junior year. Yes, baby fat, I said, until the age of 16! I didn't start really developing until about the age of 17, when my looks drastically changed. Throughout high school, I was still trying to be a tomboy, but also fit in with girls my age. I wore my brother's baggy t-shirts to school, I hardly wore any make up, (if ever) and I didn't style my thin, stringy hair. I kept my hair long and natural and usually threw it in a bun. I was completely awkward in high school and never really had a crowd or a clique that I fit in with.

I was friends with everyone, nice to everyone, and somehow, very secure in who I was. I was so kind to underclassmen, that I was voted in as Homecoming Queen by the students. I found it fascinating and a proud moment to be Homecoming Queen, when I wasn't popular, didn't party, didn't drink, and was not an athlete. My peers had nominated and voted for me, simply for being kind and accepting, and treating everyone as an equal.

I was a fantastic student in high school and easily acquired good grades. It would have been simple and seamless for me to apply to colleges and likely attend. When that time came, I just didn't have any interest in college. I didn't know what I wanted to do in life, and I didn't want to decide at 18 years old anyway. My parents were willing to help with community college, but I didn't want to commit to a life career, and I did not want them to spend money on something that perhaps wouldn't come to fruition. I felt that if I committed to a certain area, and changed my mind, that they would have wasted so much money, and I would have wasted my time and effort. So, instead, I took some average and fun classes at a community college in Salem, Oregon and I didn't take it very seriously. For example, I took art, drama, aerobics and some math and writing classes. I had no direction, but I wasn't concerned about that either.

After hopping from job to job, dabbling in just about everything, (restaurant hostess, coffee barista, receptionist, an eye doctor assistant, grocery clerk) I finally landed on the idea of going to beauty school. I was told that it was good income, independent and flexible hours and fun. So, I enrolled. The school took payments while I attended. My dad was somewhat happy that my new career was only going to cost me $5,500 up front. He loaned me the money to attend, and I promised to pay him back every penny within 5 years of graduating. I paid him back in 6 months. I never missed school and I naturally enjoyed it and excelled. During this time, I was working at a coffee shop in Salem from 6:00 am to 12:00 pm, then driving an hour to school, and attending class from 1:00 pm to 7:00 pm, then driving an hour home, going to bed, and doing it again the next day. I did this for 8 months, working tirelessly to achieve my end goal. Once again, thanks to my Dad and Mom for that deep rooted training in determination.

In September of 2005, I became a licensed hairdresser. I started working immediately on the same routine. I would work the coffee shop in the morning, from 6:00 am until 12:00 pm. At 1:00 pm, I would leave the shop, and go to the salon I worked at to serve clients until late into the night. Early on in my career, I had no clients, so I would try to chat up my coffee shop customers to come see me, or I would end up sitting at the salon waiting for walk-ins and phone calls. I was constantly sitting in my chair reading book after book, waiting for that phone to ring. Sometimes, I never helped a single client. But I might have read through a whole book. I put in a lot of hours waiting for clients and spending time advertising or recruiting. I was one of the first hairdressers in Salem to recognize the value of online advertising (it was fairly new to have internet access) and somehow managed to launch a few website ads. My original advertising rep thought my website should be www.salemshotteststylist.com, so that's what it was.

After working at the coffee shop for two years and doing hair part time, I was addressing the urge to commit myself to just doing hair and building my business. I needed to devote myself to my career, but I was terrified to leave my guaranteed income at the coffee shop and take this huge leap. I didn't have to. God took care of it for me! After 6 years at the coffee shop, the new manager told us that our holiday schedules would be based on our seniority. Perfect. I was second in seniority. I had been a hard worker there for 6 years. When I saw that I was going to be scheduled for Christmas Day, I approached her and told her that I would not work Christmas Day and that my commitment to this shop had earned me the grace to have that holiday off. She disagreed and told me that I would either work Christmas Day or quit. I quit.

While I was also freaking out about this, I decided that it was the best thing for me. I could be at the salon anytime I wanted and take clients all hours of the day. It forced me to take my career seriously and focus. If this hadn't happened, I don't know how long I would have been a coffee shop barista full time and hairstylist part time. I may never have had the nerve or the strength to take this huge leap of faith.

Before long, I was growing in popularity and my business as an independent stylist was thriving. The other stylists at the salon kept asking where I was getting all my new clients. I was handing out coupons at the coffee shop (with the owner's permission) and running internet ads. I was also sticking my business cards up on any bulletin board I could find. Pretty quickly into my career, I had already paid back my dad the business loan and was making a great income. I also recall him saying "where did you get this business sense from? It surely wasn't me". My mom was a little entrepreneur, so I think she has graced me with her personality and business mind. It seemed that this was where I was meant to be.

I leased a station at 2 different salons for 3 years, and finally decided that I would really like to have my own salon. I already had a vision that included pink, classic glam, and chandeliers. I had started recognizing what was and was not working in other salons, so that I could make good decisions in my salon and tackle issues head on. I had a business model and plan in my head ready to go. I set in motion whatever I thought I needed to make it work. I applied for my business loan with the SBA (Small Business Administration), I found what I thought was the perfect location, and I started buying what I needed on resale and storing it, so I would be ready to go when the time came. I began telling everyone that would listen about my beautiful future salon and what I would do with it. I just didn't know when it was going to happen.

After 9 months of back and forth, and endless paperwork with SBA, my loan was denied. I had spent nearly all my free time creating profit and loss statements, a business plan, a financial plan, and much more. I taught myself how to create the documents that the bank was asking for with computer programs and research. I had invested all my time and resources into getting this loan, so I could start my own business. I thought that without the loan, there was no way for me to start a salon. I was devastated, but for the hundredth time in my life, I knew that God had a better and bigger plan. On my way home, I drove by a salon building that was vacant and listed "for lease". It makes no sense to me now, why I stopped to grab the phone number. I didn't get my loan. I was literally driving home from the bank after collecting my documents back. But God works in mysterious ways. I called the landlord immediately. The place was pretty much ready to occupy. Plumbing and lighting were already there, and I just had to doll it up and make it my own. Believe it or not, the rent on this place was so affordable, and I had already bought everything I needed, that I signed the lease the next week and started making my dreams happen. The nine months I had spent preparing for a salon paid off. I had nearly all my furniture and equipment purchased and being stored. Anything beyond that, I could pay for. I would put every penny into making this salon happen and that's exactly what I did.

The man I was married to at this time was helpful financially. He had applied for a credit card, to assist in the minor work, that I could pay back when I opened. I did all the painting and upgrades that way. His family helped me paint and decorate. My long-time best friends came to my aid, hosting painting parties, helping me hang décor and install cabinets. It took a village, and I could not have done it without the help and dedication of these friends and family. It was a fun and joyful time, and I beamed with pride as I watched my dream come to life. This was my first business, and I worked my butt off perfecting it. I was making every construction decision and I did the hard labor myself. I installed flooring, hung lights, painted, hung mirrors, stocked retail, hired stylists, and started working on promotions for the business. I learned how to design my own website and online booking. I didn't have any extra funds to be paying anyone for anything.

I put in late nights and hours on a computer and figured everything out myself. I wrote and printed my own leasing documents. I found a basic generic outline online and edited it to my liking. I had to alter it more times than I'd like to count. I met with stylists constantly to recruit. I was hands on in every step, and never did shy away from getting dirty. Everything I did to build my salon, I did by learning along the way and putting in endless and uncountable hours of hard work. I think this experience, and doing it over and over as you'll see, is what was preparing me for God's plan later. I would learn so many business skills in the trial and error of doing everything myself. I learned how to fix plumbing, unclog sinks, wire and hang lighting, install cabinets, design my logo, update my website, advertise online, plan events, and manage my books. (All of this, by the way, will come in handy later. God was already working on His bigger plan, and I had no clue. When I reveal where I have ended up, you will see God's mighty plan all come together.)

I brought stylists through and tried to describe to them how beautiful everything would be and how I would run my salon. I had 5 stylists on board before I even opened the doors! The inside of the salon was ready, and all I needed to do was paint the outside. I didn't know how meaningful this would be, but the day before I opened, my mom came to help me paint. We shared some hard lemonades, some secrets and some laughs. My parents had been divorced for quite a few years, and she was dating and trying to find herself again. I was always giving her advice and helping her rediscover who she was. Our relationship was changing, and we were starting to become more like friends. I didn't always get along perfectly with my mom (we are both hard-headed, strong-willed women), and our relationship was starting to take a turn toward something great.

Up until this time, our relationship had been very strained, because of some things that happened with my parents and their divorce. My mom and I were finally at a point where I felt that we were starting to move on from our painful past. This day of painting was full of surprises and bonding that we hadn't had in a long time. Sort of when a mom finally realizes her child is grown and will make her own decisions. She takes on a role of friend, more than mom. We were starting to get there. She really wanted to be part of my next chapter, and volunteered to help with the finishing touches, so I would be ready to open on time.

CHAPTER TWO

THE HISTORY OF GLAMOUR SALON

ON MAY 5TH of 2009, I opened Glamour Salon for the first day. The stylists were excited, I was proud, my family was supportive, and clients were impressed. It was the beginning of a 12-year adventure with this business and we were off to a good start. As soon as I opened my salon, I could feel that I was meant to do this job. I enjoyed being an owner, hiring great people, and creating a beautiful atmosphere for clients. I also thrived on watching it grow and the stylists becoming more successful. It meant I was doing something right.

Glamour Salon went through so many changes throughout the years as we grew, went through hardships, expanded and adapted. After a few years in my South Salem location, around 2012, I had decided to subdivide one part of the building and expand one part to accommodate a small bootcamp style gym. Then, when they needed to expand and move into a bigger space, I renovated yet again and opened my own clothing boutique in its place. Owning a business is not an easy ride, almost ever. There are changes to be made, to adapt to the world changing. Often. I reinvented my salon nearly 6 times in the 12 years we were open.

Glamour Salon and its partner store "Le Pink Boutique" were fun. I was dabbling in so many new ventures, becoming a little entrepreneur. The boutique was popular, but my location wasn't the best, and I was starting to get distracted with so many businesses that needed my attention. These shops didn't run themselves. I was working hard, not smart. I was not paying enough attention to my salon and was making changes without informing my stylists. I also was starting to notice some unappreciation for what I was doing to make the salon successful, and I realize now that it was a vicious cycle. I didn't feel appreciated, so I didn't go the extra mile. Because I was holding back, the stylists were also feeling neglected. All in all, there was some intense turmoil that began brewing in the salon.

The months that would follow were painful. This was one of my first experiences with women who talked behind your back and acted like a friend to your face. It has become a cliché in the salon industry, and I have spent most of my adult life trying to reverse that. I've continually tried to remind women that I will not tolerate drama or gossip, and I certainly will not partake in it. But, nonetheless, as hard as I tried, I cannot change the character of certain people. I had one stylist, Alicia, who was constantly 'stirring the pot'. She was ungrateful, demanding, snide, snarky and a gossip. She played both sides of her friendships, pretending to be a good friend to me. The kind of woman who talks to you about an issue, hears your side, agrees with you, then goes to the other party, tells them everything you said, agrees with them, then comes back to you and reports what they said! It was toxic and childish behavior. It was ruining the positive vibes in the salon and creating chaos and havoc on a regular basis. She was pretending to be an advocate for the girls in the salon, helping me to understand what needed to change, but secretly taking my words and making them gossip. Then encouraging each person to believe that I was a horrible business owner, only out for myself. This was all happening right under my nose, while I was thinking that the salon was a success, and everything was ok. This was also happening right after my mom had died, so I was distracted and unfocused. As painful as this behavior is to everyone involved, this was not normal or acceptable and I had a hard time believing someone would willingly be so vindictive to me. I had harbored anger and bitterness towards this woman for years, and finally had to forgive her for what she did to me and accept that it was part of my story and the foundation for my strength. It is reiterated to me that I didn't ever want to be this type of person, and this was exactly why. I also was finally at the realization that her behavior is more hurtful to herself than anyone else. I forgave and moved on, but I imagine she is still just as unhappy, creating chaos in her own life still. I have to be thankful that this was done to me, because God used these moments to strengthen me and reveal to me where my character lies and where I want it to lie.

Eventually, in the middle of this catty drama, one of my stylists, Megan, decided to open her own place. She told me it would have a different business model and only one stylist, her best friend was leaving my salon to come with her. When a stylist tells me they have a great opportunity and they are leaving to do bigger or better things, my response is the same. "Congratulations, I hope you do amazing, and I wish you success." Unlike other salon owners, I don't change the locks, remove them, fire them and slander them. I don't try to burn bridges. It is every stylist's dream to have her own salon. It was mine! So, when someone gets that opportunity, it's important that they know that I do support them, and I empower them! Long story short, I encouraged her, helped her, even gave her my contacts and connections, and she secretly recruited and took each and every stylist at my salon. All the time, she was reassuring me that she had no interest in taking my stylists or even renting stations to them. It was the most shockingly deceptive and backstabbing thing any woman could do to another.

Behind my back, she recruited almost every stylist in my salon to come to hers. The ones that didn't want to leave, still did, because that's what everyone else was doing. Alicia convinced them that once I lost most of my stylists I would have to close. She even made a Facebook post about my salon, laughing and saying I could never survive, and I would have to close my salon permanently. My entire salon walked out on me.

Even the ones that claimed to be my friend. Even the ones that watched me slave away every day making the salon a happy and fun place to be. Even the ones who knew that the last year of my life was the hardest, with losing my mom, a divorce, and two car accidents. (The car accident's were not my fault, I must throw that in there.)

I went from being at the top of my game to a complete and total failure. I spent days crying and trying to decide how in the world I could possibly rebuild and bounce back from this. It was so painful to watch the girls I had brought together go off and do their own thing together, and the only person left behind was me. It was completely and utterly humiliating. It was the ultimate "mean girl" drama. It was way worse than being picked last at kickball as a child. It was the final stab in the back, and I probably should have called it quits in the salon business. I was not cut out for backstabbing, catty women. I've never been like that myself. I was shocked that this kind of vindictive act was done to me, when I had put so much time, effort and care into building a beautiful salon for these women. Throughout the weeks building up to this, every single girl there was behaving normally and acting like my friend. Behind my back, they were all plotting to leave their notice on paper, on my station, when I wasn't around. No one even had the guts to tell me to my face about this plot. And not one of them thought about telling me it was coming.

In hindsight, I realize that I was not being a good salon owner, but I definitely did not deserve this. I did not deserve the type of cold-hearted treatment these women were giving me. Alicia came to the salon on her last day before moving out and vandalized my salon. After finding out that she did this, no one seemed at all concerned about continuing to share a salon space with her. The entire situation seems like a bad dream. Who in the world would act like this and do this to someone they previously claimed to like? What adult has this much hate in her heart? And probably in that moment, my heart hardened just a teeny tiny bit. This was one of my life events that God allowed, to learn resolve and determination. To be faced with despair and not give up. To learn that instead of giving up, to persevere harder. Writing this story and reliving this no longer hurts, as I come to the realization that God really did have a plan for my entire career. Everything, every last detail had to happen exactly as it did for me to be prepared, strong and ready for the fight I would later take on for this very salon.

After about a week of pity party and bawling, I decided that not only would I not close my salon, but I would also double down. I would reinvest everything and build my salon back up from nothing again. The girls that left wanted nothing more than to see me close my salon and be ruined. It was a matter of pride that I refused to let them do this to me. I was going to relocate my salon into downtown. Stylists were always eager to rent downtown, with more traffic and more opportunity. My clothing boutique would do better with the walk-in traffic and location upgrade. Instead of closing, I would adjust my business plan and completely rebuild. I was not giving up. It just isn't in me. I think one of my huge character flaws is pride, and there was no way I was going to let these vicious women close me down, and then laugh at my expense. Closing would not only satisfy them, but also crush my ultimate dream of being a salon owner.

In the end, what really happened, is that these women unknowingly empowered me. They became a crucial part of a story that hadn't been written yet. They became the first step in God molding me to be ready for what He had in store. If I acknowledge and accept that God allows everything to happen to me for His purpose, I am left with only one option. To thank Him for the trials, even though I don't know why I'm enduring them. If this is the mindset I have going into any situation, I am rejoicing regularly and praising God for his goodness (whether it actually feels good or not). This is the ultimate act of faith, and He blesses those who are faithful.

I gathered myself together emotionally and charged forward. I can admit that this took a huge toll on me, but I didn't stay down long. My God has me. He always lifts me up. I wish my enemies would figure that out. I am in no way a victim in this life, but the amount of disgusting and two-faced women I have encountered is shocking. I have always been an open and real person with every woman and person I meet, which makes me very vulnerable. And in return, more often than not, I am faced with a person who turns out to be phony, fake and when the relationship no longer suits them, vengeful and hateful. This is true even to this day. My future without a salon, knowing I will not be faced to encounter women like this on a regular basis, is encouraging. My success no longer depends on anyone who can turn their back on me when it suits them. Praise the Lord!

In searching for the perfect downtown location, I found an amazing spot with an amazing landlord, Troy, who worked with me every step of the way. You will continually hear me say that when God has a plan, He will make it happen. Sometimes, you have to work hard at it, or try harder than you want, but God never says He is going to hand you your desires. My mentality is that I will go fast and hard and dedicated, until He absolutely closes the door. God knows me, He made me for goodness' sake, so He knows how I am. He knows that I am going to pursue what I think is my goal, until He makes it absolutely impossible. That being said, this new space was twice as big as my last location. It was a huge, two-level space that needed to be completely rebuilt. It was essentially a warehouse. Many times, I said to myself "What am I doing, taking this on? This is a huge undertaking." I also had only 2 stylists left, making it hard to validate building a salon this size. But something in me told me to pursue it. My mantra became "build it, and they will come." Three times, I was faced with a hurdle financially that I didn't see a solution for, and all three times, I took them to Troy, and we worked it out. That man was a blessing. He saved my business, and he did so when I needed it the most. As everything kept working out, I knew God would allow this to happen. I don't know if Troy is a Christian, but I hope he knows that he played a role in my story and God used him to build me into who I am today.

We built out Glamour Salon (again) in the heart of downtown. Scott (my husband and soul mate) and I did a LOT of the work, and we redesigned the entire space late into the mornings nearly every day. I also had that killer gang of friends that always came to my "painting parties" and helped me paint the salon (seriously every location except the last). Stiffy, Jessica,

Liz, Laura and Sara are my best friends, and have been with me through every up and down of my life, always being truthful, transparent and unconditional friends. They were always the first to step up and ask, "When is the painting party?" every time I relocated!

The first floor was my clothing boutique, and the upstairs loft was the salon. Immediately, I started getting interest in my stations again, and within the first year, I was almost to full capacity with 10 stations! Well, well, well, isn't God good? I went from thinking about closing, to expanding!! By my 2nd year of being in the loft location, I had been full on a rotation of girls almost the entire time. Stylists come and go, for good and bad reasons, but the salon was even more successful than the first location. I was building stations to accommodate stylists and had to expand my already huge space multiple times.

In my 3rd year at the loft, I had gotten even more interest in the salon and actually needed to expand the loft area to accommodate more stylists and service rooms, so even though I was 5 months pregnant with our first son, I was laying flooring, painting, moving furniture and remodeling my salon. I created private spa and salon rooms in that area, so we could offer more services and be more exclusive. Glamour Salon had started building a pretty great reputation. I had started carrying hair extensions in the salon and was solidifying my career as an extension specialist. I had even been hired by a huge national company to be an educator. My business was thriving, and I knew I was becoming a great salon owner. The lessons I had learned when my first salon walked out on me, carried over to this new salon and I was now running a business more professionally and with respect from my stylists. At one point, a casting agency had reached out to me about a game show for businesses. She and her team had skyped interviews with the entire salon trying to cast us in this new game show. The producer loved us, and we were picked!! Unfortunately, the show was never picked up by a network and it all fell through. We all lived in that glory for months, thinking we were going to be reality tv stars!

While being a salon owner and hair stylist in the loft, in the year 2015, I was contacted through my salon's Facebook from a news outlet. AJ Media had reached out, with the following message:

> Hello Lindsey, I'm a journalist with AJ+, a digital news network in San Francisco. We are working on a fun story for the elections where we meet people with the same name as candidates. You and Senator Lindsey Graham, as you know, have one thing in common. We would like to meet you in your salon to chat with you about what it's like to have the same name as Lindsey. I'd love to talk more with you about the concept. I really hope you're on board. You can reach me at *****.

I had no idea what to expect from this. I had no idea who AJ Media was, or what they stood for. I just know that it seemed like a fun opportunity, and I love being on camera, so what the heck. I was not interested in politics whatsoever (crazy, right?) so I was also a little nervous that the reporter would ask me political questions and I wouldn't know what he/she was talking about. I even asked her if I should research the senator Lindsey Graham first. She assured me that it would be more fun than logical or even realistically political. She was right. The video was cropped and edited to be fun satire, comparing my views on issues to the Senator's views. Everything from his lack of a first lady to gun control. We joked about what I would do with his hair, and what policies I liked and didn't like. I had fun with the interview, and I was, as usual, not shy. I really didn't know much about the senator or his beliefs, so the video was made to be more humorous than anything serious. It was launched on their Facebook page, as well as YouTube.

After it was released, I discovered how cruel the internet can be. This was before I had been in any media or news, ever. My friends, family and I were enjoying watching the number of views grow but disturbed when we started reading the comments. They were a lot like what I experienced with cancel culture. People were targeting my looks, how I dressed and my overall appearance. I was called names, and people were quick to label me a "bimbo", "idiot", "ditz" and more. They would comment on how I was simply a hairstylist, and had no right having a political opinion, let alone on a media site. My friends and family got defensive, calling out keyboard warriors for their harassment. They tried explaining to people how hurtful it is to call someone names that they've never met. They tried to tell them who I really was. Keyboard warriors do not care. The bullying continued and I quickly learned to A: stop reading the comments or B: understand that these people didn't know me, so there was no reason I should be hurt by their comments and name-calling. I had to explain to my friends and family that I didn't need them to waste their time trying to defend me. They wouldn't make a difference. Looking back on this event, I now realize that even this small event could have probably had a big impact on preparing me for the cancel culture I was going to endure 5 years later. The process of watching people who didn't know me attack and label me without merit, was something I had to brush off and ignore, for my own sanity. In 2020, when I endured this 1,000 times over, I may have already been more prepared than I realized.

While the salon was doing great in the loft, and we were growing in popularity, we ran fundraisers and events for the community. We put on an event called "Pretty Princess" where young girls could come get pampered and uplifted for the day. We had pink balloons, face painting, cupcakes, little girl pedicures and manicures, princess updos, and prizes. It was an event that moms always asked about every year. It made the girls feel special, and it gave the stylists something fun to do, while trying to earn the moms' business. It was always satisfying to do something in the community that people loved and acknowledged. It made us stand out from the other salons. We were involved with our guests and the downtown vibe.

One of my favorite clients of all time was a sweet woman who always had encouraging words for me, always prayed for me, and was a joy to serve. She and her daughter went on mission trips to Haiti to help and serve orphan girls. When I heard some of her stories about the conditions over there, and what these little girls were going through, my heart hurt. I had a child now, and it changes your level of relation when hearing how other families and children suffer in less fortunate circumstances. I wanted to do something, but going to Haiti was definitely not something I could consider. I had two young kids now, so I couldn't get away. But I knew I could still help. My friend and stylist, Lissy and I took on a fundraiser for orphans in Haiti, through a local church. We committed to giving 10% of our proceeds to a girl's orphanage in Haiti through the church mission group. At the end of the month, we attended their women's night and presented a check for over $1,000! We kicked butt that month and took as many clients as we could to raise money for these little girls. In return, we forged close relationships with some of the women at the church, built our clientele and enjoyed great uplifting conversation empowering these women!

The boutique however, was not a success, like, at all. I was not cut out for brick-and-mortar retail. Around this time, online sales were the new rage and almost all the downtown boutiques had closed down. With a combination of lost revenue, constant reordering, staffing issues and online sales competition, the boutique was doomed. I was so frustrated trying to keep it open and eventually was thrilled with closing it. My life was starting to get too busy. We had our first baby growing up fast, and I was pregnant with our second. We were getting ready to build a beautiful home out in the country, and I needed to get to a place where I had a business that ran without my constant supervision. I really wanted to have time for my kids, and not be consumed with business at all hours. I struggled with which direction to go for some time, even asking my landlord to let me out of my lease. I thought I was cornered, but I also knew that I needed to do the right thing and honor my commitment. The decision became clear very quickly.

I closed my clothing store, put everything on clearance, and leased out the bottom to a local furniture and home decor company, and that worked great for the last two years of my lease. They were fabulous tenants, and the salon started running more smoothly. It was such a huge relief to be less busy, less stressed, and more available for my salon and my family. In every possible way, this decision drastically improved my quality of life. The expansion upstairs went great, and I was now once again at full capacity with seemingly happy stylists. We sailed along wonderfully for two years this way. When my salon lease was up in 2018, I had a decision to make about our salon's future. Change was on the horizon again, and as my lease was getting ready to end, we had yet another killer business opportunity laid out right in front of us!

While running Glamour Salon successfully, I was approached by the owner of a very large tanning salon franchise. I have known him and his wife since I was in my early 20s. Originally, the plan was to buy the downtown tanning salon and combine it with my hair salon. It was a perfect business model. After meeting with them, we decided to buy our first tanning salon, but in a different location. It was such a celebratory moment because, ironically enough, I was the very first employee that they ever hired for this franchise back in 2008. The first store opened on Market Street in Salem, and I was in hair school, looking for a new job. I called about the ad, went into my interview, and was hired on the spot. Fast forward 18 years later and now I own a store! It was a fun and surprising turn of events. It seemed meant to be. We continued to purchase stores on this franchise and became involved in the company. We enjoyed meeting the other owners and going to the events.

We had purchased two tanning salon franchise stores in the time frame I was in the loft. When my lease was up, we had decided to also buy the originally planned downtown location and move the two businesses together, my salon and the tanning salon. It was still such a great idea... on paper. This is where my life got more chaotic. I had plenty of stylists, and I had grossly underestimated the space in the tanning salon. When I had finished completely renovating that entire store (new floor, new paint, new walls, new lights, etc.), I fearfully realized that I made a HUGE mistake. The space was crammed. The landlord and superintendent were grade A jerks. The mall we were located in was nearly vacant, probably because the landlord was a jerk. I had just moved my entire salon and I could tell within a few months that this was not going to work. After all the hard work we had just put in, and moving everything over, it was devastating to think about how poorly this was going.

Shockingly, the stylists made the best of it, and seemed to

take a positive attitude, making the space work without lots of complaints. I think they knew that I was stressed about the move and not happy, so they built me up. Even I was ready to admit that it was not working out the way I wanted it to. I had to make major adjustments and ask some stylists to share stations so that everyone could feel like they had adequate space. It was a pretty stressful time for me, and I was pleasantly surprised at the support I was getting from my stylists. I'm sure they didn't expect me to move the business again. Ha! Think again ladies! We made that space work for a year, but I was not happy with the situation at all. I was struggling with coming to terms with it, when this fantastic location on the corner caught my eye. It was right as you enter downtown, all windows, huge, and had been vacant for a long time. You see where I'm going with this, right?

During the stint in the loft the salon, I had started working for a national hair extension company educating and traveling to work at hair shows. It was pretty much a dream come true. I was working alongside other professionals and teaching other artists how to master their art. I was flying across the country to do this and was even sent to New York for four days. As I was doing this, I started acquiring hair extensions through this company on a wholesale level and had started selling hair extensions in my salon. I had tripled my business in hair extensions and was becoming widely recognized as the premiere specialist in Salem. It was so successful; I decided to market my own brand and begin selling them to other stylists and other salons. I worked nights on end once again, creating a website, e-commerce site, and working with an artist to design my brand and logos. As I was doing this, I was also simultaneously buying more and more hair to keep in stock, so I could become a retailer in Salem and sell nationally. Beauty Couture Hair Extensions became a huge success, and I was already outgrowing the previous location, trying to stock and store all my inventory!

Even though the thought of building out again was maddening, I had to see this new potential space. The timing of this opportunity was horrible. The day that I was supposed to go view the space, Scott's dad suffered an injury that had him unconscious in the Salem hospital. We had no idea what had happened to him, and we had no clue what his medical condition was going to be moving forward. We were told that his wife found him seizing in their living room, after coming in from her garden. He suffered a blood clot that reached his brain and doctors could not confirm when he would wake up or start breathing on his own. Scott was staying positive, as was his younger sister. They stayed with him and waited patiently for him to wake up. There was nothing anyone could do but wait, and Scott's family was all there. He told me to go to my appointment at the vacant store. I didn't even want to go considering his dad's condition, but I also knew that he probably needed some space to comprehend what was happening. I made it back to the hospital after my meeting in very little time, in love with the new spot, but knowing that right now, the most important thing was being there for my husband and supporting him however he needed. I guess he needed a distraction. He asked me to tell him all about it, but I couldn't do it with enthusiasm.

The next day I was supposed to have clients at the salon and his dad was still unconscious on a breathing tube. He insisted I go to work, and that he would call me with updates. I went to the salon, and halfway through the day, Scott called to say that they had decided to remove the breathing tube. It seemed that everyone thought he would either wake up or begin breathing on his own within hours. The feelings I was hearing from him were that his dad had a good chance of recovering within hours after the tubes were removed. But my heart told me otherwise. Scott said not to worry and not to come down. Everyone at the hospital was still being very positive and seemed to believe that Mike would be ok. Before hanging up, Scott said he would call me to let me know when his dad woke up. I hung up the phone feeling confused. I looked at my clients and my fellow stylists and I told them what was happening. We all knew I needed to leave, NOW. I cancelled their appointments as my assistant said she would finish the ones I was working on, and I drove as fast as I could to the hospital. When I got there, I knew that things were not good. Mike's wife and his immediate family were in the room, and the extended family was outside in the waiting area crying. I quietly walked into the room and held my husband's hand, so he would know I was there. I watched the family crying as they watched Mike struggling to survive without a breathing tube. After just a few moments, we watched his dad take his last breath. I had made it within minutes of being there for my husband when he lost his father. I think about the ramifications of that moment had I not been there, as his wife, to experience his loss by his side. In his moment of need, he was so hopeful, but God had whispered to me that I must go. God's still, quiet voice guides us when our own minds try to trick us.

Watching his family mourn for Mike, I was reminded of how painful it all was for them. The agony of losing my mom was exactly how they were feeling at these moments, and it hurt so badly to know that they were feeling it. I ached for them and tried to imagine my husbands' anguish as he suffered the biggest loss of his life. Throughout all of this, my husband begged me to act on the salon location. He could tell that it was the right move and wanted to expand into this new space. He said that I should do whatever we needed to get it going. In this tragic time, he was so supportive, and has always supported my dreams.

This salon was my dream, my career, and I couldn't accept the location we were in. It was not right. After seeing the space, I fell in love. This was my forever location. It was unbelievably perfect. It was previously an office building, so there were rooms already divided, all window front (a stylist's dream). There was a huge waiting area, and existing rooms for tanning beds. We put all our savings into building what I promised my husband was the absolute LAST location. Little did I know, at this time, it would indeed be my last, but for very different reasons. We spent $80,000 in renovations on this space. We added plumbing, paint, chandeliers in every suite, track lighting and a custom reception desk. I spent an additional $20,000 on new chairs, shampoo bowls, lighting, furniture and décor. You heard me. We spent one hundred grand on this gorgeous salon. It was worth every penny. When I say I put my blood, sweat and tears into my business, I mean exactly that. I contracted out a lot of jobs in this salon, but demolition was something I could do. I could tear up carpet, take down shelves and demolish the old reception desk. During demo, I was pulling shelving off the wall, when the wrong piece broke off. A shelf came flying off the wall, and into my face. I had no idea what happened as I hit the floor. My assistant was there with me and asked if I was ok. I said, "I have no idea. I don't know what happened." As I took my hand from my face, a steady stream of blood pooled onto the floor. She asked me what was bleeding and I had absolutely no clue. Turns out the shelf had hit me square on the bridge of my nose, busted open the skin, and broke my nose. The painter came by with rags to help stop the bleeding and she panicked. She said, "I'm calling an ambulance!" In this moment, with my nose broken, my consciousness questionable, and blood soaking the rags through, I somehow was thinking logically. I said "Please don't. I don't have insurance." Good Lord.

She insisted on driving me to the emergency room. That was probably a wise decision. The bleeding would not stop, and my bone was showing through! We scurried about the parking garage trying to find my vehicle before I remembered that I had a rental car. The poor girl was running around trying to find my black SUV, and it wasn't even there to begin with. At the ER, I was bleeding internally, and the blood was pooling and coagulating in my face and throat. I was throwing up blood in the waiting room, and the nurse finally said, "Ok, let's get you to a private room." Four stitches and some pain medication later, I was good to go. The next day I was back at the salon for demo. We had a schedule to keep.

The entire city was talking about this salon, the first thing you see in downtown Salem, all lit up and shining, with chandeliers adorning every window. My business was a raging success. I had my office for my hair extension company, Beauty Couture Hair Extensions (www.beautycouturehair.com for you stylists reading this) selling local and shipping national, and I was finally able to stock more hair than any other retailer in the area. Stylists knew us as the best hair extension retailer in town and clients now recognized my salon as having the best stylists in town. We were #1 rated on google, yelp and Top Three websites and search engines. I had to start moving tanning beds out of rooms to let more stylists rent them. I had been through 3 locations with this salon, and I knew I would be here forever. I couldn't expand any more, I had every inch leased out. After everything I had been through as an owner, every build out, every mistake, every lesson, I felt like I had finally made it. The salon was full of independent stylists that took care of their own business, so I didn't have to micromanage anyone. The place really did run itself. Scott had just partnered and built an incredible gym in Woodburn that was guaranteed success. We had four tanning salons, all doing well. I was now pregnant with our third baby, and the timing could not have been better. Our businesses were booming, and we were at the top of our game, and I was ready to chill out and enjoy the successful life we had built.

CHAPTER THREE

LOSS

IN JULY OF 2009, just two short months after opening my original location for Glamour Salon in May 2009, my first husband showed up at the salon in the middle of my workday. I got a big, bright smile on my face at the surprise visit. My husband said to come outside, that he needed to talk to me. I gleefully walked out, and saw my dad waiting in the parking lot. I also saw my older brother. The look on their faces will be something I will never forget. I stopped smiling. I looked back and forth. My husband hung his head to avoid eye contact with me. I started bawling and said "Who is it? Who is it? Is it Jake (my little brother)?"

I knew someone was hurt; I knew something was wrong. In that exact moment, I needed to know because my world had stopped, and I didn't even know why, how or who yet.

"Mom was in an accident. She died."

That's all I remember hearing, as I fell to my knees, in the middle of a parking space in front of my business, just like they do in the movies, screaming. I covered my face and wept with so much pain, I couldn't imagine it would ever go away. It was a moment you wish you could take back. Two minutes ago, my life was fine. But now, I have undeniable and final knowledge that I will never speak to, hug, kiss or touch my mom ever again. This kind of loss is nearly unbearable. And it is the absolute worst in those first 24 hours, when you deal with every stage of grief, while also being in complete shock and horrendous pain.

The details slowly unfolded throughout the day, and as they did, I became devastated over and over and over, like the news was brand new with every new detail. When my brother first said "accident", I assumed she was in a car crash. I was desperate to see her body. I demanded that someone take me to the scene. I was in complete denial that it was her. Hours later, I was devastated yet again when I found out more clearly that her accident was in a plane, not a car. I had already run through the worst scenario of how this car accident had happened and was beginning to let that sink in. Now I had a whole new version in my head trying to picture her death. These are surprising and sometimes odd things that you do when you lose someone close. You allow yourself to try to imagine their death. I'm guessing that psychologically we do this, so that we can accept it and begin to comprehend closure. My head was dizzy, trying to comprehend where and how this could have happened.

My mom had died in a small Cessna plane crash in California, on Mammoth Mountain. She and her boyfriend, the pilot, died on impact. On the other side of the state, another family was mourning the death of someone we had never even met. But they lost their lives together. For the next few days, we went about completing the horrific jobs that come with losing a loved one. Notifying family and friends, planning a funeral, picking out a stupid casket. The entire time, shaking your head, asking yourself if it's real. I was still insisting on flying to the mountain to see where she died. There was so much of me that could not accept this. As we sat with the funeral director, he had asked us about an open casket. This was such a blow to the mind. I had said that I needed to see her. I still could not believe it unless I did. But an open casket? How severe were the injuries from a plane crash that her body was ok to view? That's when I regretted opening my mouth. He outlined her injuries so we would not be shocked when we saw her. Hearing someone describe the pain and fear that your mom would have endured during the last seconds of her life is a moment I wouldn't wish on anyone. The details were so horrific that I had to leave the room. When I returned, everyone had decided that we could see her after they spent some time making her presentable. But an open casket was not a good idea.

When it came time to view her body, I had no idea what I would feel or what it would do for me or to me. Seeing her body gave me closure. But as I lay there, willing her to move or talk, caressing her hand, I knew she wasn't there. Not just that she was dead, clearly. But that who she was, was her soul, her heart, her being. Not her body. She was in heaven with Jesus. It wasn't comforting, I was still in shock and angry for losing her. But as peace came to me over the years, having that last moment where I could look at her body and know that God had taken her soul to heaven, would comfort me. I had the clairvoyant moment where I knew what everyone knows after they've lost someone. Our body is just a vessel. What makes us each unique and alive is the soul and heart that God gave each human being in His image.

Hundreds of people came to my mom's funeral. She was so loved and adored. Her smile would light up a room and her snort laugh made everyone in the room laugh. She was wild, fun, a jokester, the life of every party. Everyone loved her. At her funeral were her fellow flight attendants, church friends, family friends, my friends, my brother's friends, and people who barely knew her, but loved her light. My mom was obsessed with kiss marks. She had them on shirts, shorts, suitcases, purses, nightgowns, cards, bumper stickers, etc, etc... When she was working as a flight attendant, she would kiss the outside of the plane near the door with bright red lipstick and claim to be "blessing the flight." Her co-workers would later tell me that those lip marks would be on there for weeks. For a short time, they would find her kiss marks on planes after her death and smile. Toward the end of her service, everyone was given the chance to go to her casket and say their good-byes to her. Without any encouragement, the flight attendants began kissing her casket and leaving kiss marks all over it. She was buried, covered in love and affection, from a crowd of people that loved her.

There are no days in my life that this tragedy does not affect me. Whether good or bad, honestly. There are days that God uses this to remind me of certain things or bring me painful joy. There are days that memories of my mom are more painful than others, and there are days that my heart somehow breaks as largely as it did that day. There are also days when my mom makes me smile and a fun memory of her surfaces out of nowhere. This often happens when I'm interacting with my own children, and I recall her fun personality and everything she did to create a beautiful childhood for me and my siblings. This tragedy became a part of me, a part of my story, and a part of who I am today and why.

Years back, around 2002, long before my mother's death, I had decided to get a tattoo on my right wrist that would encompass my faith in God, and His protection over me. Something I could look at in time of need. I had been through an abusive relationship (we will get to that) with unthinkable heartache, and a renewed faith that God will endure with me through everything. I settled on Isaiah 41:10. *"Do not fear for I am with you. Do not be dismayed, for I am your God. I will strengthen you and help you. I will uphold you with my righteous right hand."* It has been the message I have needed through so many of life's hardships. It has been the perfect way to start a prayer when I'm in need. It has been the promise of my Savior over and over and over. It has been fulfilled every time. When my mom died, I remember standing in the first shower I could bring myself to take, having one of those heart-breaking moments where the devastation just overcomes you for no apparent reason. I read my wrist and God gave me peace. He would get me through this.

As my family began unpacking my mom's things, I came across an old box of my belongings from my teenage bedroom (1995-1999). One item was a picture bought from the Christian bookstore when I was young, probably 16 years old. It was the root meaning of my name, it was the origination of my name, and at the bottom, there was a scripture assigned to my name. *The Scripture was Isaiah 41:10.* As I painfully went through my mom's things, there she was with God, plain as day, comforting me. This had been packed away for 5 years and who knows why my mom had kept it. But of all the beautiful and powerful Scriptures God had written for us, the one I had chosen to tattoo on my right wrist was the one that had been written for me all those years ago. God is so good. This Scripture on my arm was also about to get me through a hard decision that I had to make.

I was unhappy in my marriage, and I did not want to be married to my husband, Josh. In regard to this particular relationship, I never should have gotten married. He was not my life partner, and I knew it very quickly after the wedding. I had been through another disappointing relationship right before Josh, where I was being used and taken advantage of by a man with no motivation or pride. I had had it with men who had no goals in life. I was immediately attracted to Josh's good qualities but overlooking the foundation of what would make a good lifelong marriage. We were entirely different people and not in the way that opposites attract. Although he was a good man, he was not the man for me, and I had been open about my desire to leave the marriage multiple times.

After my mom's death, it was solidified. Life was short, and I did not want to be unhappy. I wanted to live a full and beautiful life with someone I was truly in love with, and that I felt God had made for me. We had no children, and I wanted to finalize a divorce before we might have brought children into it. I had previously told Josh that I wasn't happy in the marriage,and I thought we should divorce. This was met with the decision that he would change; do the things I wanted and overall make different choices. But I didn't want to be the kind of wife that had to change her husband to appreciate or love him. I wanted him to be with someone that loved him as he was. But that was not me.

I was also facing extreme judgment and disdain from my family members, who thought they knew best and that my desire to leave my marriage was simply a mental concern, especially after losing my mom so suddenly. It was hard enough to make a decision this large, especially after losing the one person who would probably support me wholeheartedly. But to have the rest of my family treat me like a mental patient, was heartbreaking. Everyone had decided for themselves who I was supposed to be with, who I was supposed to be, and what the best decision was for my life, regardless of what I thought. When I took this step to end my marriage, I was forced to face it almost completely alone.

I knew that when it was finally time, it was going to be one of the most difficult things to navigate and without the support of the only family I had left. Making it harder was knowing that my mom would have had my back. She would have listened, understood and reinforced my faith in knowing what was best for my own life. No one else had to live my life, so no one else understood how I felt or had the right to tell me what the rest of my life should or had to look like. Interestingly, some of the very people trying to tell me how to live my life, are now people who come from broken homes, have unhappy relationships or have made their own horrible marital decisions. In the end, I was always right about one thing: I do know exactly what is best for my life, because I am the one who lives it. No one else.

Throughout this struggle, God made something very clear. That my relationship with Him, was with Him alone. No one else had the authority to tell me where my life was going, or what was right for my purpose. I was never called by God to divorce my husband. That was my decision. God probably would have had me not marry him at all, but I never really asked. I was intent on going about my life in the way that I wanted to. I also was intent on proving to everyone that I could have a normal life, get married, have kids and be happy. I had lived such a colorful and painful life the last few years, it was as though I needed to prove to everyone, including myself, that I could make normal, adult, responsible decisions. Getting married was the first step in my new life.

I also learned that the struggles I do endure are entirely my own. I had always counted on family and friends to help me through situations, comfort me and tell me that I was making the right choice and I would be ok. In this decision, everyone told me the opposite. I was ostracized by many of my friends for divorcing Josh. I was slandered and gossiped about.

My family treated me like a psych patient. I felt forced to go see a psychiatrist who was baffled by why I was even there. In three sessions, she criticized the people that shamed me and said, "You are not a crazy person for wanting to be happy." Before seeing her, I was made to feel as though I was once again a complete screw up, and didn't have the right state of mind to be making big decisions about my own life. I got very little sympathy for what I was enduring in this decision. I had no support from family and very little support from friends, some of whom decided to "keep Josh" in the divorce, especially after he started lying about me. It was a clear indication that I had to be strong completely alone.

In this trial, I learned to count on myself, my own decisions and convictions and stand my ground no matter what anyone else was saying or telling me. I made this decision on my own, without anyone else's direction or opinion, and yet, everyone felt that they were entitled to help make the decision for me. I was forced to be strong in my direction and stick to it, knowing it was the right one, while being told by everyone around me that it was the wrong one.

Finally, after three previous attempts to leave my marriage, I moved out in October of 2009 and filed for divorce. The details are fuzzy and noneventful, but it was a quick process in legal terms, and although there were emotions involved, I was ready to move on. This book isn't really about this part of my life events, so I don't need to detail them out. But everything we do in life is all part of God's plan, and this is one of them. Divorcing my husband was an event that forced me to be strong, stand up for myself and be confident in making a decision that was unpopular, but right.

My ex, being too proud to admit that his wife left him, decided to spread a rumor across town that I had been cheating on him and left him for another man. This story is so incredibly untrue. I was NEVER unfaithful to him, and I did not deserve to be slandered for any sort of thing. This type of behavior will become a pattern in my life that has gotten me to a point where my self-worth does not lie in what people THINK they know about me. This was the beginning of my having to realize that people can and will say whatever they want about another person and there is really nothing you can do to stop them. You must recognize your truth, stand by it, and pray that someday it is revealed. Ironically enough, 12 years later, the very thing he accused me of, he has now been accused of multiple times.

CHAPTER FOUR

MY SOULMATE

I'D LIKE TO take you back to my younger years, so you understand my relationship with my current husband, Scott. When
I was 18 and he was 22, we attended the same church, and he
was often dating the pastor's daughter. He would show up here
and there, based on their relationship. We were friends first of
course, always joking around with each other and goofing off.
It was my belief that he was out of my league and I was happy
with the fun times and attention I got as his friend only. The
girl he was dating was beautiful, fit, smart and sweet. She was
the type of girl you idolize and try to be like. I was nothing
like her; I was still awkward, very prude, and definitely not as
attractive. I was still learning how to do my make-up and dress
like a girl. Remember, I had just hit puberty a year before!

This was around the era that instant messenger came out
on AOL. (Young people, think: Texting. Except you had to log
onto a computer and type on a keyboard. And that computer
only worked on dial up. So even starting a conversation took 10
minutes. Yeah. Life was rough.)

We started messaging late at night, spending hours on
the computer joking and talking as friends. Scott was in the
middle of another break up with his girlfriend, this time fi-

nal. We had established a great friendship and were spending time together outside of church and had start messaging quite a bit. Out of nowhere, he wrote me a poem and it outlined his feelings of romance for me. Woohoo!! I was shocked and twitterpated! I could not believe that this gorgeous, kind, funny man was interested in me! We soon became a couple and made great memories that year and had a blast! I won't bore you with the childish drama, but we ended up breaking up after only 6 months. I was still young and insecure. This was my first adult relationship, and I had no clue what I was doing. I could sense heartbreak on the horizon, so I dumped him before he could hurt me.

Apparently, he would later say that I was always the one that got away. God had a plan even back then. If Scott and I had stayed together, he wouldn't have his son from his first marriage. And honestly, after you read about my young adult life, you will see that God had plans for me on the side, and those plans would never have included Scott. We wouldn't have made it through the life I experienced together. We were meant to be apart.

Not long after my divorce, I reconnected with Scott on social media, which was also a newer thing. Myspace had been the social media platform to be on for years. Now everyone was jumping over to Facebook. I caught up with him there. We caught up on life; where we both were, what we were doing and our life changes. I had the nerve to ask him to meet me for coffee. Rebound? No. I had been eager to leave my first marriage for over a year. Emotionally, I was healed and had been ready to move on for quite some time. Or maybe I wasn't. Either way, it worked out as God planned. We immediately fell back in love. He was instantly the man I remembered, the love I had lost and the comfort of someone I had known forever. After seeing him for the first time in nearly ten years, I couldn't even eat my dinner. I was so enamored with how handsome he still was, and how witty.

Funny story: that first night we ended up at dinner, not coffee, and the night went on and on. We did catch up, we laughed, we smiled, we found silly things to do to keep the night rolling on. Finally, he walked me to my car, and I wanted to think of somewhere else we could go so I could stay with him. I didn't want our date to end! But I knew he woke up early for work, so I didn't want to keep him up late. What I meant to ask was "Are you tired, or do you want to go somewhere else?" What came out of my mouth was "Do you want to go to bed?" His eyes got really big, as I turned red and blubbered out what I was trying to convey. Good thing he already knew me well enough to know that it was one of many awkward Lindsey moments, where I speak before I think. I do this often.

Nine months later we were engaged. One year after that we were married. That was 10 years and 3 babies ago. I had no intention of remarrying, especially so soon after my first marriage, but I knew for sure that Scott was my partner for life. My family didn't support my divorce, so you can imagine how badly they thought of my dating someone again. The isolation from my family forced me to connect to Scott on a deeper level and focus on our life together. My family bond was falling apart and would continue to for years but God used that time to ensure that Scott and my relationship was solid and our family together would be our focus moving forward.

Scott and I began building a life together that involved jobs, kids and businesses. Over the course of our marriage, we have had our ups and downs with businesses. He had a degree in sports science and medicine and was an excellent personal trainer. So we have opened and sold multiple gyms. We also opened and closed a few other businesses too. I failed at a clothing boutique, he failed in a partnership boot camp gym. We were very driven entrepreneurs and along the way of course we made mistakes. But we never stopped striving for the best and reaching for the top. After every failure, we would encourage each other, be faithful, and try again.

As Scott and I began our relationship and our life, he had his hands full. I was still grieving the loss of my mom and struggling with a defective and unproductive mentality of "life is short". I was living on the edge, being careless and trying to almost literally live life to its fullest every day. Luckily, he was along for the ride to an extent. But at times, my carefree mentality caused some strain on our relationship, and we worked through it quickly. We were a sure thing, and there was no doubt in either of our minds that we were meant to be together. We both declared that indeed, we were "soulmates."

Shortly into our dating relationship, it got frustrating for us both how far apart we lived. He lived about 45-50 minutes north of me, in Canby, Oregon. He had bought a townhome there. I had moved into my mom's old house. Get this. As you recall, my mom died suddenly in July. I had left my house with my previous husband in October. I had nowhere to go when I left my ex-husband. The family I still had left was not supportive of my decision to divorce. They would not offer me any emotional support or enforcement, so I wouldn't dare ask to stay with anyone for any amount of time to get back on my feet. My ex had shockingly decided to take all the money in my salon account, including my mom's life insurance payout, and transferred it to an account I couldn't access. Even though I assured him I had no intention of doing anything like that, he did it to me and it wasn't until I threatened him with an attorney that he gave me some of the money back. Looking back, I am now frsutrated that he felt entitled to half of my mom's life insurance. But I was so desperate to get out and move on that I let things go that I should not have. With no money to get a place of my own, I decided that although it would be horrific, I would move into my childhood home in Turner, where my mom had lived the last few years without her family. After months of the bills being unpaid, I knew I would have no heat or AC, no electricity and who knows what other shape the house would be in. But I would have a bed and a place to call mine, where I could clear my head during this time of uncertainty.

Lo and behold, my God was once again watching out for me. I packed what I could and moved my belongings into my mom's room, which was once my parents' room as a child and teen. The electricity was still on, the heat was working, and the water was running. It was a miracle, really. One of the first things I did when I got into that house and settled, was take a bath in my mom's restored clawfoot tub that she adored, poured a glass of wine and had a really good cry. I had a beautiful new salon, and a bright future, and my mom would never see it. She helped me paint the outside of the salon, and helped me decorate but she would never watch my business grow and she never even got her hair done at my new salon. Even though I had friends, I felt very very alone. I couldn't talk to my dad or brothers about how I felt. They would express only disappointment in my decision and belittle me. But in my heart, throughout this, I KNEW I had made the right decision. I knew that I was not happy with my life and that doing what was best for my life was overall, my choice. And I had made the right one. Even at the moment where most would see as rock-bottom, I was confident in my decision. For a girl living in an abandoned house, newly single and feeling isolated, I still felt peace.

"For God did not give us the spirit of timidity, but a spirit of power, of love and of self-discipline." (2 Timothy 1:7)

Moving into my mom's house, and seeing that it was functional and livable, to me was a sign that God was going to bless me for making the hard choice that I know was His plan for me. I knew that He was providing for me in my time of need. Throughout my entire life, it has always been this way. God had never abandoned me or forsaken me. And there were many times I did not deserve His goodness. But in this instant, I did need Him badly, and He was there, as usual. I looked at my right wrist and smiled. Isaiah 41:10 was giving me the pep talk I needed.

Living in my mom's house was clearly not a long-term arrangement, and now Scott and I had started growing a very real relationship where we were trying to see each other every chance we could. After about a month, and finally getting my money back from my ex, I decided I should get a small apartment. After being in my apartment for a few months and the commute to see each other getting harder, Scott and I decided together to rent out his townhouse in Canby and move him into my apartment. That was hilarious. Myself and my yorkie, Scott and his boxer, and every other weekend Scott's son from his previous marriage. It was a full house! Chaos is the only way to describe it.

We rented out the townhome to a few different people, all

great tenants, but the last one was interesting. Even though he had signed a year lease, after 4 months, he simply told us that he was moving out. He broke his lease, owing us tens of thousands of dollars. He left the place completely spotless and vanished. He and his family went completely off the radar, with no forwarding address or contact info. Who breaks their lease, knowing they'll never see their deposit again, but cleans the place spotless? Ironically, this man has now resurfaced as a follower on my Instagram page to support me! We could not find another tenant, and the property had lost its value hugely. We made the tough decision to just let it go.

We filed for bankruptcy and let the bank take this house too. It was a sinking ship and a huge financial burden on us. These are those times in your life you look back on and say, "Oh those were those ups and downs my parents always talked about!" Neither of us were happy about having to lose a house, but after attempting every route, we knew we had to. Early in our relationship, we went through a lot of financial burdens and mistakes, but it never broke us. We have been each other's support system through it all, knowing that together we can get through anything! Money is no exception!

In 2009, Scott was working for WebMD from home, doing online consulting when I met him. I thought he liked it, but time would tell that he did not like it one bit. He was basically cold calling customers to coach them in wellness, to decrease their insurance premiums. People dodged his calls, lied, hung up on him and treated him like he was a telemarketer. In reality, he really did want to help people. If I were being offered free support from a certified trainer with a degree, I like to think I would take it. But he was starting to dread it and felt like his career was going nowhere. I had a huge portion of my salon that I was not using and it could have easily been put to better use. He and another trainer at WebMD had been chatting and dreaming about opening their own gym someday. It was perfect. In 2011, we remodeled the huge space I had to create Fit Studios, a boot camp gym. It was awesome!! Think 'orange theory' but we did it first. It was instantly successful, widely talked about and a perfect addition to the neighborhood. My clients joined and their clients came to my salon. It was a great business venture. After a couple years, they needed to expand and move into a larger facility with more equipment. The new space was secured, the move was scheduled and instead of a gym, I planned to use the space we created to open a clothing boutique. It was one of my most exciting ventures. I was constantly shopping, gathering distributors and acquiring merchandise. I got to design the shop however I wanted and made it incredibly girly. Throughout this process, people close to me would always say "Your mom would be so proud of you." That never gets old.

We had accomplished so much in the short years we had been together. Scott had endured most of my hardships with the salon by my side. We got through them together. We succeeded together. We failed together. We struggled together. We expanded together. We have been tested as not only life partners, but also business partners.

In 2020, after years of building and rebuilding our businesses, we had finally felt accomplished and ready to settle down with our kids and enjoy our years and years of hard work. Glamour Salon was now in its permanent location, Scott was running his tanning salons and we had just moved into our custom forever home, designed entirely by us. Our lifelong dream together had been to build our forever home on acreage. In 2017 we bought some land. In 2018, we designed a home and in 2019 it was finished. We moved in one year exactly before government lockdowns. In 2020, we had both felt that in the 10 years of very hard work and dedication to our marriage, family and businesses, we were in a place that was finally settling. We could enjoy our life, focus on our kids and allow ourselves to have the life we had given up so much to create. We had sacrificed so much to get to this place of peace and security with ourselves. With the older kids being 6 and 3, I had finally decided to expand our family for the last time. Now, to convince Scotty.

CHAPTER FIVE

COMPLETING OUR FAMILY

HAVING OUR LAST baby was a huge deal. He was due in March, and I was enjoying the idea of being completely done with that stage of my life (making babies), settling down with our kiddos, going on vacations and being a mom. I was only working three days a week doing hair, so I had plenty of time. We had saved for three years to buy a boat. I was raised boating and we couldn't wait to start that family tradition with our kids. I thought I was done after our second child, Oakley, our little princess, and told my husband I wasn't ready to do anything crazy to permanently stop that yet though. We tried out just the two for a couple years. Then I wrote my husband a poem about wanting a third baby, how I would announce it and started the guilt trip any chance I could. It worked of course. In the end, my husband is an angel, and he knows good and well that we made freaking awesome kids. So, we stopped preventing.

I don't remember how long it took, but one day my stick had two lines. I jumped for joy and told my husband. I immediately called my doctor and got a blood test to confirm. I'm a loudmouth and I simply cannot hide my emotions, so I blabbed to anyone who would listen and pretended it was a top secret to each one. We told all our family and started making plans immediately. The next workday, while at the salon, the nurse called me and told me that I was NOT pregnant. That my hormone blood levels did not show a pregnancy. I argued with her because the line on my stick was very much there and still was. Pregnant chicks can vouch for this: we study the heck out of those sticks, and we save them for reasons even we don't know. That line is either there or it's not. It was there. She basically told me, that if I was pregnant two days ago, my hormone levels were already dropping, so I was likely miscarrying. It was the kind of pregnancy that would have gone completely undetected if I hadn't been obsessed with testing. I was losing the baby as quickly as we had made it. This is medically referred to as a chemical pregnancy and it happens way more often than you'd care to know. I had to go tell my husband, friends, co-workers and family that I was no longer pregnant and mourn this 48 hour dream we had been dreaming. This was November. God is good all the time, I told myself. This was part of His plan. What is He up to, I wondered?

In late January, I got pregnant again. I peed on that darn stick and two lines came up!! I only told Scott. Because of my last experience, I peed on a stick again the next day. No line. Once again, I had a chemical pregnancy, and this time, I barely shed a tear. I was becoming jaded to the idea that I would have a third baby. I was certain that if I did get pregnant again, I would be waiting anxiously for the line to go away. No woman should have to experience this kind of loss, or this type of attitude toward pregnancy. It is supposed to be a time of joy and celebration, and yet women experience miscarriage more often than we acknowledge or admit. It is heart wrenching and most women endure it privately, ashamedly and alone.

Sometime in the next month or more, well I'll be darned. I got two lines again. I only told Scott and I did not do it emphatically. I told him with a half-smile that, well, I was pregnant, but we would see. I kept getting two lines, and after a few days, I finally made a doctor's appointment. I did a blood test, and to my joy, the doctor called to say that my hormone levels were very high and that it looked to be a viable pregnancy. I cried from joy and was certain that my heartache was finally over. I waited weeks and weeks to tell anyone! I was slightly cautious when I did, but secretly I felt confident. When I saw my doctor, she did a fetal heartrate monitor and happily told me the heartbeat was strong and steady. Ladies and gentlemen, we had a baby!!! That weekend was Easter and I had it all planned out to announce my baby now that we had confirmation. A little Easter basket, each egg representing a family member, and a new little egg no one would recognize, announcing baby Graham. We did a photo shoot, we dressed up and we staged our little eggs. I told social media that we were having a baby! And everyone rejoiced with us. I posted the poem I had been dying to post for months now, every time we lost a pregnancy.

In life sometimes we know when things aren't just right and I felt like this was something that was worth the good fight. I felt in my heart that our family had room for another little Graham and maybe soon. One night we were lounging and out of the blue I looked at my husband and said "Babe wouldn't another baby be cool?" He looked around and said no way our house is a mess. Secretly I think he was just putting me to the test. So I waited some time and one night out on a date I looked at him again and said "Gosh babe another kiddo would be just great." He said "No I think two will do."

But I thought to myself why? Why shouldn't we have three? We make such beautiful babies you and me... Then one night as we had some adult drinks leisurely, my husband turned and he gave a special look to me. He said "Well I guess another wouldn't be so bad." And I knew he was right because he's such an amazing dad. I thought "this is my chance!" and as quick as I could I put in motion what I thought would be the plan. We prayed and we hoped that this was a go, but after a loss and so much time I thought this was the end of the road. But God had big plans for our little family as you can clearly see. We are blessed and excited to announce the arrival of baby number three.

The next day was the first ultrasound and my husband was swamped with work. I told him he didn't need to come; I was a pro at this. I would bring home the pictures and celebrate later. But we would know exactly how far along I was and that was exciting. Trigger notice: the ultrasound did not go as planned. I lay on the bed while this sweet tech did my images. He stayed quiet. I told him I should be about 7 weeks. For those who don't know this, a baby's heartbeat starts around 6 weeks. I had heard it two days prior on a doppler machine, so I knew I was past that point. In the ultrasound I would be able to SEE the heart pulsing in my little baby's gummy bear chest. I was watching intently to see it bubble up on the screen. Let me tell you how this went. I watched the screen, I watched him hold the images still. I watched him take pictures. He made no small talk. I watched for that little familiar flicker that I knew was supposed to be there. I told him (pointedly) that we should be able to see the heartbeat. He nodded and said something vague like "Usually. Unless you aren't far enough along yet." I told him I had heard the heartbeat days ago. He nodded without looking at me or even acknowledging that confidence I was exuding.

I very certainly in that moment understood exactly what was happening. I got very quiet and the tears welled up in my eyes. I sat silently in pain, the agony building, knowing exactly what was happening in that room and no one wanting to say it. I watched him intently, looking for the signs I knew were there, trying to read his expression that would say it all. He continued to move the instrument around, taking pictures, going about the routine, which hurt even more, because in my heart, I knew he was wasting his time. I knew that he knew that too.

I knew by his silence that he did not want to tell me my baby had died in the last 48 hours. As I choked up and quivered, I said "I don't see the heartbeat. I do not. I know what it looks like, and I don't see it" then began bawling hysterically. He hung his head and said "I'm going to go get your doctor" without making eye contact. These techs are not supposed to tell the patient anything. They are supposed to operate the machine, take the images and measurements and give them to my doctor to analyze. Most of them are educated more than enough to know what they're seeing, but they are not legally allowed to inform the patient. Afterward, I felt terrible for him being faced with this situation. I was crying in the room, alone, and he knew that I was aware of what had happened, and he didn't have the authority to tell me, assure me or comfort me.

At that exact moment I knew that I was right and that in mere moments a doctor was going to walk in and I was going to be told for certain that my baby had died. But my heart already knew. While I was waiting for the doctor to come back, I called Scott and told him through sobbing and tears, almost in a scream, "There's no heartbeat. There's no baby." He was shocked beyond words and his logical mind could not comprehend how two days ago, there was and now there wasn't. And I had told him not to ome. So here I was, alone, trying to understand what had happened to our baby and what I was supposed to do now. It was horrendous, as doctors piled into a room and each one gave a medical opinion regarding this pregnancy, each one trying to gently tell me that this was no longer a living baby. Each one agreed. It was over. During the confirmation ultrasound, I looked at an image that should have resembled a little gummy bear. It was a messy pile of nothing. I was actually staring at the left-over collapsed body of what should have been my third baby.

God is good, all the time, right? There is a purpose for this pain, right? God will never allow me to suffer long. I will call out to you, Lord, and you will rescue me from despair. And, boy, was I in despair. I was starting to wonder if I was being punished for some decisions I had made earlier in life. We'll get to that later. But my faith reminded me that God is not karma. God does not punish. He very gently comforted me during this time and reminded me that He had a plan. I was no longer sure that it was a third baby, but I was trying to be strong anyway. I had a girlfriend going through almost the exact same thing. We had pregnancies days apart and miscarriages just one day apart. At least I had someone who could understand and relate. She had been through a much harder loss in 2016, and I was praying just as hard for her to have a baby as I was myself. Having a close friend to talk to, who was going through exactly what I was made it a bit easie.

A few months later I still was not preventing, and now my cycle was off. My body didn't know what to do because I had been pregnant now three times in the last year. My hormones were crazy and I just lost track of everything. Every part of me knew that if I did get pregnant again, I would be restless the entire time. And yet in August we went on vacation and at the end of it I was trying to squeeze into this cute little dress and my girlfriend said "Lindsey, your boobs!! You are pregnant!" And I knew she was right. My body has started changing already and I was oblivious. I was trying NOT to think about being pregnant. The moment we got home, I tested, and the "you're pregnant" line came up darker than the other line. It wasn't even questionable, and it was immediate. I was decently far along. You would think, at this point, I would be massively skeptical, not convinced and probably bitter. But somehow I knew, I just knew, this was a baby that was going to make it. This was my rainbow baby. He made me sick, tired, cranky, swollen, angry, hungry, sick, sicker and more uncomfortable every single day he grew in there. And I was okay with that.

For this pregnancy, my doctor agreed that she would let me have an ultrasound every week if I wanted. She knew I was paranoid and terrified. I needed to know that the baby was not just in there, I needed to know he was alive. I needed to know every week until I felt safe. During one ultrasound I had a different doctor, and my mother-in-law was with me. We were excited to see my baby move. As the instrument hit my belly, baby was squishing and unsquashing his little body, almost like he was dancing, just for a second though. We laughed and smiled. The doctor said he looked good. I asked, "Is there a heartbeat?" The doctor said, as lighthearted as he could muster, "You did see him moving right?" After feeling like a complete nimrod for a few moments, I found the humor in the moment. He showed me the heartbeat and I was relieved once again.

When I was about 5 months along he gave me the scare of my life. I had not felt him kick in an hour or so and I knew that was an important thing to keep watch of. I was also still waiting to lose him. I was terrified. I started moving my hand around my tummy, sort of pushing on my sides and giving him little nudges. When he didn't respond, I got more aggressive, standing up, dancing, jiggling my tummy. Nothing. I read online to drink cold water, that it could wake a sleeping baby. I chugged it. I did all these things late into the night, for hours, starting to panic and telling my husband I was getting deeply concerned without trying to be paranoid. I finally called a nurse practitioner and she advised me on a few things I had already done. Then she told me to go to the ER. To be safe. The ER covered by my insurance was 45 minutes away. I packed myself up at 11:00 pm and headed there in terror. Was I going to find out tonight yet again that I had lost a baby?

My heart was saying no, but common sense kept running through the facts. He had not moved in a very long time. If he was sleeping, I had certainly done everything safely possible to wake him. I was struggling to see through my tears on my drive, praying and begging God not to take this one. I had already started to talk to myself about how I could handle this, what would I do? Scott was back home with the two other kids, so I would be alone again if something had happened. How would I tell him? How would I tell the kids? The devastation was already taking over with my natural instinct preparing myself for the worst. I was 2 minutes from the hospital when he kicked me as hard as he could. He was awake, and now turning flips and kicks so that I would know that there was no doubt. He was there and he was ok. I had to pull over my truck as I bawled in relief and called Scott.

On March 6, 2020, I gave birth to this beautiful boy Ranger, and I sobbed uncontrollably when they laid him on my chest. In the back of this book, you will find a raw picture of the undeniable joy of motherhood, snapped the second the nurse laid him on my chest. Friends were shocked that I shared this photo on social media. It is a stolen moment of the pure angst, relief and joy that belongs to a mom who has just done one of the hardest things women were made to do. I am proud of that first beautiful moment that I held a baby I was never sure I was going to have. After we lost Scott's dad, I told my husband that if we had another baby and it was a boy, we would, without a doubt use Scott's dad's name as his middle name. The baby's middle name would be Michael.

When we found out that baby Ranger was finally going to stick, I was so excited to be able to name him after Scott's dad in honor of him. The other boys in our family had family names, and it felt so perfect to be able to give Michael a namesake. Ranger came out absolutely perfect, happy and content. It wasn't until the next day that I looked down at his toes and saw that he had webbed toes on both feet! Scott's dad had webbed toes and Scott's grandfather had webbed toes. Scott and his two sisters did not and neither did Scott's first son. Trigger, our first son also did not have these hereditary webbed toes. But baby Ranger, conceived after Michael's death and named after him, also inherited his genetic webbed toes. It was a comforting moment for everyone to see that Scott's last son took after his own father. It was also to us a sign from God that Michael was still close to our family and watching over us.

Our family was complete. For my entire maternity leave, I enjoyed those precious moments. I knew he was my last baby; I had my tubes tied at the hospital and I wanted to remember every little breath, every cuddle, every coo and the way he smelled. We took our last baby home and started watching something on the news about this supposed pandemic. There were whispers of a lockdown, which was fine, because I got more time with my baby. Or so I thought.

"Every good and perfect gift is from above" (James 1:17)

CHAPTER SIX

MY COLORFUL PAST

GOD HAS ALLOWED me to endure many hardships to become the person I needed to be in this lifetime. Although I will never know when His plan has come to fruition, I can only enjoy His blessings along the way, knowing that they have been given in return for my faithfulness throughout all my trials. As a young adult, I turned my back on God, making choices that did not glorify Him and choices that disappointed my parents. The stories are so intricate that I couldn't possibly fit them all into one book. Some of them are so discouraging that I wouldn't even want them in print. But some stories in particular need to be told because it has now played a huge role in the formation of the courage I have now. It is the reason I believe God has prepared me for this.

When I was 20, I found myself independent, and ready to experience life. Not in a good way. In a life where I had previously found myself making mature, responsible decisions I had suddenly done a complete 180 and decided that I needed to try everything. I am not proud of those years, but I do not regret them. As I've said, God uses these experiences to shape us into exactly who He needs us to be when He calls us to glorify Him. You will soon see that I am not who you think I am, and I have done more than you could have imagined. But hopefully, God will reveal to you how He used my decisions and failures to grow me into exactly who I am and why I am proud of who I am now. This is the part of the story I struggle to make public, not only because I am ashamed of what I was capable of, but I am ashamed of who I let myself be. I knew God and I knew He was disappointed in me, but it didn't stop me from taking His grace for granted. While making these horrific decisions, I would recognize that God saw them, knew them and would forgive me. I continued my behavior anyway and told God that eventually, I would come back around to Him. But right then, I was having fun. Until I wasn't. My choices had severe consequences.

In 2000, my mom and I went to a group interview for Southwest Airlines. We both had outrageous personalities and unending smiles. We were both hired on the spot. I went to training first, so that I could start my career young. She selflessly waited one month for her training in Texas, while I began. At the age of 20, I now had a great job as a flight attendant and was enjoying the glamorous life, flying around the country, meeting people and having fun. I loved the job; I was fantastic at it. I was the flight attendant who wrote her own songs to the announcements and sang them for passengers. Jokes, absolutely. A smile at all times, you bet. I was enjoying it too much. After flights, I was enjoying drinks with my crew, even though I was underage. I had developed a "Sure, I'll try it" attitude and took it to the extreme.

Partying became a hobby and doing the job was starting to get in the way of that. I wanted to have fun on my layovers more than I wanted to be in full character the next day. Drinking was becoming a huge part of my life and that led to more intense partying. I had put my job at the bottom of my priority list and as a result, I lost it. I had been late too many times, failed to even show up but nothing could change the rules that I had not followed and I was forced to leave. I hadn't even been a flight attendant very long before I had allowed the lifestyle to suck me in. My mom was saddened to lose what seemed like something that had bonded us. Passengers loved to find out that a mom and daughter team were flying with them. She stayed on with Southwest Airlines until her death.

I was in fact, a flight attendant when the twin towers were struck. I was on a layover in San Diego and woke up to phone calls and texts asking me if I was ok. I had no clue what my friends were talking about and I turned on the news to find out. I am just now realizing that in this moment of my life, God was still using me, even though I had turned my back on Him. He was still working in me without me realizing it. In that time, on that day, I was supposed to get back on a plane and fly all day. Even though airplanes were being hijacked and flown into buildings. But nothing in me was terrified when I clearly should have been. I was in shock, awe and disgusted, like the rest of America, but something inside of me told me that I needed to be a brave face for the passengers. I needed to be on that plane, showing them that we were going to be ok. Nothing can ever describe the feeling in any airport that day.

September 11, 2001, if you were flying anywhere, you were freaked out like crazy. There were no more flight schedules. Everything was chaos. There was not a scheduled plane departing, landing or flying as planned. As a flight attendant, you showed up to any gate at all, and if you were cleared to fly, they put you on a plane, and when the plane had three flight attendants, it flew. When you landed, you found another plane that needed a flight attendant and you got on it and flew. I had no idea where I would go that day, or where I would end up. I was dealing with passengers who were completely terrified and anxious, and we were doing all we could to keep them calm, identifying that a tragedy and fear existed, but somehow assuring them that they would be ok. Which is something we couldn't promise.

I felt like a hero that day. I really did. I would show up to a gate and the agents were so happy that not only would I fly, but I would also work nonstop as long as they needed me. When any flight attendant arrived at a gate and the passengers would see that their flight was going to be able to leave, they clapped and cheered as they loaded up. Some flights had been delayed hours and hours, just waiting for a flight attendant to show up, able and willing to work.

As you can imagine, most flight attendants did not want to fly that day and even if they did their families had discouraged them from doing so, out of fear. Even though I had failed myself in this career, and have no one to blame but myself, I knew I had made a difference in that day alone and it is a day in that life my I'll never forget.

Now unemployed after my little airline shenanigans, after what I thought would be a lifetime career, I was having to start all over and decide what my next step in life would be. I was distracted though, by my lifestyle, and not focused on my long-term goals or careers. In this moment of weakness and desperation, I chose a job that completely encompasses how far I had fallen away from God. After watching my bank account dwindle and having no hope of anything great on the horizon, I joined some of my girlfriends in their place of work and became a dancer. And I don't mean a ballerina.

Even as I watched myself dive into this demeaning and detrimental life choice, I apologized to God. I knew He was disappointed in me, and I knew that He knew that I was going to do it anyway. I also know that He knew that I was His child and I was going to come back someday. And He was gracious enough to give me this chance to make my own mistakes, my own poor and harmful choices and let me learn. And when the time was right He would use these choices for His good. I knew in my heart that God was reaching out His hand to me, and I could see it but He knew I wasn't ready to take it. Yet instead of walking away from me, He kept it out the whole time, waiting for me to realize how badly I needed it. That time was far, far away and I had many more mistakes to make.

The lifestyle of a dancer brought about more bad decisions than I had anticipated. It's not surprising now, looking back, that I was introduced to drugs early on. It was almost a given. I was still obviously in my "try anything" attitude and meth was now on the list. If you've never met someone who has used meth or seen it firsthand, you need to know how real it is. It looks bad in the mugshots yes, but it is far worse in real life. I was addicted almost immediately. Before I could stop it, it was a natural part of my life. Instead of working to earn a living and pay down my debts, I was working now just to fund my addiction. I had lost an alarming amount of weight and my friends were growing concerned about my health. I was still the same silly fun loving person but now a drug addict. I had friends that still stuck by me and watched me painfully deteriorate. I stopped making my car payments and lost my car, I moved into a small dirty house with some other dancers. I was barely working and of course I could not hold a relationship. When someone tells you that you'll lose everything once you start using drugs they aren't kidding. It's dramatic.

I had only been using for 3 months before I had lost nearly everything that previously resembled my life. I was hiding the drug use very well and lying about my weight loss to most people. At least I thought. In fact, during this time in my life, I attended church with my parents at times, still holding on to that last bit of God and praying still that He would forgive me for the sins I was currently committing and with no intention of stopping. At a church service one Sunday a man caught my eye. Even though you will soon see why he was not my destiny, you will see that God used him to close one chapter of my life.

At the still immature age of 21, I fell victim to the manipulations of a man who portrayed himself as a wholesome Christian man but was instead a violent, abusive predator. I met Mikey in church service. He had a great smile, a shy demeanor and a polite manner as he impressed my dad and stole my heart when he began courting me. He appeared to have so much to offer as a man, it was easy for him to manipulate me into being one of the weakest people I have ever known.

He was older than me, owned a business, drove a nice vehicle, went to church and was well groomed and dressed. He could win anyone over during a dinner or gathering and was able to hide his true colors on a dedicated basis to nearly anyone. He fooled parents, women, church members, pastors and children. When anyone met Mikey, he always left a great impression. This was how I fell quickly for him after meeting him at church. I went on a few dates, told him exactly who I was (not the drugs) and what I did for a living. This should have been a clear red flag. He didn't like it but still seemed to be interested in me.

One night I was at work, and I called him to say hi. He was

on his way to a young adult group at church. When I told him I was working, it slapped me in the face harder than I expected. THIS was not who I am. I thought I was a good person, and I was supposed to be a Christian. I wanted to be married, have kids, live a respectable life, have a good career. What I was doing was NOT going to get me where I wanted in life.

If I wanted to be in a happy relationship with a good, caring Christian man I wasn't going to get that being a drug addicted dancer. The person I had become was so far from the person I imagined I would be that I could no longer even know who I really was deep down. I wasn't just failing my family, and God, I was failing myself. I walked out. I never went back. I started looking for a new job the next day. I didn't quit for him, I quit because I had goals in life. I hadn't lost sight of them; I just didn't prioritize them. I realized I wasn't going to reach them in the state I was in. The choices I was making were taking me away from my goals. And now, with the idea that I could meet a great guy and start over I was ready to make better decisions that directed me that way.

Did I hope that by leaving my job, Mikey would consider dating me seriously? Yes. I immediately felt that weight lift as God began to start His process. At the time, I thought that God's plan was this man. I was very wrong. God did have a plan, but it was another way to humble me, strengthen me and show me grace and courage.

After giving up dancing, I still struggled with giving up drugs. I knew I needed to hide it more now that I was in a relationship with Mikey. So I asked my dealer to make the drugs into pill form, so I could disguise them, monitor my doses, and keep my little secret for as long as I needed. This is how I know now that God was in control and not Mikey. I wasn't making changes for a man; I was making changes because God had convicted my heart. He was starting to move in my life again. If I was only hanging on to get a guy, I would have given up my drug habit immediately. Mikey still didn't know I had a drug problem.

I was still content keeping my drug habit and I was doing a great job of concealing it from everyone. If I were to give credit to a man for helping me get clean and sober, that wouldn't be the case. God was the one who deserved all the glory. For His timing was different and His purpose was more intentional.

One day at my new job as a coffee barista, I was praying that God would help me in my life and direct my choices. I was still not happy (shocking). He very clearly told me to quit using drugs. This is not surprising, of course God doesn't want His children using drugs; they become a false idol! I bowed my head in the coffee shop between customers. I asked God to cleanse me and help me to be and stay strong. I knew what I had to do and I begged God to give me the courage. He did.

In that exact moment, what will always be shocking is that I took my pills, full of meth I flushed them down the sink and I never used again. Once again, a monumental moment in my life had happened and I was all alone. Only God to give credit to, only God to share in this miraculous turn of events. At a coffee shop, on a normal day in the afternoon, by myself, God healed me. He told me what to do and gave me the strength to do it. I obeyed, and I was never tempted again to a point I couldn't resist. Trust me, Satan tried. I had no one to even celebrate or share this with. I had lied to everyone about my drug use and told them I quit months ago. I smiled, I cried and I thanked God all alone for the miracle He had just done in my life.

To this day, I've never met another person who had quit methamphetamines cold turkey. I am told it is unheard of. But God did it. He spoke and it was so. I imagine there are countless other drug users who have experienced that power of God in being healed from their addiction. I will always remember the feeling I felt as I watched the pills run down the sink and knowing that this part of my life-the dancing and drugs, was completely over. In a year or so, I will have hit rock bottom and God could finally bring me back. But I had much more pain in store for me yet.

"Because he loves me, says the Lord, I will rescue him; I will protect him, for he acknowledges my name. He will call upon me and I will answer him; I will be with him in trouble, I will deliver him and honor him." (Psalm 91:14)

Unfortunately, Mikey was not the man I thought he was. After very little time dating, Mikey slowly started his process of gaslighting and manipulating me. For those who have never been in an abusive relationship, it rarely ever starts with physical abuse. The abuser must first diminish your personality, target your strengths and create confusion. They must make you question your own sanity (gaslighting), which would then allow them to be the authority to tell you what is real and true and be certain of. It is a smooth and slow process and so subtle that even strong women can fall victim.

It starts with small criticisms. With Mikey, he targeted my faith and my appearance, two things I had previously been confident in. (They go for your strengths because your weakness already presents itself as vulnerable. In order to truly break you down, they must remove all belief you have in yourself.) Mikey was continually berating me for my choice in Christian music (yes, he believed that he was the all-knowing about which Christian music artists were the most appropriate to listen to.) He berated me for which church members I connected with (no one would ever be as good a Christian as he was.) He scolded me for listening to false prophets (only he knew which pastors were above reproach and should be listened to). After he had most certainly made me feel inadequate to make my own faith-based decisions, it was of course, imperative that I seek his council when making those decisions moving forward. As you can imagine, Mikey made sure to bring up in every argument that I was a stripper and drug addict so I clearly did not have any authority to be making faith-based decisions in any fashion. Although I had been clean and sober for 6 months, to Mikey I was always going to be a "cheap whore." Faith torn down: check.

Then he began harshly criticizing anything surrounding my appearance. I wore too much make up. So, I cut back on makeup. Then he would praise another woman for how well she took care of herself. You guessed it, she had beautiful make up. He would tell me I dressed like a slut. So, I started wearing more conservative attire. Then he would criticize me for not caring about my appearance. He told me how I should do my hair, what color it should be, and how much I should work out. According to him, I was always overweight, where he was always in great shape and much healthier. He would buy us hearty dinners then guilt me for eating it. If I went to a gym, he would accuse me of going somewhere else or accuse me of going to the gym to meet a guy. If I did start working out, and looking good, he would tell me it was for other men and I was doing it to get attention. Or I must have been cheating on him. Confidence in how I look completely diminished: check.

After I had gotten clean and finally confessed to Mike that I had been addicted to drugs, he used that against me as often as he could. Every time I was tired or sad, or just not acting like myself, he accused me of using drugs again. He said he knew that I was still an addict and using behind his back, which was never true. Please keep in mind that I have given God full credit for curing my addiction. Why wouldn't this man be proud of me for accepting God's grace and giving God glory for my salvation from drugs? Wouldn't a Christian recognize and rejoice in that with someone? Mikey never praised God with me. He used my past and my sins to further deteriorate my faith and my confidence. One day in a Chinese food restaurant, I got up to use the restroom. When I came back, he started accusing me of using drugs in the restroom. He demanded to check my pockets, my purse and do a body search in the middle of the restaurant. When I continued to deny it, he started screaming at me, causing a huge scene, and then refusing to leave. It was humiliating.

Next, he isolated me. He told me all my friends were sluts, that they were a bad influence on me. He told me that by continuing friendships with them, I was still the same person and would never change. He told me who I could and could not be friends with at church. (He probably didn't want me getting too close to any woman who might see through his charade and give me guidance.) I definitely could not be friends with any other male or he would accuse me of sleeping with them. I soon found myself very alone, very belittled and very cowardly. My friends did not like him, saying he would make inappropriate comments to them. Oddly enough, he would always tell me my friends were "whores" and I should not hang out with them. But when he needed to, he would also tell me that they were much better women than I was, that I should be more like them and that he should have dated them and not me.

I found out right away that all his ex-girlfriends were of course "crazy." When I started seeing Mikey, his last girlfriend was still leaving notes on his front door, written as though they were still dating. He assured me that he had dumped her months ago and that she was still obsessed with him. "She was crazy." I was the new girlfriend and I would soon find out exactly why these women were crazy. He was still stringing them along, pretending to still be interested while finding a new partner. He was telling her he still loved her, while telling me she was psycho. He would later do the same thing to me. He would later do the same thing to his wife, and later do the same thing to his new girlfriend while his wife divorced him. We (the exes) would later discover that he had been doing this his entire life, since high school, to every girlfriend, for nearly 30 years. As I met and bonded with these women, I felt less stupid for the person I allowed him to manipulate me into being. Most of my life the things he did to me are still under the surface and still cause emotional trauma at times.

As soon as he had me right where he needed me emotionally, he began physically abusing me. Instead of just screaming at me and calling me names, he began throwing me against walls, throwing me on his bed and holding me down, pushing me, and at the very worst, strangling me. All these fights started because in some way or another, he was convinced that I was cheating on him, or some other extraordinary offense, that was never true. For example: one day I had let him pick me up the night before from home and had no car. So, when he went to work, I had to stay at his apartment until he got home. Pathetic. It was depressing and boring, and I needed SOMETHING to do. I decided to walk to the nearest Hollywood video, which was quite far. I didn't care though because I had all the time in the world to go get a video to rent. I left his place, in my pajamas in the rain. I got a video, walked back to his place and watched it. When he got back from work, he asked me where I got the video. I told him I walked to the store. He immediately accused me of either having a man over or getting a ride from a man to the video store. In his irrational mind, there was no way on God's green earth I would walk to the video store. There was no changing his mind. I was either taken there by another man or given a ride by another man. The more I tried to defend myself the angrier he would become because in his psychotic mind, I was clearly lying.

He would now check my cell phone for unknown phone calls. When I wasn't near him, he would call the numbers and see if a guy answered. There were times I had calls from an office or a business and if a male receptionist answered his call, there was no convincing him that it was a business. Ironically, all this time he was still communicating with his ex-girlfriend and lying to me about it telling her he still loved her.

One night even, she called his cell phone at 1:00 am. I knew her phone number by heart of course. He denied that it was her number. This is an extreme gaslighting situation. He told me the number I was seeing was not hers. It was someone's from church. I was crazy. It was not her phone number. But, no he would not call it back at 1:00 am because that's just rude. But no matter what, I was a psychopath and there was no way it was her phone number. He was trying to make me feel crazy and incoherent. He had me bewildered that he was trying to convince me of something I knew to be absolutely wasn't true. I couldn't believe that he thought he could get away with that. Needless to say, that ended with a physical brawl as well, as he turned the tables on me and began berating me for checking up on him and looking at his phone.

At a gas station one day, Mikey bought me a pocketknife that hung on a keychain. He told me it was to protect myself. I'm glad he didn't buy me a gun because I did end up needing that knife to protect myself...from him. One night, he was raging at me for some unknown offense. I was denying his accusations as usual. The more I argued with him, the more outraged he became. He had already thrown me into the wall in his bedroom and taken my shoes so I couldn't leave. He would often take my car keys or my shoes when he wanted to assault me because then I couldn't run from him. He could continue to berate and abuse me as long as he liked. On this night, I had somehow gotten past him and gotten my car keys and was trying to leave his apartment. When he was enraged like this, there was no rational argument. He wanted to be right and telling him he was not made him angrier, because then he assumed you were now also lying. Basically, there was no winning. In the end, I was always going to be hit, thrown or pushed, no matter what I said. My defense became only one option. Try to leave. Grab my car keys and simply run. He didn't want the truth, he didn't want a lie; what he wanted was to take out his anger on my physically and I knew that there was nothing that would stop him.

I was begging for my shoes and begging him to just let me leave. It was never enough for me to walk or run away. He needed to hurt me to feel complete. He would never let me leave. I had my car keys in my hand and was near the door when he slammed it shut, almost taking my hand off. I went to run for my shoes, but he got back there first. So, I turned and headed back to the front door. He threw me against the front door, and I was curled into a ball in a defensive position. I remembered the pocketknife on my key chain, pulled it out and held it in front of me and asked him one last time to please let me go. He refused and came lunging at me. I can't remember if I stuck it out or he lunged into it, but either way, it went straight into his thigh and came back out when he backed away. He grasped at his leg, looking horrified that I would do such a thing to him, even as he was lunging to beat me up.

I ran from his apartment in my socks, while he was already calling the police to tell them I stabbed him. He called the girl he already had next on the line, and she hurried over to take him to the hospital. Yes, he called another woman he was already seeing and brought her into this drama. From his story alone, I was contacted by the police and told to turn myself in. I humbly and ashamedly called my dad, the retired police officer, and asked him to drive me to the station. It was protocol, but it still was one of the worst moments of my life, seeing my mom sobbing and my dad in pain, as I was handcuffed and taken to jail. I was forced to spend the night in jail with other criminals, while I waited to see if my parents would post bail for me. I was interviewed by an officer, and upon seeing my bruises and suffering, he determined that I had defended myself and no charges would be pressed. I was released the next morning.

Everyone involved hated the other. I was the girlfriend who stabbed him. He was the boyfriend that had me thrown in jail. We were a mess and we should never have been together in any form. This vicious cycle is so disturbing it's hard to even put it on paper. After not very long, I was calling to check on him and he was calling to make peace with me. For some disgusting reason, we always thought that we could make up and make it work. I was just damaged enough now that I didn't know any better. It took some time, but we got back together. Toxic relationships are somehow harder to break away from than we think, especially when it's not our own to judge.

CHAPTER SEVEN

ROCK BOTTOM

IT WAS IN this relationship that God finally allowed me to hit rock bottom. We were still continuously off and on, always breaking up dramatically and then resolving things just as quickly. Our friends and family were sick to death of this relationship, but no one knew how to cut it off. We were broken up again when, less than a year into this relationship, I became pregnant with his baby. It was not the happiest moment in my life and I knew that it was not going to be a blissful family I was gaining. Even when I took the test, we had been broken up the day before for the hundredth time. Even knowing who he was and knowing what a miserable life it had been with him so far, I thought in my ignorance that maybe this would change things. Maybe he would respect me as a woman now carrying his child. Maybe he wouldn't hurt me, knowing his baby was in there. Maybe he would appreciate me as a mom and a woman who could bring a child into this world.

I did not plan to be pregnant with this man's baby, but I knew I could make the best of it. I cannot believe I allowed myself to hope this much. I was so wrong. When he finally answered my phone calls and I told him, he went straight to his usual accusations. He told me I was a lying cheater and that the baby was definitely not his. Then he told me I was just a liar and I was making it up to get him back. Then he told me the test was fake. He told me his last girlfriend did the same thing. Then he told me that if I really was pregnant, to go get rid of it.

My senior debate in high school was on being PRO LIFE. I was raised prolife. I was raised a Christian. I am a believer. I don't believe in abortion. I believe it's murder. I was not going to have an abortion, that was for certain. But as the weeks went on, Mike gave me every manipulation tactic he had. First, he told me that he would not stay with me. That he was leaving me, and I would be left to raise the baby on my own. I was ok with that. He didn't like that answer. He said he wouldn't be able to imagine his child being in existence without him. Then he told me that if I did have the baby, he would come after me, show the courts how crazy I was and take the baby from me. He assured me that I would never see or have custody of my baby if I had her. That terrified me. I knew he would do it too.

He continued to threaten me that if I had the baby he would make my life miserable, take the baby, do anything he could do to make it impossible for me to care for my own child. I knew he was right. On paper, I looked like a nightmare. I was an ex-stripper, an ex-drug addict and now had an arrest on my record for stabbing him! No one would allow me to keep my baby! And maybe they shouldn't! After everything I had done and who I now believed I was, I was sure that I couldn't be a good mom. But the truth was very different. God never gives us more than we can handle. God would have come through for me and for my baby.

When none of these tactics worked, he finally knew exactly what to say based on what he knew about me. He told me that this was not the way he wanted to start a family. He told me he loved me and wanted to marry me and have kids, but he wanted to do it "right." He said he wanted to do it the Christian way. He said we should have an abortion quietly and secretly, then we could get married and then have kids, do everything in perfect order. That's what he really wanted. This stuck. He had me. I still wanted that fairytale life. I still thought we could have it. I was so abused, disoriented and delusional. He had broken me down into a nothing of a person. I didn't have faith in myself. I couldn't think for myself. I couldn't trust myself with any of my own decisions because he had convinced me that I was a horrible person. I wasn't a Christian. God despised me. In fact, why was he even with me? I didn't deserve him after all the things I had done. I was LUCKY that he wanted to marry me and spend his life with me. I wanted him to be happy and I definitely didn't want to have a baby and see her taken from me. I was terrified, petrified and he made me believe that the best possible option for both of us was to start fresh.

God help me, I caved.

Even though I knew this was the ultimate sin and would bring pain upon my life forever, I was so weak and pathetic, I would do anything to save myself from the nightmare that would have occurred if I had his baby then. I also knew in my heart what a horrible man he was and I imagined that if I did have this baby, he would take her and he would hurt her, and ruin her, like he has me. I knew that my baby would be doomed for a painful life if he took her from me, and I would have to watch it happen. How stupid I was. I was living in a nightmare. We argued about it daily and I kept thinking I could change his mind. I tried to come up with baby names. I named her Cadence. I looked at baby clothes as if she were really going to exist one day. I kept putting off making any kind of appointment. I knew I should not do it. I knew it was wrong.

I was incredibly sick those first weeks and my mom figured out I was pregnant pretty quickly. She was trying so hard to be happy for me while knowing what a horrible person Mikey was. I think she was just as terrified as I was of having this man's baby. We couldn't celebrate because I knew he wasn't going to allow me to have her and I couldn't pretend she wasn't there, because my mom knew. I was stuck in this terrifying limbo of having life inside me and dreading what her life would be like and dreading having any kind of positive emotions about it. I was trying to delay booking the appointment in hopes that he would realize what he was telling me to do and stop demanding it. I was praying that he would see through his own selfish motives and spare me. Spare his own baby. See, the real reason he didn't want me having his baby is because everyone would then know that he is not who he said he was. Having a baby out of wedlock would be proof to everyone that he was not the devout and perfect Christian that he wanted everyone to believe. He was trying to bury me and bury our baby. He succeeded in both. He didn't change his mind.

We were celebrating my birthday party at a restaurant with my friends and family when he pulled me aside to tell me that he took the liberty of booking my appointment for the next day. Happy Birthday to me. I had to go back to the table and pretend to be ok. I had told no one of his plans. I was dealing with this completely alone. That night I lay in bed alone, put my hands on my tummy and I cried out. I prayed to God. I begged for forgiveness in advance. And I told my baby I was sorry. Between sobs and comprehension I knew that I was going to go through with it, even though I did not want to and I didn't believe in it. I don't know why I wasn't strong enough to stand up for us, to say no and to take the hard road. I don't know why my convictions didn't take over. I was so weak and unable.

I am disgusted at this person who would do something she didn't believe in and allow someone else to control her body. I look back at her, and I know there was no way I could have stopped her. She isn't the same person. She was brainwashed. But I can't help but berate myself for allowing myself to be her. I have to constantly remind myself that God couldn't stop me. It had to be my decision, the free will that He blesses us with and I was just not strong enough.

The next morning, my mom knew something was wrong. She knew what I was doing and where I was going. She also knew that she couldn't stop me and that if she tried to stop me, it would all be too real. She had to pretend that she didn't know that I was leaving to go kill her grandchild. I will never forget the look in her eyes, as she said goodbye to me that day, waiting for me to fall into her arms and confess it and change my mind. I know that she wanted so badly for me to confide in her so she could help me, but I walked out and told her I would be ok. As I watched her eyes fill with tears, I knew I would not be okay.

Mikey, this man, this disgusting, vile, pathetic man, "had to work" that day, but he would hurry back to be with me he had said. Liar. He wouldn't even stay for the appointment that he made, that he forced me to go to that would kill his child. He dropped me off at the front door. He didn't even walk me in. As I continually tried to reach him to come he kept saying he was still at a job site. This happened for hours. I now think that he went somewhere nearby, waited and was just going to come pick me up when it was finished. I also think that he still believed I was lying and that nothing was really going to happen. That I was putting on a show.

I was confiding in another woman there and sobbing quietly. She tried to comfort me by asking me if I really wanted to do this. I didn't but I knew that I had to. The strong me = now realizes that I had other options, even deceptive ones, but I was too scared and too weak to think clearly or rationally. I could have pretended to abort my baby, left him, hid away and never spoken to him again. I could have told him that the baby was someone else's. I should have never told him at all. Unfortunately, I was not cunning like that and I was too weak and deflated to think for myself. The nurses had to medicate me more than usual, I was in such despair. I find it interesting now, that with that demeanor, not one person suggested I NOT follow through with this decision that clearly was not my own. I was told it wouldn't hurt. Liar. They tell you whatever they must to keep you in that chair. You're sucking a human life out of my body and it's not going to hurt at all? When it was finished, I was put in a wheelchair to leave. I was numb and I was broken; I left there a shell of a woman. I felt completely empty.

Mikey magically arrived just in time to pick me up. The nurses helped me into his truck. That's right, he didn't even get out to help me. He waited in the driver's seat until I was loaded in by nurses. When the door was shut and we started to drive off, his first words to me were this: "I can't believe you just killed our baby. I didn't think you would actually go through with it."

Let's not be shocked that in that moment, of course, he could do nothing but make sure he was guilt-free of any wrongdoing, and I was once again the sinful villain in this story. In the absolute worst moment of my life he made sure to berate and abuse me for an action that he instigated and demanded. I couldn't even yell at him or argue. I had nothing to say. There was no fight in me. I was drugged, miserable and the worst human being in the world. I deserved everything he said. When I woke up from an awfully long and painful nap, the reality of what I had done had sunk in. I did NOT want to feel what I was going to be feeling the rest of my life. I wanted to brush it off, ignore it, pretend it never happened and move on. If I wallow in this, it will certainly kill me. And it almost did. (More on that later.)

I told Mikey, now, we could do things right like he had said. I had done the one thing he wanted me to so that we could be a family and start a family the way he wanted to. We could start over. We could put this behind us, get married and start new. His response: "I hope you're kidding. I would never marry you or have a family with you, after what you just did."

There it is folks. In a nutshell, the very tactic used to get me to do what he wanted, was also now the excuse he had for never having a future with me. I had been duped into killing my own child.

Believe it or not, we attempted to stick it out. We tried to get through it. I read statistics on couples that go through an abortion together, how often they do not stay together. I was determined to beat it. But the fights got worse. I blamed him for the baby and because he had tricked and deceived me, I was no longer buying his "perfect Christian" act. I was no longer blind to his tactics and even though I wasn't strong enough to leave yet, I was at least starting to see clearly. I started fighting back. I started lashing out myself. I had nowhere to channel my anger and no one to confide in. At this point, after everything I had done, I was too ashamed to let anyone help me. I really was the disgusting person Mikey had been telling me I was for the last three years. Mikey did not care one bit how hurt I was by the loss of my baby. He didn't care one bit how it was affecting me and how it had changed my life forever. He did not care that I was crying myself to sleep every night, mourning. He really was thrilled to be moving on and had escaped his true character being revealed. He was already attending a new church, and meeting new people, including new women. (Women who were much better than me, he would tell me, who hadn't killed their babies.)

If I wasn't damaged enough already, I was now. He was the only person I expected to help me through this struggle. He was the only person who knew. I told my mom a week later, casually, that I lost the baby in miscarriage. She pursed her lips and held back tears and asked me if I was ok. She knew what I had done and was waiting for me to be ready to tell her. If only I had been humble enough to lean on my mom, she could have been there for me, given me a shoulder to cry on, mourned with me and gotten me the help I so badly needed. I would call Mikey regularly to cry and tell him how badly I was hurting. I didn't know how to recover from this. He was trying to move on from me and he wasn't being shy about it. He wouldn't break up with me but he continued to make his own plans, meet new friends and I was never invited. He often ignored my calls, even when I was desperate and begging. My abortion was destroying me and I was in the darkest place I had ever been.

One night I was alone, in deep mourning over my decision. I had alienated all my friends. I was still keeping this secret from my family. (They knew the truth, but were waiting for me to open up to them.) I was feeling hate for myself and hopelessness for my life. I was having an unbelievably bad night and over the phone he told me he didn't have time to come comfort me. He was going into church group. He hung up on me. I was alone in my apartment, I was depressed, I was a murderer, I was disgusted with myself and all I wanted was to stop feeling. I texted him and told him that I would no longer be a problem for him. I didn't want to be a problem for anyone anymore. My parents had to be so disappointed in me by now. I was appalled with myself. I went through my medicine cabinet and saw that my allergy pills were labeled with a warning about causing drowsiness. I took as many pills as I could and went to bed.

Mikey casually told my dad over the phone that I was being crazy and acting suicidal. That my dad should probably go check on me. At this time in my life, I really was behaving crazy and acting irrational most of the time. That man didn't even bat an eye that the next day I would probably not exist, but it might interfere with him meeting a new girl, his next victim. My dad found me, took me to the hospital and it's pretty much a blur but I imagine they saved my life. I know I was still walking and talking, but that's about it. I have a few vague memories of being in the car with my dad and saying something, then looking at his face and knowing that whatever I had said didn't make any sense. I remember him trying to ask me what I had taken but I didn't want to tell him. I was incoherently mad that my dad was having to take me to the hospital. This wasn't his fault. I wanted Mikey to take care of me. I wanted Mikey to suffer with me. I wanted Mikey to suffer the consequences of what he did to me. Not my dad.

Afterward, I was answering the hospitals questions about suicide patients. They needed to determine whether I needed to be checked in somewhere more permanently. Even though I had done something that could have caused my death I knew I didn't want to die. If I had died, I wouldn't have known any different. But now that I had survived, I realized what Mikey had done to me. What I had allowed him to do to me. I realized that there was not a lot lower I could go. I wanted to live. I didn't want him to have the benefit of knowing he had broken me.

Killing my baby had ruined me. That is why I am not just pro-life; I am adamantly and passionately pro-life. Not just for the babies God created, but for the women who suffer when the reality hits them that there was a human being God created and a mother meant to raise him. And that mother took his life. It was when I had my first son that I realized the impact my abortion had on my life. I had already asked for forgiveness from God. I had already forgiven myself. But as I looked at my newborn son, I realized that there was a person that should have existed that did not. There was a life, a laugh, a future, someone God wanted to live, that I took away from myself and the world. I now had the knowledge of what a mother's love was, and it hurt me more looking at my child, knowing that I had another child whom I will never know or hold. I wonder what her personality would be like, her eyes. I wonder about her laugh and what God would have planned for her. This type of agony can never be portrayed. You simply must have endured it to understand it. I know that not only do abortions kill babies, but they also debilitate their mothers.

Women suffer severe and life altering regret and remorse when the realization eventually comes that they had taken their own child's life. I am pro-life because I am pro-woman, and women empowerment means protecting each other and uplifting each other. I will never meet a woman, a mother who can say she "regrets having her baby." But I know for a fact that I regret with all my heart taking my child's life.

This plays a major role in why I am also completely against the feminist movement. Women involved in this movement think that they speak for ALL women. They think that what they believe is what all women believe. This is not true. They preach that it's our bodies and our rights. But what they don't stop to consider is that the biggest advocate for women is other women. Our job is to support and empower each other. Our role in each other's lives is to speak proudly of our friends, highly of our co-workers and strongly for other mothers. Without judgment and hostility. The feminist movement does the opposite. It tells other women what they should believe and what they have to stand for. It also mocks and berates a woman's natural role. The most beautiful gift that was given to women by God is the ability to bear children. Painful or not, it is something that we rejoice in and experience. It is something that no man ever can. It's why we endure periods and cycles and hormones our entire life. The beautiful and courageous blessing of carrying, nurturing and bringing our children into the world with our own strong bodies. The feminist movement mocks this.

In a feminist world, women parade around in vagina hats, carrying bloody fake babies, and rejoicing in their right to kill their own babies. They celebrate their "right" to terminate a pregnancy at any stage they like simply as a birth control. They believe that all women feel this way. When they are dancing around, praising themselves for their movement in the right to terminate pregnancies, they don't seem to care one bit that some women are not able to even have pregnancies. One out of three women have experienced miscarriage. Thirteen percent of the women in the United States are infertile or have experienced difficulty getting or staying pregnant.

If the women's liberation movement is to support, endorse and encourage other women, why would any woman publicly celebrate the right to kill their baby, knowing that another woman is home crying at any given moment that she cannot even carry a baby? How is that women empowerment in any capacity? Does a woman have a right to terminate her pregnancy for any reason at all? In my opinion, no. But the United States has started to say "yes." And women are rejoicing and posting on social media the number of abortions they have had, bragging if you will. And the women reading it who have miscarried, had still-born babies or can't get pregnant are devastated by this news. These women are in excruciating pain every day, asking themselves what is wrong with their body,that they cannot experience children like so many of their friends and family. Then they see another woman rubbing it in everyone's face that they are enjoying the "right" to kill the baby growing in their body. It's appalling and heartbreaking. The feminist movement has harmed women far more than they have helped women.

"Before I formed you in the womb, I knew you. Before you were born, I set you apart." (Jeremiah 1:5)

After this episode, Mikey put on his best show of character and pretended to be concerned for me, and somehow roped me back in but not for very long. I was still bound to him because of what we had been through but I was starting to see hope in a future without him and I began dreaming of the day I could break away for good. I had started interacting with people regardless of his opinion and even reconnecting with friends I had previously had to push away because of him. I had a male friend, Brian, that I really trusted and cared for. At one point I had briefly dated Brian but after everything I had gone through we both agreed that friendship was our route. I didn't have romantic feelings for Brian anymore but I knew he was genuine and I trusted him. He also came through for me so many times when he didn't have to. There were a few nights that I wasn't well, that he let me come sleep on his couch just so that I wasn't alone. He was always kind and respectful. I was not allowed to speak to Brian because Mikey told me so and if I did, I would most certainly be accused of sleeping with him. I had been reaching out to Brian and he was supportive and fun and made me remember who I could be without Mikey. He was just a friend and he was a friend that I needed at that time. Brian was like a guardian angel. He knew all the things I had been through and done. He never judged me or condemned me. He was there if I needed him, in a platonic way. He owed me nothing but he went out of his way to keep an eye on me and help me when I asked.

The very last time I let Mikey put his hands on me was the time I thought he was going to kill me. He had accused me of sleeping with Brian and cheating on him and this time, he was not going to take no for an answer. He threw me on my couch, face down. Held my face in a pillow and pounded me with berating questions. No answer I gave was going to be right. I had allegedly slept with my male friend. I was a cheater. I was lying. I was in love with him. Why would I do this to him? Why was I such a whore? These are the things that were being screamed into my ear as I lay helpless. In my apartment, alone I kicked, screamed and threw my own furniture if I got my hands free to try to make the neighbors come upstairs. No one was there to save me. I prayed and sobbed as he held my face into a pillow, demanding that I confess to something that I didn't do. He wouldn't stop and I was sure he was going to kill me so I did something I've never done. I confessed to whatever he was accusing me of. I told him I did sleep with Brian, and it was amazing, and that we were in love. I had been in love with Brian for months and lying to him. I couldn't wait to start a new life with this man. He was sweet and kind and wonderful and more of a man than Mikey would ever be.

None of this was true of course, but something in him clicked. It's like he was more at peace knowing that he was finally right. That I really was guilty. He could accept all my lies if they were presented as truth. He calmed down. He acted like a wounded dog and sobbed as if I had caused him more pain than anyone in the world. It was so pathetic and weird. It solidified that he had been mentally ill this entire time and I had never recognized it. He was a narcissist in every way. He was a sociopath. He was now content in being the victim and allowing me to wallow in my decisions, hoping that maybe later I would apologize for the acts of treason I had just admitted to. (Even though he had been doing these things to me the entire time). In his victim mentality he left, tail between his legs and waited for me to call him like I always do. I didn't. I was free. He had left without any more of a fight and I felt truly free. I was so close to thinking he would kill me and I could not go through it again. I also had a new feeling. Confessing to things I never did but was always accused of was freeing. I survived. From that moment on, I knew I was going to survive.

> *"See, I have refined you, though not as silver. I have tested you in the furnace of affliction." (Isaiah 48:10-11)*

I was never the same, however. This event along with the others had caused permanent physical damage to my body. I can't rationally handle pain inflicted by another person, even on accident. Not long after this incident with Mikey I was rough housing with my older brother at home, chasing each other, just goofing off. We ran around a corner and he shoved me to the side, playfully of course. But I had fallen too hard and fell into the wall with my shoulder. He started laughing and even though I was not hurt and I knew it was an accident, my body went into convulsions and I started hysterically crying. He ran to me, concerned that I was badly hurt. He asked if I were ok and I told him yes but I could not stop crying, almost hyperventilating. I had no clue what was wrong with me or why I was crying when I knew I was ok. And I knew my brother hadn't meant to hurt me. I realized later that this would be an ongoing issue my entire life. If I fall or hit something or hurt myself, it's no big deal. But if someone, even my own kids, accidentally hurt me even just a bit, my body goes into a panic and I have to go into a room privately and cry, so I don't freak people out. It's like, even after all this time, I still suffer from traumatic emotional scarring. Although I hate it, it reminds me where I've come from, what I've endured and to be thankful for the man I am now married to.

This is also why I have continued to battle mask mandates. I cannot wear a mask without bursting into a hot flash, feeling suffocated and struggling to compose myself. I feel my blood pressure rise and my hands get sweaty. I start panicking almost instantly. When you've experienced a situation where your breath has been taken from you and you struggle to survive, willingly forcing your body into that same situation is not healthy. It's also dangerous. When I had been in the very few situations where I absolutely had to wear a mask, even for a moment, it has been detrimental to my emotional wellbeing and my natural health. To reveal to other humans daily why I struggle with mask mandates should not be something I have to announce in a grocery store or any public place. I shouldn't have to explain myself. Masks are for communists and I will never support them in any way. But there are hundreds, if not thousands of women who suffer this along with me. And it is not fair to make them lay out their violent past and painful history to have to justify their exemption. We shouldn't have to go to a doctor and try to really explain why a mask is a symbol of sufferance for us. I will continue to fight for those women and anyone suffering PTSD or trauma due to the hinderance of their natural breathing right. I'm on a rant. Back to my demon of a boyfriend.

Mikey still thought he had a hold on me. He called repeatedly and apologized. He came over, he stalked me. He tried to tell me it was my fault for angering him. He tried to tell me he just was so upset and wanted me back, that's why he did it. Somehow, I had broken free. And while he permanently damaged me, the strength I found later is why God allowed this man to make an impact on my life. Mikey did things to me that will forever haunt me and will forever be the reasons I believe in some of the things that I do.

> "Don't be surprised at the painful trial you are suffering as though something strange were happening to you but rejoice that you participate in the sufferings of Christ, so that you may be overjoyed when His glory is revealed." (1 Peter 4:12-13)

CHAPTER EIGHT

FINDING MY STRENGTH

AFTER OUR BREAKUP, Mikey quickly moved on to another sweet woman in another state who didn't have enough time with him to realize what she was getting into. It was an online relationship, and she didn't see the real person hiding inside. Mikey used the same tactics on Rebecca that he did with all his previous relationships, and she discovered too far into the marriage that his abuse would never stop. He was mentally ill. I received a random message from Rebecca in 2017, telling me that she was Mikey's wife and she was divorcing him. She asked me if I had any experience with him that involved abuse. It was a heart stopping message. I was in the middle of the salon when I read it.

I had wanted so badly to find this woman years ago and tell her about Mikey, that he was not who he portrayed. I wanted to warn her and tell her to run for her life, literally. But Mikey had always painted his other ex-girlfriends as "crazy" to me, so I knew he had probably already told her about me and she would never believe me. I also told myself that it wasn't my fight. But it became my fight very quickly. Rebecca and I talked, and I told her everything. Mikey had been abusing her in front of their three children for years, and she was trying to get free. My heart hurt so badly for those kids. I knew how dangerous Mikey was, and how he could manipulate and hurt people mentally. I couldn't imagine the damage he was probably doing to those children. Rebecca was now asking me to testify in court against him.

This man had caused me more harm than any other human I know. He had caused me to do things that were not in my character. He had ruined parts of me that will never repair. He had changed my life in so many negative ways. He had hurt me in every way possible, so many years back. How in the world could I face him after 15 years and not fall apart? Yes, I was a different perso, and I was much stronger because of him, but could I really get on the stand in court and speak about the terrors this man caused me? I told her I would. Then I told her I wouldn't. Then I bought a ticket. Then I cancelled it. Then I thought of her children and what they were being forced to endure with this demon of a father. And I said yes. I bought my ticket. I told myself I could not back down. I told myself this would be the closure that I needed.

Rebecca had found three other ex-girlfriends online and all three, including myself told stories of Mikey's demeaning behavior, gaslighting, manipulations and mental, emotional and physical abuse. He had been treating women this way his entire life. I wonder how many other women have survived this man. I was the only one who could or would testify. I had to sign a legal affidavit under oath testifying to what Mikey did to me. When Mikey's attorney gave him a copy, that man had the audacity to write me on Facebook and tell me he was "confused" by my testimony and wanted to chat about it. He actually thought, after 15 years, it would be that easy to manipulate me into having a conversation with him.

A part of me really wished I had messaged him back, just to laugh at his security in thinking he could still work me over. But the logical thinker in me simply ignored him and forwarded the message to Rebecca's attorney. After all, he was intimidating a witness. His message reminded me that his behavior was still exactly as it was 15 years ago, and he was still treating other women this way. Over the next few weeks, I started receiving anonymous threats on my Facebook messenger. They were harassing, demeaning and threatening. They made fun of my looks and called me a drag queen. I knew it was someone he had recruited to try to intimidate me, perhaps his new girlfriend or one of his family members. It didn't work. It gave me resolve. I wanted him to see me on that stand, speaking up against him and doing so strongly.

The night before and the morning of testimony, I was undeniably a mess. I couldn't sleep, I couldn't eat and my stomach was upset with nerves. I got nauseous in the airport and in the courthouse. My eyes were saggy and black. My face looked sunken. I was a woman terrified and emboldened all at once. I found myself looking at that tattoo of Isaiah 41:10 on my right wrist repeatedly. I took the stand. I spoke my truth. I stared at him throughout the testimony and that weak little mouse of a male never once lifted his head to make eye contact with me. He couldn't even look at me. He was the victim now. I was standing up to him, speaking out against him, and there was nothing he could do about it. I drove my eyes into his face as I walked out of the courtroom and he hung his head the entire time.

I exited the courthouse with my chest puffed out, my head held high and a new breath in my lungs. The color came back into my face. My eyes brightened. My smile restored. I had done the bravest thing in my life up until this point. I had finally told my story and closed the hole in my heart that this man created. I believe that this moment was a moment God gave to me, to show me what I am capable of. He gave me the ability to face a person that scared me more than anyone, and to stand up to that person. Fifteen years ago, I believed that this man could kill me if he were given the right opportunity. Today, I would stand in a room alone with him, knowing that God would protect me and strengthen me. I am who God has made me today, because of the pain He has allowed to happen. It has made me stronger, bolder, clearer headed, more logical, more free thinking, more aware of people's behavior and tactics. Had I not been through everything with Mikey that I had, I would be more judgmental, never knowing what abuse victims and abortion victims go through.

I have never been a "holier than thou" Christian. You

know the type, right? Their faith is strong and pure, but they have never made extremely bad or painful decisions and cannot relate to those who have. Their sin is that they believe they are perfect Christians. They obey the rules, but they don't always have a true relationship with God. They unfortunately treat other Christians as though their faith always supersedes anyone else's. I was a "really good Christian" in my youth, and I could easily have been a person who thought that they were without sin and self-righteous. I probably would have been judgmental to others who had made bad choices and fallen away from God. Like the choices I had now made. But I could have been. I was on a path in high school of being a well-behaved person, and without knowledge of real human desires, sins, behavior that can cause them to make poor or bad decisions in their life.

I was a little bit unsympathetic to the issues people have in their life, living with the idea that well, they made their own choices. Well, now so have I. I have paid for those choices. But I don't have to suffer for them. God has forgiven and restored me. His grace has saved me. I no longer look down on people who have made life choices that I haven't, because I know we are all human. We are all capable of being manipulated, convinced and scared. We are all capable of being in the wrong place at the wrong time. We are also all capable of surviving things that God knows will be used for good. I believe that there are a hundred ways God is going to use my story for good. I also believe that one of them was so that I could testify to people, especially women, with the confidence that I can relate. I am no better than anyone I meet. God has allowed my story to transform into one that is not above reproach. When I witness to women about life, I don't speak from a pedestal, I speak from their perspective, as a person who has experienced it.

When I was about two years recovered from my meth addiction and back into a relationship with God, I walked into a movie theater bathroom to find a woman at the counter, washing up. I knew instantly that she was high on drugs. I knew it because I could recognize it from my own experiences. God allowed that. As I grabbed the door to leave, God stopped me.

I felt compelled to speak to her, to witness to her. I couldn't have done that if I didn't know what she was going through. I couldn't have done it had I not been there myself. I could relate, and that gave me a reason. I walked up to her and said to her face "I know what you're doing. I used to do it too." I began telling her about how God saved me, how He gave me the strength and desire to quit. I told her that being clean is the best decision I had ever made, and that God could help her too, if she wanted. She started crying, hugged me and told me she wanted to stop. This was no act; the Holy Spirit had taken over my words (I cannot remember anything I said) and had placed me in this restroom to allow God to save her, working through my life. I prayed for her as she continued to cry. She promised she would seek help. She gave me her number and I prayed that I had truly reached her.

The next day, I called her house to check in on her. Her mom had answered and told me she was not available, she was sleeping. Her mom asked me who I was. She said, "Are you the girl from the bathroom?" I told her I was. She started weeping and said that her daughter had come home from the movies, told her about her addiction and asked her mom to help her get clean. She was sleeping because she was coming down and withdrawing. She told her mom that God had sent someone to help her and told her she needed to quit. Just like that, God was using my pain to save lives. He was taking my bad and making it His good. I checked in on that girl multiple times. She never used again as far as I know. She got clean and started her life over.

Just this year, at a restaurant in Scottsdale, after meeting for a business dinner with a fellow patriot, I used my life lessons to stand up for someone else. I was walking to my truck, which was parked much farther away than I would have liked. I was driving around looking for spots and could find none. My faith told me that God wanted me in that spot for a reason. Instead of cursing that I had to park far away, I told God that I would be open to whatever His reason was for me being exactly where He wanted me. There's always a reason, my friends. After dinner, and walking all the way back to my spot, right in front of me was a couple, dining outside, just ten feet from where I was parked. I noticed something was wrong right away. The man was standing up, flailing his hands at her, screaming obscenities and stomping around. She was quietly sitting at the table with her head straight, making no eye contact with anyone. As I got closer, I smiled at them walking by and neither smiled back. I watched the man scream within inches of her face again and storm off. It hit too close to home. This was how I was treated while I dated my abuser, Mikey. Of course, he would never have behaved this way in public. This man's rage was terrifying and he was displaying it in full daylight for everyone to see.

Mind you, no one else was outside to see this except me. But he had no problem with me seeing it. I walked past and got to my truck, unlocked it and put one foot up. Nope. That voice said no. I took a deep breath and walked back to the woman. I sat at her table, looked directly at her and said, "What did you do wrong this time?" She laughed and sniffled. I said, "Let me guess. You're wearing too much make-up; your skirt is too short. You didn't say the right thing at the right time." She stopped sniffling to look up at me. "Yeah, pick one."

I reached over, grabbed her hand and gave her as much comfort as I possibly could. I told her she deserved better. I told her this wasn't normal. I told her this was not how it was supposed to be. She nodded and squeezed my hand. I told her to be strong and when she was ready, I hope she would leave him. He made his way back, and Patriot Barbie was out now. I had found my courage. I would never allow a man to treat someone like this in front of me again. He asked me who I was in an angry, violent tone, littered with cuss words. I told him quite politely that it was none of his business, that it was between her and I. Let's just say that did not go over well. He continued to berate her and now scold me.

He kept looking at her for support as he challenged my authority to be there, holding her hand and giving her strength. She continued to ignore his shouts, and I think I saw her head lift a little higher as I continued to spit my defense at him. He thought he would come over and scare me away. I stood my ground. I spoke to only her. I boldly defended myself, and I would NOT take his crap. I refused to answer to him or answer his questions. I said, "This is a public sidewalk, and I can be friends with and encourage whatever woman I would like to." He accused me of being paid to be there. Yes, he said someone was paying me. Wait, what? He assumed there was something in it for me. I got through to her a little; I know I did. Their families finally came out of the restaurant and asked what was going on, as they were leaving. He continued to use vulgar language to describe me while I smiled pleasantly and told them I was simply making sure she was ok.

I gave her one last bit of encouragement, right in front of him, then stood up, hugged her and started for my truck. She grabbed my shoulders and looked directly at me and said, "Thank you. No one has ever done anything like this for me." I think it was her adult son, who said to me as a I passed, "Thank you so much. I'm so worried about her." I was saddened to hear that she really was in a dire situation, and no one could free her. But I also know what that's like, and that it has to be her choice alone. I pray for her, and I pray that God protects her before it's too late. I regret that I didn't get her phone number so I could check up on her and encourage her. I urge you to make these human connections when you can. If you see someone in trouble or hurting, reach out and be the voice that encourages them. No one else might be doing it. God gives us the strength and courage to do these things on a daily basis. He also lays out the plans.

Like I said, why did I have to park so far out? The answer was beyond clear. Had I parked anywhere else, I would not have been there for this woman. Where have you been in life that lets you be God's vessel? What have you experienced that God can use to help someone else? Why does God put you exactly where He puts you every single moment of your life? He has given you a story, and it is our job to use it for His purpose and glory in every situation.

"Blessed is the man who perseveres under trial, because when he has stood the test, he will receive the crown of life that God has promised to those that love him." (James 1:12)

God allowed me to be a drug addicted dancer who fell in

love with an abusive narcissist, who convinced me to abort my own baby, which led me to act unnaturally and eventually question my existence. He didn't want this for me, but I chose it, and He waited patiently while I figured it out. When I was finally at rock bottom, His hand was still there, outreached, and since I couldn't pull myself up, I had to take it. Then, God nurtured me back to health and love and life. In a church that praised God, during a time of prayer, I finally gave my baby to God. I gave God everything I had done in my life. I begged for forgiveness and it was given. I begged for healing and it was given, slowly. I begged for new life and it was given.

I didn't even have to ask, but God gave my pain purpose. He had His work cut out for Him, making all these heartaches for good. He picked me up from the pile of dirt I had buried myself in, He brushed me off and then He polished me and I was like new. But because He allowed me to experience the things I have, I am the person He needs me to be, to glorify Him. I cannot witness to you or anyone on a pedestal. I have no place there. I cannot testify to you from a place of perfection. I cannot tell you that God is good and can heal all wounds, without having two handfuls of my own. You cannot look at my life and imagine that it's perfect and ask how I would know anything about what you're going through. Sister, I've been there. And now you know it.

As much as I would have loved to keep this dirty dirt tucked away in my closet of skeletons, this is the path from which God has saved me. This is the journey of pain and heartache that God let me experience so that when I tell you He is almighty, you don't have to believe it, you saw it, as clear as day in my life. You don't even need faith; you've got proof! Look at what God has done for me. You can't get much more evidence than that. Amen friends. Jesus has forgiven the grossest of my sins, made me new and TOLD ME I am His. His grace has been a beacon in my life and for every deed and sin, I have been blessed ten times over, because of His grace. Whew, preach it girl. My God is so stinking good.

"For nothing is impossible with God." (Luke 1:37)

I still don't know what God's plan is, through all of this. Maybe it's this book, maybe it's something bigger. Maybe it's something that won't happen for years to come. But I know that what we have been through must be used for His glory. He must have used this time to strengthen me, empower me and bring me closer to Him for a purpose.

When God called me to write this book, it was divine. I have never been a person who "hears God speak." But He gives me signs, and I pray for the correct interpretation. I don't think there is any room for doubt that I was called to write this book. My Aunt Lori and Uncle Dene are devout Christians and strong believers. Aunt Lori gave me a book on my 40th birthday called The Eye of the Storm, by Ryan Stevenson. It's a book written by the Christian song writer and singer, about his journey in life, his calling to make music and his walk with Jesus. My aunt said that I had been through a storm, and she thought I would like it. That wasn't all. I opened the book on my flight to Oregon for work. In the front she had written, "Lindsey, we thought you might enjoy this book of hope and faith, and maybe encourage you to write your story." I had been told once or twice that I should write a book about this last year, but that didn't seem like God speaking. I have a hard time differentiating what I want to do and what God is calling me to do. In this situation, I believe it was one and the same. I do like to write, so I sort of tucked that away in my head.

Throughout reading his book, I felt myself connecting to Ryan, absorbing his emotions and pain, and thinking of my own pain in life and my own storm. I read about Ryan continually asking God to reveal his purpose and plan for his life. I began bowing my head on the plane and praying the same prayer. "Please God, reveal to me your plan. Show me, tell me clearly. Let there be no doubt. I need concise signs of what you want me to do with my story." It seemed like God had used me to do this big thing last year. Something that only a handful of other people had gone through. Why would He have my life go that direction without a bigger purpose? Amen people, I hope you know what He did next. He told me, within 24 hours.

I got to the salon and a client I hadn't seen for 6 years had booked an appointment online. Janet and I caught up and she filled me in on her life. I took a breath when she said, "I also published a book." This was the second time today that someone has mentioned writing a book to me.

A couple hours later, between clients, I was reviewing an email by Breaunna, a Christian woman who had written my press release, announcing my move and the huge announcement that I was having to close Glamour Salon. At the end of my press release, she announced "expect big things from me". In a phone call with her, she told me that she included that sentence because she could foresee something in the future with my story, "like a book deal." I was stunned. This was it. This was God, being as blunt as he can be without setting a bush on fire. He was telling me to write a book. He was telling me to tell the world about Him and His unconditional love for me and how determined He is to bless me through this trial. But because I'm an imperfect human, I told God, "One more sign. To confirm. I need one more." My co-worker laughed and said, "This wasn't enough of a sign for you?" We finished up at the salon late, and I went to my friend Jessica's house, where I stay when I visit. I laid down and checked my messages.

A patriot from Florida, Rory, was regularly checking in on me, praying for me and my family, reaching out and offering support and encouragement. I couldn't believe my eyes, when I opened a message from Rory, sent at 11:43 am saying "Hey Lindsey, just dropping in to say hello. I had an idea that popped up which was to do a continuous podcast or write a book about everything you went through. Thoughts?"

My God is so unbelievable. He gave in to my demands and gave me a final last sign. I was going to write my story. My story is ongoing, and always will be. As I write this, I can only tell you about my blessings so far. God is still working miracles in our family's life, and my faith tells me that God has so much more work for us.

"For I know the plans I have for you, declares the Lord, plans to prosper you and not to harm you, plans to give you hope and a future. Then you will call upon me and come to pray to me, and I will listen to you." (Jeremiah 29: 11)

CHAPTER NINE

THAT SALON OWNER FROM OREGON

"Have I not commanded you? Be strong and courageous. Do not be terrified, do not be discouraged, for the Lord your God will be with you wherever you go." (Joshua 1:9)

IN MARCH OF 2020, when governors around America started locking down their states, including small businesses and schools, I disobeyed. After only 6 weeks of being locked down, I was done being told I couldn't earn a living. The story I'm about to tell is what I and my family endured in the days, months and year that followed this crazy decision. As I had not intended, the story also covers the journey of my life before all of this and how God's plan has been revealed throughout my life. How God used my past experiences to prepare me for this battle. Before I start, I want to make sure that YOU, the reader understands that nothing I did was of my own doing.

Apparently it was brave, strong, bold and inspiring. I've been told by many Americans that I am their hero. But I do not take any credit for the stand that I took. Something in me took hold and gave me the strength to fight this giant, against all odds. God used me in His glory, to stand up for my family and you. I genuinely believe that everything that has happened to me in my life has been part of a bigger plan, to strengthen me for this specific battle. God knew what He was doing when he picked me. I didn't, but He sure did.

> *"The voice of the Lord said 'Whom shall I send? And who will go for us?' And I said 'Here am I. Send me." (Isaiah 6:8)*

I never felt a "calling" to take this stand, I never believed I was doing God's work at the time. But some very amazing people who have come into my life because of this believe that I was. Looking back, I am disconnected from the woman I see in pictures, on the news, and in news articles. I don't recognize her as being me and I think that's because God was hard at work in me, that I wasn't even making my own decisions. If there is any part of this book that strikes you as cocky, or self-indulging, please know that I am not speaking of myself. Everything I did in this battle, I did so with the strength of God, His blessing, and only through His Holy Spirit. If you are a believer, you will know this is the truth, because if I did not have God with me throughout this, you will know that I would have failed, and I could never have endured. This story also has a happy ending and that proves that God is present as well. He has turned this nightmare into a dream. He had a plan the whole time, and although I couldn't see it, my faith kept me going. My belief that God had a plan for us allowed me to continue when everything in the world told me to quit.

> *"The Lord will fight for you; you need only be still." (Exodus 14:14)*

You think you are about to read the story you saw in the news about the brave salon owner, who defied the governor and stood up for Americans. But you are really about to read the intimate details of my personal life and what I was enduring and battling behind the headlines. The emotions and pain that came with what I did. You are also going to read about the greatness of God, and how my unwavering faith got me through. You're about to read a series of events that, with faith, leave NO doubt that God has, throughout this year, placed His people exactly where they needed to be in my life to bless me. He has lined up every detail of this story in a way that cannot be denied,.His plan is being revealed. My God is walking with me. He is present and active in my life. He is almost showing off. (That's a joke). You're about to read my testimony. This is the real story of how I became the Patriot Barbie.

Here is what happened, not what you saw on the news, not little bits and pieces, not hearsay and not mainstream media. Here is what happened to my business, my family and me personally. You aren't going to like it...at first.

CHAPTER TEN

STAY AT HOME ORDERS
(MARCH 23, 2020)

FOR THOSE READING this book years from now, that didn't experience this historical event, let me explain.

There was a virus, called Covid, that was much like the cold or flu, that was contracted in a similar way, through bodily fluids, cough, sneeze, etc. When the news of this virus was released, the scientists behind the study of it had no clue what they were dealing with, and continually changed the rules surrounding this virus almost weekly, sometimes daily. In the beginning, they claimed that the virus lived on surfaces and could be spread by touching things that those who were infected touched. They also claimed that the virus was spread through the tiny particles in someone's mouth and nose fluids. Those particles could "float" in the area for up to 30 minutes, and anyone essentially walking through them could contract Covid.

So they encouraged everyone to wear masks, covering their nose and mouth everywhere they went, even outside. They assured Americans that by wearing a mask, you were "protecting others," which made you a good, caring citizen. "Your mask protects me and my mask protects you". It was BS, to be nice about it. It was conditioning people to believe that we all control each other's health, which is clearly not true. I can't walk up to a stranger and remove the cigarette from their mouth, because I know what's best for them, and I control their health. Right? It sounds fun, and I would record it, but I don't think it would go over well at all. It was also a way for the government to assure us that they knew what was best for us, and they were protecting us. "It's for your own safety."

As the mask propaganda was being regularly promoted, it was still just a suggestion that most were not on board with. Meanwhile, mainstream media was promoting fear, that hundreds of thousands of people were dying from this virus, and that staying home was the best option to save lives. "Staying home" was the government and media's solution to curing a virus.

Let me pause right here really quick to say that the entire concept that anyone other than GOD Himself can control a virus is asinine. No one is God, no one has His power or his control, especially not the stinking government. So from the very first time I heard the Covid crap, I said to myself, "This is ridiculous. Why is the government and media trying to tell us how to control a virus? That's impossible." I immediately saw through the agenda and propaganda. I was awake, if you will, and I was buying little to nothing of what they were trying to sell. I watched as the scientists continued to change their story, discovering that it doesn't really live on surfaces, while half of Americans were buying bleach spray and spraying down their freaking grocery bags and food every day. Wearing gloves, isolating themselves from friends, even family. Refusing to hug or kiss others. People were hysterical with fear, it was working!

This virus, which no one knew anything about, was changing our lives, emotions and normal behavior. As the hysteria built and the media pushed the primal fear into humans on an hourly basis, it was no surprise that the government used this time to authorize a complete act of tyranny, insisting on a complete shutdown of almost every state in the U.S. Across the nation, governors went into press conferences saying, "All non-essential businesses must shut down." Oregon's order was a "stay at home." Meaning, people Americans, humans, were not allowed to leave their home without having an essential job to go to or to go out for medical care or food. Who decided whose job was essential? The governor deciding to enforce this order. His or her OPINION of who was and was not essential. Spoiler alert: a governor's position was essential in all 50 states. Imagine that.

The people telling their citizens that they cannot work, cannot go to school, cannot socialize with their friends and family, cannot leave their house, cannot earn a living gets to do ALL those things. Every governor collected their paycheck and benefits, did press conferences, and continued with their lives. Multiple photographs came out in the media of governors breaking their own rules, attending functions, enjoying life events, all against the very rules they were threatening to enforce. By the way, the penalties threatened by breaking these rules included: a class C misdemeanor, jail time, citations and more. Not one governor suffered any penalties for breaking their own rules. While tax paying, hardworking citizens were being threatened daily to obey and comply without question. After all, "It's for your own safety."

As the rules continued to change, they came up with a term called "social distancing." Seriously, they made this up. This was never a thing before 2020 or at least not that you had ever heard before. Social distancing meant that you would remain 6 feet away from another person at all times because the droplets in their saliva could float around 6 feet of them and you could contract the virus. This would all be very funny because it's so stupid, but it's not because people believed it (still do as I write this,) and it altered the way human beings treat each other and how we interact. It's been devastating to natural human interaction and our emotional well-being.

Months after this virus was identified, doctors and scientists believe they pinpointed the exact moment that Covid came into the U.S. (so ridiculous,) and that is when the hysteria started being promoted and the news stations had continuous tickers on the bottom of their screens showing us how many people have died from Covid. Here's what is sketchy and alarming. Because the government declared this a "pandemic" hospitals and treatment centers were given excessive funding to accommodate Covid patients. So if a patient has Covid, the hospitals made more money. Someone could walk in with a tummy ache, and hospitals would test them for Covid, without any symptoms so that if the test were positive, they would profit. This person could be perfectly healthy and show no symptoms and that hospital made money off them AND now that ticker at the bottom of the news has another scary number to add to the pandemic watch.

As humans built up immunity and began disobeying the ridiculous isolation rules, we started becoming less affected by the virus. People were getting stronger, their bodies were doing what they were supposed to, what God designed our bodies to do, fight it off. Less and less people were dying from Covid. Those numbers were fudged anyway. I know a woman whose husband died in a motorcycle accident. He was decapitated. They took his headless body in and tested him for Covid to "rule it out as cause of death." They stated on his death certificate that he was positive for and had died from Covid. Another number to the hysteria. I know another woman whose husband died of a heart attack. The hospital tested him for Covid and, he was positive. They listed his cause of death as Covid-19 not a heart attack. We were told that hundreds of thousands of people had died FROM Covid, but more than likely they died WITH Covid. Their cause of death was something completely unrelated, but when listed as Covid-19, the hospital received more money. What a scam.

When more people started testing positive and requiring no hospital care, it became a little too obvious that most Americans would completely survive Covid. So, the new propaganda became to strike fear into Americans by running a daily positive test ticker. So, instead of watching a fearful number of how many had died, we were now watching the news run up the alarming numbers of how many people were walking around with Covid. All the while, pushing propaganda to get people to test! After all, you could have it and be spreading it without knowing. You could be killing people!! Get tested immediately to protect others. Yes, scientists were NOW saying that you could be completely symptom free, healthy, and carrying Covid, while spreading it to others. How disgusting and selfish of you. Since testing was being done in mass, of course the number of positive tests were also going to increase. New ticker, new alarming numbers, more panic. Well-done government and well-done news channels.

In the midst of all of this people were starting to wake up, starting to defy and starting to want their rights and freedoms back.

March 23ʳᵈ was a day that brought devastating news to millions of Americans. Governors had shut down all small business, only allowing huge, big box "essential" stores to remain open. Here are some almost comical "essential" stores: Sex shops, weed shops, abortion clinics, gas stations, all big box stores and home improvement stores. Those who could not operate but many would definitely consider essential (if it were about health) were gyms, health facilities, salons, tanning salons, restaurants, small clothing stores. Correct me if I'm being naïve, but in the midst of a "pandemic" (i'm sorry but I cannot say "pandemic" when referring to Covid-19 without quotations. It just wasn't a "pandemic", and it never will be. I cannot call it that in good faith.). In the middle of a "pandemic" that mostly killed unhealthy, older and obese people, I think gyms would be pretty dang essential. That's just me.

What I have said from the beginning, and will continue to say is this, *"Everyone's job is essential. Not because of what we do or how we do it. Because it's how we make our living."* I believe that with every ounce of my being. Every person in America had a right to keep their job, keep their business and keep their social activities exactly as they were. We have a right to make our own health decisions, with accurate and truthful information provided to us to do so. When governors shut down their states, they did so with bias, targeting small business owners.

Those who were actively employed perhaps didn't worry as much, since unemployment and bonus pay was being pumped out and hyped up. They were taken care of. It was the small business owners who promptly had a panic attack. People like myself and my husband. Let's lay down the concepts for people who do not or have not ever owned a business, just so that the mindset of panic in this situation doesn't appear exaggerated.

A business owner pays lease on their space. They typically

pay utilities as well. Some businesses have equipment or electronics that they owe payments or overhead on. And lastly, small business owners pay their own insurance policies.

That's just the business. Please keep in mind that business owners also pay for their own responsibilities with the income provided by the profit of the business.

Typical Americans have a mortgage, two car payments, home insurance, car insurance, home utilities, childcare or school, taxes, credit card debt, and of course the expenses of daily living: food, gas, clothing, cosmetics etc.

When a governor unjustly and unconstitutionally declares that a business cannot operate, the expenses of that business still exist. The owner must still pay for everything that month. Let's say business expenses are $10,000 and the business also profits $10,000. That money is what the owner uses to live off and put away for retirement or invest.

The business is forced to close in March. In April, the owner still owes its $10,000 expenses but the business is not earning any money. So the owner is now in debt $10,000 for a facility that can't operate. (Hopefully, he has it in savings. Probably not. Most Americans don't get wealthy running small businesses.) The owner also doesn't have any personal spending money to pay his mortgage, bills or family needs. Why? Because remember, the governor told him his business wasn't essential, so he hasn't been able to make any money! In May, where is the owner going to get the $10,000 he owes for last month's rent and now this month's rent? His family is now into month two of being unemployed and broke. The business didn't open. It didn't make money. In fact, now its June and he owes another $10,000 to ensure he isn't evicted from his lease, or his equipment isn't repossessed or his utilities turned off.

Now, looking back we know that some landlords did a forbearance on lease. That means simply that the tenant doesn't have to pay the rent until the end of the period. It was about 3 months in some areas. But please remember that in 3 months, that business owner wasn't making any money, now he owes $30,000 all the sudden. Where will he magically get that money after not being able to work for three months? The government promised bail outs and PPP loans and SBA loans, but some owners did not get those or they did not qualify. Some owners got some but not enough to cover these back expenses. Most business owners are driven, hard workers who strive for their goals and want to earn their living fair and square. Most of us were not interested in handouts from the government. We just wanted to work, like always.

Now that you have some concept of the disastrous out-come of a business owner being told to close, please keep in mind that my husband and I owned 6, yes SIX businesses. That's six leases, six overhead expenses, six utility bills and six places not bringing in our family's income. We also had just spent our savings to build our forever home on some property. I had just, 2 weeks prior, gave birth to our third child. I also just signed a loan on a new SUV to cart around those little nuggets.

Let that dramatic number sink in for a moment. With that concept in mind, you might understand why we felt very strongly that being closed any longer than 6 weeks was going to devastate our family. Looking back, I hope you can see that it did indeed devastate millions of people. Why hundreds of thousands of businesses have closed. Why Americans are sick to death of this tyranny. Why, only 6 weeks in, I was ready to take it head on.

CHAPTER ELEVEN

PRE-OPENING

IT WAS AROUND the end of April, I started getting anxiety about what was going to be the future for my family if we continued to be closed. Democrat Governor Kate Brown was stringing her state along, making no promises and lots of threats. We had no clue when her highness would allow us to open. I had had it. I was at the point where I wanted to cautiously take action.

My first step was to call around and see who was enforcing what rules, if any. After all, if I were going to open my business, I wanted to know who was coming for me first and if they actually legally could. My little investigation was highly informative. I sat in my office and started making these important calls.

I called Oregon OSHA first. They had already been in contact with me. A vindictive ex-stylist left on horrible terms and became adamant at hurting me and harming my business. Right after I had my baby, she sent me a cold and callous good-bye via text message, left my clients hanging and skipped out, after being my apprentice and colleague for 2 years!! I didn't realize this until she did this to me, but she is the type of woman who praises and accolades you to your face but the moment you turn your back, begins to slander and demean you to anyone who will listen to her. It's the opposite of women empowerment. Her actions hurt me more than anything else I was going through at the time. In this time of fear and uncertainty for everyone, she could not help but try to somehow slander my business and reputation while she sat on her unemployment with no success in sight. I feel so sorry for her. She spent years with me, watching me speak kind words about other women, building them up and trying very hard not to berate or belittle them. She had to know that I was a good friend to her and anyone I encountered. She had my friendship and she not only refused it but trampled on it. I'm sure she has her own version of how things went down but there isn't a whole lot to say to defend yourself when you are the one actively looking to ruin someone's career and reputation after you left them. Actions will always speak louder than words.

She reported to Oregon OSHA that my salon was still "completely operational" behind closed doors. The report is humorous, because she had not had access to my business for months, and couldn't validate anything, but alas, she was just eager to validate her existence by trying to bring another woman down. I politely replied to Oregon OSHA that the report could not be validated (this is true) and didn't warrant a response.

They agreed and the case was very quickly closed. In truth, there was some client action going on in the salon by other stylists and some of it by me, and I won't apologize for that. I am not ever going to apologize for doing what I had to do to support my family. After that experience, I started wondering if OSHA was really the organization that was being told to enforce the "mandate" and if so, wow, they must be getting a lot of tattle tale phone calls.

On hold with OSHA, their voice recording said something like "We do not enforce stay at home mandates or business closures. I jotted this down and waited for a real person. I asked the real person about the recording and the capacity of OSHA to enforce anything. Her response was essentially that they do not enforce the "stay at home order" and that complaints should be filed with the police department. Interesting.

I called the police department who told me that they also do not enforce the order. All potential violations should be called in to the sheriff's department. I reiterated to this operator that OSHA told me distinctly that I should report businesses to the police department. She was insistent that the information was false. They would not take reports on business violations.

Next, of course I called the sheriff's department. You guessed it. They do not enforce the mandate or order. The man I spoke to told me he didn't know who I should report to. Keep in mind, I am humored by the whole concept that if someone isn't obeying the mandate or a stay-home order, that a neighbor could actually be looking for a way to rat out their friend or neighbor, or in my case, a disgruntled laid off hair stylist. I imagined what it would feel like to be a Karen.

The last phone call was to Oregon Health Licensing to ask them if a hair stylist's license could be suspended or revoked if they were caught violating the mandate. The response was "no." Furthermore, I downloaded the licensing handbook and looked for anything resembling a statute or rule that would apply to this very unique situation. I found none. I was confident that yet again, no form of discipline could be instilled upon me legally, should I decide to, you know, work for a living.

I did a live video in a hair stylist forum on social media. I thought it was important for my fellow stylists to know that not only did I firmly believe that we had a right to work, but that if we did, there really wasn't any legal ramifications of doing so. My question was, "Why aren't we all working?" I knew that I wasn't ok with just sitting around, going into debt. My clients needed me and even though their hair wasn't essential, my ability to pay my bills was. I had been reading the frustration of other local stylists who, like myself did not understand why our salons weren't deemed safe, but these huge grocery stores were. It makes absolutely no sense to anyone who is paying attention and thinking for themselves. I thought if I could show that we could open without consequence, that others might join me in standing up and fighting back! I was very wrong.

After this chain of phone calls and my live video, I made

the decision in my head, firmly, that I was going to open Glamour Salon and I was going to work. There was no doubt in my mind that it was my God given and American right.

At this point, the salon was privately leased property. I had the right to do whatever I wanted with it, in accordance with my lease agreement. Which happened to be with the city of course. I was paying rent on this space to be able to operate a business and being told I could not. I told the stylists quite bluntly that I was not going to be monitoring the premises. It was not my job or responsibility to uphold or enforce this mandate. If they were going to come in and assist clients on their own, I wouldn't know, and I wouldn't care. I also was clear about my feelings surrounding it. I did not support the order and I was not convinced any governor had the right or authority to tell us we can't work. With the salon being accessible to those who leased, I would presume that some girls utilized the facility to do a client here or there. And I don't blame them one bit. They were single moms, bread winners, and even ex-military. They were women who depended on their clients to pay their own rent at the salon, their own mortgages, feed their kids, pay their bills. These women deserved to have a safe place to work. I had been told that other salon owners were monitoring their salon, and made sure not one stylist could even get into it to get their supplies, let alone sneak a client in. I couldn't imagine playing a role in their lives where I assisted in taking their income away. I wanted to be someone they could count on. I wanted them to know that I would always support their right to earn their living, with or without permission from the government.

Before I publicly opened, I had mounds of extension clients desperate to get theirs removed or fixed before it broke their hair off. I obliged. Who was the governor to come between a consenting stylist and client? We both knew the risks and we both agreed to complete the transaction as consenting adults. And darn it, I had a family to care for. "Sneaking clients in" every couple of days is not what I would call a steady income. Nor was it sane to believe that we had to sneak around to do fair commerce in a facility that we pay for and support. I had previously worked 3 days a week, solid hours and with an apprentice. During this period which felt like the speakeasy of hair salons, I could only manage one client at a time, spread out and one or two days a week. I certainly was not the only stylist who was calling a bluff on this so-called pandemic. But no one could operate to their potential under those kinds of circumstances and it was time to open completely. I was not making my regular income and I was definitely not happy with having to act like a criminal in doing so.

At one point, there was a police officer in the parking structure, and someone came in, alarmed, and terrified that we were going to be arrested. They were sure that he was there to watch us and monitor what we were doing. I couldn't imagine for the life of me, what kind of charge an officer could possibly come up with to arrest a hairstylist for doing hair. How is this America? As the days went on, and huge box stores and corporations were open, I realized that there was nothing less safe about our salon than a superstore holding 500 people. Having to smuggle clients in just to make some income here and there was ridiculous. I was furious that it was something we had to hide and feel guilty about.

Right before shutting down, I had 25 stylists leasing at my salon. We were at full capacity and at the pinnacle of our careers! When the mandate went into effect, two stylists had their own studios in the works, so they left to get that going. Why pay rent on a station in my salon that they were no longer allowed to use? Shortly before the shut down and within days of my birthing our third baby, three stylists had done some very inappropriate things and acted unprofessionally so their leases were terminated. As we went into this lockdown, I had "fired" and lost 5 stylists.

My apprentice, as you recall, Brittany, had up until this last month been a "friend," a good apprentice and someone I thought had respected me. I had valued her and everything she brought to the salon and my business. We had fun at work, we laughed, we got along great. I thought she was a friend to me. I found out the hard way that I was wrong. She was completely two-faced and only out for herself. I found out after she left that she had been gossiping, stirring up drama and causing friction in the salon, behind my back. Even though I have forgiven her for some of the horrible things I'm about to tell you, I need to tell this story because it is the kick-off to this horrific year and how people I once trusted became an enemy when they should have been an ally. Brittany had decided that she longer benefited from the business relationship we had agreed upon for almost two years. She decided this while I was in the hospital giving birth to my baby. While coming home from the hospital, she informed me that she was not going to serve my clients as promised while I was on maternity leave, that she was going to another salon, and "thanks for all the opportunities."

For months, we had agreed and signed a contract that she would help manage my clients while I was on maternity leave. She would be paid well for serving them and her work in helping to manage my schedule. She was handed over a full clientele for a month that she never had to work for or earn herself. For both parties, it was beneficial. I knew that my clients would be taken care of and kept in the salon. She would be earning a great income during the month I was gone and would not need her to assist me. Instead of discussing her concerns about this arrangement, she waited until I gave birth to my last child, was home cuddling and loving on him, to rip the rug out from under me with no apologies.

She stole my maternity leave from me as I struggled to re-book clients, apologize and prepare myself for a new apprentice when I returned. She also posted on Facebook that my baby had birth defects. As you recall, baby Ranger has webbed toes, which is hereditary and passed down from Scott's dad. This was something that was beautiful to us and I had been excited to tell everyone this cute story. She posted on Facebook "You know what's disgusting to me? When women drink their entire pregnancy and their baby has birth defects. And they call it cute." She took something that was precious and beautiful to our family and our new baby and made it vicious and ugly. Not only is this statement untrue, but it's also slanderous and hurtful. Also, why? I had never done anything to intentionally hurt her. I accepted her hateful and sudden resignation without mean or angry words. Why would this woman take to social media with a purpose to hurt me, knowing I was at home with a new baby? This story is shocking, I know. These are real things that horrible people do to other people. Clients and friends were reaching out to me in disgust at her behavior and absolutely shocked that an adult would say such a thing. During my entire pregnancy, we had talked about how blessed I felt to have this baby. I was so excited to be in a place in my career where I could take the time off to enjoy him, knowing she would help me out while I was gone. We had spent months nailing down every detail, so that when I was on maternity leave, I could enjoy every minute with my new and last baby. She knew how important it was to me and her behavior makes it that much more painful.

> "Even my close friend, whom I trusted, he who shared my bread has lifted up his heel against me. But you, oh Lord, have mercy on me; raise me up that I may repay them. I know that you are pleased with me, for the enemy does not triumph over me." (Psalm 40:9-11)

I was appalled at what she was doing but wondered if God wasn't telling me that I should have removed this person from my life a long time ago. I just didn't have the heart or courage to do it. I also now think that for what I was about to do, God did not want her to be a part. She was someone I did not need by my side, and she would have been detrimental to the cause. I was continually giving her the benefit of the doubt. But in hindsight I am so glad she was not by my side during my stand. She is not the kind of person I wanted to be associated with, knowing what I know now and she would have tried to capitalize on the events for her favor. God once again was looking out for me, but in a way that was painful at the time. She deserved to be told she couldn't work at my salon, for how she had been behaving months ago, but I was not going to terminate her contract. I give people way too many chances and grace, especially when they don't deserve it. But even as I was weak and forgiving, God was at work, removing the people in my life that did not need to be there.

So here I was, right after my baby's birth, instead of enjoying every second like I had planned I was forced to deal with these unprofessional girls causing major problems in my salon. During the lockdown, Brittany publicly admitted on Facebook to calling OSHA on me, trying to get me fined or shut down. She went so far as to tag the salon. Then she told anyone that would listen that she supported my right to work and was "proud of me" for standing up after I opened. Give me a break. Can you say frenemy?? While trying to do something I believed in, something I am now proud of, something to save my life's work, I was now also dealing with crazy chicks and the emotional damage they cause to everyone around them.

I had a private Facebook group for the stylists that lease at my salon, called "The Glamorous," so we can communicate easily and share things. To about 20 artists now leasing at the salon, here is exactly what I posted on May 2nd.

"Ladies.... my conviction is real and strong. Liquor stores, dispensaries, abortion clinics and adult shops are open. Massive retail stores are open. Kate Brown just reserved her right to extend this until July.

It is going to be a hard uphill battle, but I feel this: I HAVE TO STAND UP FOR MY FAMILY. I have to stand up for my rights. I have to open my salon and ensure that our government does not take away our civil liberties again. They can now do this to us any time they want... we stood by and let them take away our right to earn a living. I just can't do it. I've done my research and I feel confident I will not suffer great or even any consequences. I do so at my own risk, and I am ok with it. I am retaining an attorney on Monday and moving forward. If you are not taking clients, this will not affect you and when we can "legally" do hair, I'll be excited to see you!!!!

If you are not interested in taking this stand with me, I don't blame you one bit and I would encourage doing your clients at their home or yours. If you want to be a part of this revolution, please text me. We need to all be on the same page and things NEED to be handled a certain way. I'll be starting this process Monday and when I go in to work Tuesday, I will do so openly with a salon that is accepting clients. I don't expect everyone to agree with this decision or my beliefs. But I do need to do what I believe is best for us as business owners and for my family. I hope I can get most of your support because I am going to need it and I'm going to need people to rally behind me and get others to rally behind me."

Turns out, not very many of these stylists wanted to rally behind me. Interesting, because throughout my entire career, I have been someone who strives for women empowerment. I have gone above and beyond for most of the stylists, helping them build their brand, improve their skills and market themselves. I've given leniency in times of need.

I've had stylists who haven't paid rent for months on end, giving me random excuses repeatedly. I have given them the benefit of the doubt, being lenient and hoping that I'm giving them the opportunity to catch up, get their affairs in order. Only to find they've moved their stuff out in the middle of the night owing me thousands of dollars. I've put hours in where I didn't have to, to help someone build their clientele. I'm no angel, but I know my strengths and I know my weaknesses. I have always, always had my stylists' back when they needed me and encouraged them in every way. And when I needed it most, they did not have mine. Mind you, it's not that they didn't believe in their right to work. They did. They just didn't want to have my back if things didn't go well.

"To do what is right and just is more acceptable to the Lord than sacrifice." (Proverbs 21:3)

Upon opening, even though they had signed and committed to one-year long leases, four stylists told me they were leaving the salon and walked out. These are women I had known for years. These are women whose businesses were largely built by my hard work at the salon and my dedication to creating an amazing salon for them to work. Their clientele had been built by the new clients coming to my salon. They took it all for granted and bailed on me without looking back. I was too distracted at the time to worry about it. I figured it was best that anyone who didn't support this cause wasn't present for the tribulation of it. I also wished them well in their new endeavors. In my mind, I was justifying their actions by admitting that they did not have the strength to stand up for themselves, and that was ok. I would do it for them.

CHAPTER TWELVE

THE PLAN TO REOPEN
(SATURDAY MAY 2ND, 2020)

THE DECISION TO open my business 6 weeks after lockdown was most definitely not a hard one. We were truly getting anxious and desperate. Our family survived on the income generated by our businesses. It's all we did. We had worked our entire marriage, building them up to a place where we could enjoy our free time, provide for our kids and have financial freedom. Having a governor close our businesses for 6 weeks was ruining that financial freedom. We woke up every day watching our savings dwindle, our investments collapse and wondered if we would even be able to keep them after all the financial debt this lockdown was causing. We were very likely going to have to start selling off our possessions we had worked so hard for to pay down all the overdue bills that were going to accumulate.

We had started pulling money back out of retirement and investment accounts to keep the businesses afloat. Neither my husband nor I wanted the government to "save us." We did not want a handout and unemployment paychecks. Not only was it deficient in helping us, but we believed in hard work and earning your money. Even with this belief we felt forced to apply for every single grant, loan and relief that we could.

After all, we were paying the lease on 6 commercial buildings, the overhead and the utilities for all 6 locations, and dipping into our savings just to pay our personal bills. Anyone who has ever owned a business knows this lockdown was devastating. Not to mention we didn't volunteer to shut down. We didn't get a choice in the matter. We were being tyrannically TOLD that we couldn't operate. We felt we had no choice but to apply for the grants being offered. Otherwise, we would be filing for bankruptcy. Government had created this problem and was now offering the "solution." That is not ironic people. That is planned.

Turns out, we weren't getting any unemployment pay anyway! The state of Oregon wasn't prepared to offer unemployment to small business owners. People who were actually employed started receiving benefits almost immediately. Others were forced to wait months as the system crashed and overloaded (gosh who could have predicted that?). Small business owners were told to apply and that ours would be approved. False. I personally applied twice and got rejected in the 6 weeks we were closed because I was self-employed. Then I was told to reapply under the brand-new program for self-employed. Then rejected twice again due to computer error. I was forced to reapply 3 more times.

Then I just gave up. I was receiving all sorts of random rejection and approval and re-apply letters. I basically had accepted that I was not going to get any support from the unemployment department. And finally, 8 months later, in October 2020, I randomly received my unemployment for the six weeks I was closed. Scott was denied repeatedly and never offered any unemployment benefits, despite our hundreds of thousands of contributions to this agency over the years as business owners.

After 6 weeks of closure, and no end in sight, it was simple. I was going to open my salon, I was going to let my stylists who rent their stations, work. I was going to earn a living because in my heart I knew certain things. I knew that this lockdown was not right, morally or ethically. I knew that it violated my liberties, my freedoms and everything that America stands for. I just knew that I had to do it and whatever the consequences might be, it wouldn't matter. Someone had to stand up, or we were all going to fall.

> *"The righteous cry out and the Lord hears them; He delivers them from all their troubles. The Lord is close to the brokenhearted and saves those who are crushed in spirit. A righteous man may have many troubles, but the Lord delivers him from them all." (Psalm 34:17-19)*

Even though I did feel a small amount of bravery in what I was doing, mostly because everyone was saying so, I had no idea what it would become. I had no idea how brave I would need to be in the weeks ensuing.

I decided on May 2nd that I was going to open my salon the next week on a Tuesday and allow stylists to work. But most importantly, I was going to work also. I was going to take clients, serve them and collect my income as a stylist. I didn't want an "essential job." My job IS essential, and as I told you, I stated in one of my press conferences, "Every job is essential. Not because of what we do, or how we do it, but because it's how we make our living." I don't know where that statement came from, if not just the deep, true belief of every American who was suffering loss due to lockdowns. Who was Kate Brown to decide who was and was not allowed to work? Why was her opinion of essential the only opinion that mattered? Why couldn't I decide for myself that my job was essential? I've stated many times that I don't believe that getting your hair done is actually essential. I don't. We will live if we have grey hair. We will live if it gets a little long. Heck, we will live if our hair extensions grow out, break off and cause bald spots. We will. It would suck, but we would live. But no one has said, and I have never said that a hair appointment is essential. I'm saying and what I've continued to say is that my ability to work is. And I am right, you'll never convince me otherwise.

And to be perfectly honest, there isn't a pandemic in the world that gives the government the right to take that away. I don't at all consider Covid-19 a pandemic, and the truth has shown us that it wasn't. Here we are, 18 months later and the media and Dr. Fauci are still changing the rules, launching phony vaccines that don't work and trying to escalate the numbers for hysteria. But even in a true pandemic, the role of the government should always have been to educate its citizens, truthfully, and then allow them to make their own health decisions. Anyone who thinks otherwise is a communist.

In my line of work specifically, it's that simple. If you don't think getting your hair done is essential, and you are afraid you may catch Covid at my salon, you are more than welcome to exercise your rights to NOT COME IN. I will gladly take clients who want an appointment, and they will gladly support me for taking them. It's called free commerce and it's beautiful. It's based on educated adults making their own decisions to trade a service for payment and do business together. It's an American right by the Constitution and during Covid the government trampled all over it by convincing quite a few sheep that our sole job in this universe was to now be responsible for every other American's health.

With my decision to re-open and my conviction rock solid, I attended a Re-Open Oregon rally and was determined to see for myself how many people in my city were supportive of businesses being able to operate. There were a LOT! It gave me hope that I would have the support of my community.

I posted my intentions on a Facebook group, called Open Oregon, filled with likeminded individuals who no longer supported the lockdowns and closures. I wasn't paying attention really to the group statistics and didn't realize that it was a public group! I posted this:

> "I just wanted to reach out to say that I'm opening my business on Tuesday, government be damned. I would appreciate knowing that should I get arrested or need additional support, I can beg for some here. It's a hair salon. I'll be doing hair and selling retail. I'm in downtown Salem. I'm opening smart and safe and hoping to be an example. Thank you for the support already!"

This post had 594 comments, nearly all supportive and encouraging. The post was shared 128 times publicly, and I was getting more attention than I expected. I didn't realize that the post could be shared outside of the group. I thought the group was private but it was public. Anyone could share the post on their social media and they did. Oops.

What I also discovered was that the moment I made this announcement, I had basically committed to this action, and now saw that hundreds of people were going to count on me to follow through. This is an aspect that I never considered and have really never addressed, even to myself. I basically promised these people that I would do this brave thing and I wasn't even sure I was brave enough to do it. After all, there were threats of arrest and jail for those who didn't comply. I watched throughout the day as it was shared over and over. By the end of the first day, nearly 70 shares and thousands of views and comments. Uh oh. What did I do?

Shortly after my realization that this was becoming very public, the local news stations started reaching out. Was I really going to open? When? And why?

I've never been afraid of public speaking, and I've never hated attention. I am a loud, boisterous person in all elements of my life and I am not shy. It didn't scare me to interview with the news, and actually I felt that it was extremely important to shine light on the devastation this was causing small businesses and their families. Did all the people collecting unemployment realize that business owners didn't get that? That we still have all our responsibilities and no bail out? I knew in my heart that I needed to control the narraive of this story and ensure that I spoke the truth about why I was opening, and make sure that America saw the tragedy unfolding right in front of them.

As it turns out, allowing the media to hear and print the intimate details of my opening was the best decision for the journey I was about to embark on. Had I done this quietly and covertly, perhaps I wouldn't have been so harassed and attacked by both the government and my community. But I would not have reached the massive supporters across the nation that had my back, supported me and donated to my legal fight.

After my post in the Open Oregon group, I had a man reach out to me, offering his help. I asked if he was an attorney, he replied "Message me". So, I did. This is one of those times where I was responding to hundreds of messages and comments and for some reason, God led me to this one. I could have easily ignored it and moved on. Was I really going to privately chat with EVERY person who said they would help me? But I felt inclined to message him and it was the best decision I could have made that day.

Roger was well connected, involved in the conservative/ Republican circuit, well known, and highly intelligent. He told me that he would connect me with an attorney he knew well and trusted and was educated in constitutional law.

Roger connected me with Rick Day, who would later become my official attorney, and the one who filed my lawsuit against the state. Rick came onto the scene with no retainer, no promises and no idea where this act of defiance would take us. He was someone I immediately trusted and confided in. He joined my inner circle simply because he was passionate about what I was doing, believed in me and helped me without asking anything up front or in return.

I knew that he was there to stand up for what was right. I also knew that I could not have gone through with it had he had not been there. He was my council and my advisor. When I wanted to quit because I was risking my entire livelihood, he would show me how we could beat this. He never had to convince me to keep going but he did have to encourage me to continue to think logically and legally.

We both believed with all our hearts that our constitutional rights were being taken and we were fighting for everyone who supported us. Roger continued to stand by my side, making news appearances when Rick could not. Roger never asked for anything in return. Never. He simply wanted to help the good guys. God miraculously brought these men right to me; the strong and capable men I needed to lean on in the time I needed it most. I would not have gotten through this trial without both of them.

> *"This is the confidence we have in approaching God: that if*
> *we ask anything according to His will, He hears us. And if*

we know that He hears us-whatever we ask-we know that
we have what we asked of Him." (1John 5:14-15)

With my face and story now widespread in the media,
Oregon OSHA showed up at my salon before I even opened.
Aaron Colemone knocked on my window and proceeded to
lay out all the penalties I would incur should I open my doors
the next day. It was intense. I hadn't even done this brave thing
yet,and I was already about to fold. He told me that I was not
permitted to open according to the governor's mandate. Here's
where I started to realize what my life was about to become.
If I opened my doors the next day, I would be issued a citation of $1,000. I told him I would keep my doors locked and he
wouldn't be permitted in without a warrant. He said he would
indeed get a warrant. I told him "Well, you're going to have to
get a warrant then. I'm not letting you in tomorrow."

Aaron told me that after he issued the first citation, I
would need to close and if I did not, I would be issued a red tag
citation, deeming my facility unfit for business. It would mean
that my facility was a danger to the community and it came
with a $70,000 fine. I hung my head, then I shook my head,
then I bowed my head in defeat. I could not afford to lose my
business and pay that kind of fine. Even with all these people
backing me up. It was too much for one little salon owner. I
was opening so I could MAKE money, not end up bankrupt or
in debt. I guess I must have posted this update online, maybe
in the group, maybe on my Facebook. Remember, this time in
my life was a blur. I had a newborn, we were stressed about
losing our businesses and our home and now I was taking on
the governor single handedly. I was tired, excited and stressed,
all at the same time.

Either way, I made sure that the public knew that I could
not open. I could not absorb that kind of financial debt. Well,
the public had other intentions. A GoFundMe account was
created by a friend to help with my fines. It was shared. I started seeing that America was ready to fund this stand. I saw
the comments of my community, practically begging me not
to back down. Pleading with me to push forward. If I were to
close down my business again, it would mean that the gov-

ernment had won, and that their control and power over us would be imminent. I knew that if I backed down that quickly, no other business would have the courage to open up behind me. That day, I watched the funds grow, and even though it was nowhere near $70,000, I acted in pure faith.

The next day, May 5th, I re-opened Glamour Salon.

CHAPTER THIRTEEN

THE RE-OPENING: DAY ONE
(TUESDAY MAY 5TH, 2020)

THE SUPPORT WAS overwhelming. The crowd on the sidewalk brought me to tears. The knowledge that people I didn't even know were counting on me was a little intimidating. News crews had gathered outside the salon to capture the moment I actually opened my doors publicly.

Sometimes I wonder if they thought I wouldn't do it. Trust me, the thought crossed my mind. A lot. But the reality of what I was doing had started to sink in. I've told friends this: At that moment in my life and since then, I have felt as though the person who opened Glamour Salon and stood up to her governor, who continues to fight tyranny and is taking on the liberal cancel culture, is someone else. It's as though I have an alter ego and she is someone very different than the woman who is a goofy, sensitive, self-conscious mom, friend and wife. I don't know how to explain it, except that even when reading either hateful or supporting comments about me, I sort of separate myself from that person. I know what she did and I know exactly what she feels and what she stands for, I just have a hard time believing I'm her. I see her picture in news feeds and in news articles, but I don't recognize her as myself. I'm guessing that's why I kept forging forward, she took over for me. I am a normal person, a wife, a mom, a really crazy friend, a goofball, and an open book. I am just a girl who wanted to work, and darn it, I hate being told what I can and cannot do.

This other person, The Patriot Barbie, she has strong, real convictions and has nothing to lose. She stands up for her own rights, her family and her country on a daily basis. That chick is on fire for America and is a loose cannon, ready to fire at whoever dares threaten her rights and livelihood. My husband can now ultimately declare who is talking at any given point. If a political conversation starts, I am usually casually invested, and when something gets said that violates my beliefs, well, Patriot Barbie takes over. She gets louder, more vigilant and steadier. She doesn't waiver. She is a force to be reckoned with. When she's done, I shake my head and ask myself, "What just happened?" Patriot Barbie is the American who opened her salon against the lockdowns, not me.

The days that would follow were, in one way, a LOT like what I should have expected. And somehow, in another, shocking. I could envision being arrested and that didn't scare me. But what really happened was so much worse. After seeing how much attention the government agencies were paying to my case, I now expected that at some point I would indeed be in jail or that my business would be raided and quite literally boarded shut. I had been following the stories of what I now call "patriots," who had opened their businesses. There were only a couple at this time. Americans who were standing up for their freedoms and reclaiming their God given right to work and operate their business. As shocking as this sounds, there were less than a handful. In regards to opening up publicly, I was about the third or fourth in the entire United States.

I was particularly interested in the journey of Shelley Luther, a salon owner in Dallas, Texas. She opened her salon, which consisted of employees and allowed her employees to earn a living. She wouldn't name who was in her salon working and wasn't actually working herself, as she was not a stylist. She had been harassed by her local government endlessly. She was constantly in the media vocalizing what she was going through and what each day brought. Every day I watched her videos and told myself that I should be doing that too. She is brave, and she is fighting for her employees, her family and herself. Why is she alone? Why is no one else standing up too? And then it sort of slapped me in the face what a hypocrite I was, judging every business owner in Texas for not having her back. While I sat by with my doors shut also. I started researching the different authorities in Oregon and seeing who was enforcing these illegal mandates. You would think that I would have said to myself "Ok, so you're going to get all that too...." But what I really said to myself was "Well, nothing legally has happened to her, just threats, so I should be ok. Besides, the RIGHT thing to do is open up. We have a right to work. There is no way it can be legal or constitutional to take away our living." (*insert laughing emoji)

> *"Many women do noble things, but you surpass them all."*
> *(Proverbs 31:29-31)*

It's important to note that the day we re-opened against the mandate was actually our 11-year anniversary of opening to the day! Ironic, I thought after someone brought it to my attention. Eleven years ago I was a young stylist, trying to build the salon of my dreams. The dream had gotten bigger and bigger throughout the years until I finally felt like I had "made it." Then the government told us we didn't have the right to work. At 11 years, I was now watching it all fall apart. I didn't realize the importance of this date until after we re-opened. I announced the expected release of this book on the exact day, one year later on May 5th, 2021.

Oregon OSHA had told me the day before, as you may recall, that they would come to my salon if I re-opened and cite me. I learned that if you are "closed" and your doors are locked, they cannot come in without a warrant. For this reason, I had the salon doors locked. Only appointments and retail sales were going to be allowed in. Not just looky-loos. Plenty of people wanted to come in and thank us for our stand, and that was always welcomed. We needed to hear it.

I had 16 stylists still and didn't anticipate the loss of any more stylists. The ones standing by me seemed strong and ready to take on whatever came our way. The ones who were nervous just claimed that they would wait until everything was "legal" to start working again. It didn't matter to me who did what. I just knew that I did need to work.

Only four were willing to actually work on re-opening day. Their nerves were shot. They were terrified that we were all going to get arrested or worse. They had booked their own clients and I was desperately trying to get in all the clients wanting to support us.

The phones were ringing off the hook. I had three young girls volunteer to come in and help with the phones, emails and messages. They could not keep up. It was alarming. As the story started reaching national news outlets, we were getting calls from around the entire nation, wishing us well. People were so supportive and encouraging. It really was their support that kept me going strong. At one point, I was at the front desk and there were four pages full of phone messages, front and back. She said, "I keep trying to call people back, but the phone won't stop ringing!" It was surreal and again, felt like an out of body experience. Who was this brave person everyone was calling to praise?

Mail was coming in loads from people who had read or seen the story about our opening and wanting to send supportive letters and donations to the cause. Here are some of the beautiful words that were written to me:

"The severe and cruel treatment you have received from our state government, along with many other small businesses, is unfair and unjust. I know that the stand you are taking takes courage, strength and bravery."

"God bless your family and you are a great patriot. We need more like you."

"You are so brave and courageous! We stand with you and will fight for you!"

"Thank you for standing up for what is right and the

American worker. I applaud your bravery and courageous attitude. Stay strong!!!"

"Do not give up your fight! Sending positive energy to
your spirit!"

"I just wanted to let you know how much I admire you
and how proud I am of all you have done. I wish you
the best."

"I am so thankful for folks like yourself who are standing up."

I received both negative, hateful and supportive reviews on my
new public Facebook page:

"She's a true patriot and an inspiration for us to stand up
against draconian politicians."

"She is all of us. She is Oregon. She is the American
Dream... People that are mad at her for wanting to feed
her family (based on Science and Actual Facts) prove their
true alliance is with Big Brother Government and wants
welfare."

"Thank you Lindsey for fighting for what's right! You are
so brave! You are the kind of person that this country was
made of and for! God bless you and your family!"

"I love how Lindsey stands for what is right. Americans
have Constitutional rights that the Democratic party
keeps trying to dissolve and Lindsey Graham refuses to be
bullied by Kate Brown and her abuses of power."

"She is amazing and has the strength to stand up for her
rights. Keep up the good fight."

"Some people will do anything for their 5 seconds of fame,
including risking the lives of other people. Thankfully we

can rest assured that her 5 seconds are almost up and soon she'll go back to being just another boring Nazi woman."

I would like to point out that there were many, many more hateful ones. I can't find them now because I blocked the haters! Haha! They can't torment me if they can't connect with me. Bye, Felicia! But during this time, I recall constantly being berated and called names, simply for opening my business. I was a "murderer." I opened because I "wanted to be famous," or "wanted attention." I didn't need any of that. I was content with how my life was going prior to being shut down. It was the lockdowns that started a fire inside me that wanted to rage against this tyranny.

Honestly though, my biggest problem at that moment was that I did not have enough stylists to accommodate the appointment waiting list. It was actually a bit frustrating! Here I was, standing up for their right to work and the majority didn't want to work! I couldn't get stylists to work! They were all too afraid of the consequences. Again, America?

The cancel culture started immediately. I did my first ever press conference in front of the salon the day we opened. Multiple news stations were outside and newspaper reporters. Cameras were being set up and a load of microphones jammed into one area, where I was supposed to stand and deliver some sort of statement. I had never done anything like this before and had no clue what I was doing.

When face to face with the cameras and news stations, I find myself humorous now. This is what they call a press conference and it was about me. I walked out with my new attorney Rick Day, and said to them "Ok, go ahead." Rick tapped my shoulder and said, "You should start." Oops. Was I supposed to write something up for this? Rehearse? Practice in the mirror beforehand? I had never even considered that this would happen, and I didn't even know what they cared to hear about. Listen, I was just opening my business. That's normal stuff. How did we get to a point in America where my working for a living became national news? Well, I started by thanking the people standing outside cheering, the drivers honking and the online comments of love and support. That's all I remember. That one chick took over. I think she calls herself Patriot Barbie now.

After my news interviews started airing, it was confusing to read some of the comments being made. Here I was, standing up for myself and other business owners, expressing my right to work and earn a living and people were attacking my looks, my motive, my demeaner, my personality, anything they could find. I was shocked to find that so many people were offended by my lips!!! I had always been insecure about my thin lips as a young adult and when I started investing in my appearance, as I aged, I got lip fillers and became so much more confident. I have never been shy about admitting some of the fun medi-spa services I get. I got Botox, and fillers, I wear lash extensions and hair extensions. It's just who I am, I'm kind of high maintenance like that; I am open about it, and I really don't care if people don't approve. I don't tell anyone else how they are supposed to look, so why should they be judging what I do? So, my lips (so weird) became a hot topic on the commenting section. It was baffling.

This is the adult version of bullying, internet bullying and mean girl tactics. I hope these parents don't wonder where their kid got it from. I also was genuinely surprised that people felt offended by what I was doing. Why in the world was my right to work controversial? They don't have to come to my salon and I'm not telling them to. I'm simply expressing my freedoms to run my business and if customers want to be served, they are expressing their freedoms. It was so simple, but a percentage of the population had decided that because of what I was doing, they were entitled to attack and harass me based on any number of things they deemed fit.

> *"In no way be alarmed by your opponents—which is a sign of destruction for them, but of salvation for you, and that too, from God." (Philippians 1:28)*

I'm entertained now, thinking back to the cancel culture, who originally had started the social media rumor that I "was a millionaire." They googled it. Yes, googled my income. That's not real. They insinuated that I was trying to use my opening as a publicity stunt to "steal people's money," referring to the GoFundMe money that people were DONATING! Don't ask me how I am supposed to be stealing money that was gifted to me.... Months later, they were still looking for a narrative and someone suggested that I did NOT have lip fillers (yes, we are back to my lips) in my first interview and suddenly I did, later. So I had used the GoFundMe money to get lip injections. Oh my gosh, stop. I can't make this up. Look, if I'm the millionaire you suggested weeks ago, why would I need to STEAL donated money to get a $350 service? A small bit of research on their part would also see that I had an injections specialist at my salon sooooo....yeah.

Some of the more shocking cancel culture tactics involved completely falsifying information and stories about my husband and me. On Reddit.com you can be assigned a user name, and anonymously say whatever you want about anyone. So it was easy for anyone to make up stories about me, start their own narrative and even spread rumors about my family. One thread claims that my husband and I are swingers and live in a community with other swingers. It claims that we are both bisexual and that my third baby isn't my husband's. One person even fabricates an ENTIRE night, where we supposedly went with them to a swinger's club and then details about everything that happened that night. I do not, at all, understand who has the time to concoct entire stories about people and then sit down and write it publicly. What is the motivation behind telling lies about my husband and me?

I can't recall any situation where I have wronged or hurt someone so terribly that they would want to cause this kind of damage to my reputation permanently. I also can't imagine being so bored that I would take this kind of time out of my day to fabricate stories about someone and then continue to read and reply to comments about it. I feel horrible for whoever felt this was a productive use of time, and how unhappy they must be with their own life.

In this weird and unnecessary time of being a "victim," I reflected on my own behavior as a human and business owner. There have been plenty, if not an abundance of times in my life I have been hurt by someone personally or professionally. There are plenty of people that have wronged me. I'm not special. We've all been hurt and we've all hurt people. Not only is it unfortunately a common occurrence amongst women in general, but as a business owner especially. Believe it or not, I used to be a very sensitive person. Finding out a friend had said something terrible about me was like a dagger in the chest. I was prone to being hurt very easily. As you read, you'll find out why I am no longer this way.

In my life as a salon owner and female, I have endured moments I considered heartache when someone I thought loved me, someone I trusted, acted in a way that was purposefully hurtful. I can remember distinctly the ones that really did emotional damage, and although I hold no anger any longer, I can still recall exactly how I felt in the moment that I experienced it. Like many, I am guilty of wishing revenge, thinking of ways to make them pay for their actions. I mean, who doesn't love a bit of karma? Who doesn't think about the ways you COULD get them back if you wanted to?

But the beautiful thing was that I never did. I would connect with God, ask for a forgiving heart and remind myself that not only would it not make me feel any better, but I needed to focus on the positive things in life. Also, it has always been my premise to "take the high road." This way, I can sleep at night. And lastly, knowing that when the story is told later, that they can say whatever they like (truthful or not) but they know in their heart that I did not seek retribution. That made me always, always the bigger person.

Spending time harming someone else is never good for the soul and it never satisfies the way you expect it to. Don't get me wrong, if that person gets their own karma, I may smile. But I was not going to be the one dishing it out. I have never started a rumor about anyone in my life. I try very hard not to talk about others behind their back. I have never set out to ruin someone's reputation. If someone has done something to me that is unethical, unprofessional or downright nasty, I will tell the truth upon asked, absolutely. But I'm not the person blasting anyone on social media or calling and texting everyone to air their dirty laundry. I have never devoted time out of my life to enact revenge on them.

It may have taken time, but eventually, I moved on and forgave and just hope that eventually they'll get theirs. Or maybe they'll finally recognize their behavior and apologize. Watching people do this to me, taking time out of their day, focusing on this kind of hate, that is foreign to me. There are so many more productive ways to spend time, especially as a parent, spouse or business owner. While enduring the drama of random strangers making up stories about me, I was also now reading stories of disgruntled ex-stylists who wanted their moment to shine and use my name to get attention.

> *"The troubles of my heart have multiplied; free me from my anguish. Look upon my affliction and my distress and take away all my sins. See how my enemies have increased and how fiercely they hate me! Guard my life and rescue me; let me not be put to shame, for I take refuge in you. May integrity and uprightness protect me, because my hope is in you." (Psalm 25:17-21)*

I had a stylist that had barely worked at Glamour a couple months before I reopened. She was failing miserably at her other salon and could barely contain her excitement at coming to Glamour and doing well. She showed respect for me as an owner and was grateful for her opportunity with my salon. She was at my salon less than two months when she sent me a text that she didn't feel safe working during Covid and wanted to only pay half her rent since she wasn't working. Geez, we are adults, aren't we?

After explaining to her how a business works and apologizing for the confusion on her part, she quit, moved her stuff out and didn't tell me until after she had left and I had informed her that her rent bounced. I sent her a kind message telling her I hope she succeeds in her next job but that her behavior was completely unprofessional. Then, of course, when my story went national, (not when this actually happened) she got on social media and couldn't wait to tell everyone how horrible of a person I was, how I was trying to make money off my stylists during a "pandemic." And how she walked out and was so glad she did. It was incredible that she could say anything she wanted, true or not, and her post was shared over and over as cold hard truth.

Remember karma? I found out that she had to remove her post on Facebook because people were telling her what a horrible person SHE was for trying to slander her boss just to get attention. She never did hair at another salon after this, and no one would hire her because, well, she took to social media to slander her last salon owner. Would you hire someone like that? Karma. And I never once even texted this girl to tell her how horrible I felt because of the things she was posting about me. I wanted to. I wanted to, trust me. I considered reaching out to her and simply tell her how disappointed I was, that after taking a chance on her, giving her a new opportunity and welcoming her with open arms into my salon, that she would sink low enough to trash me publicly and without remorse just to get attention. But I didn't. And of course, looking back, it didn't matter. I learned quickly that anyone would really say whatever they liked about me, and since nothing can be proven true or untrue, I needed to not worry about it. I KNEW MY TRUTH. I was accountable to God only and He knew who I was.

"Do not fear them, for the Lord your God is the one fighting for you." (Deuteronomy 3:22)

Inside Glamour Salon, the day was a complete whirlwind. I remember that I did clients, a normal amount and that it was satisfying. I was doing clients while talking to friends, while managing social media, while answering questions, while scheduling interviews, while saying hi to people who wanted to support us.

I am honored to now know Brad, our first client of the day, who knocked on the door to come in for a haircut. He was the first client in the door, and he deserved that moment. In my mind, I will never forget the exact moment he walked in, and the roar of applause and shouts outside, as we became one of the first businesses in America to open up. Brad was a veteran, a patriot, and became a huge part of our story, as it turns out. He is someone that God placed in that role for a purpose.

I remember that there was complete chaos all day long as stylists scrambled to serve the clients trying to get in. We could have worked for 24 hours straight, for a week, getting clients in that were desperate to support us. It was incredibly satisfying and momentous.

I remember that no one from OSHA showed up to cite me $1,000.

It was one small victory.

Throughout the day, I was overwhelmed with news interviews, media, social media, emails, texts, messages, clients and stylists. This was something I didn't even consider. I had no clue that the media would run with my story to any extent, let alone this one and at a national level. I really was naïve as to what I was doing. It was a bigger deal than I realized or recognized. At some point in the day, someone said "Lindsey, you have $60,000 in donations on GoFundMe."

I was flabbergasted. I didn't even get a visit from OSHA. I thought they were bluffing. I couldn't imagine why they were going to let me get away with being open a whole day, unless they didn't have any legal authority. I didn't really expect people to fund my potential $70,000 citation, especially if I didn't get one. Without OSHA showing up, I was feeling way too confident. I thought it meant I was in the clear! I celebrated entirely too soon.

Things were brewing in the shadows that I wouldn't suffer until days later. Government officials were behind the scenes, having meetings about me, looking for ways to shut me down. A whistleblower later told me that a big wig in the health licensing office was meeting with another big wig, discussing my opening and was heard to say, "Just find a way to get her!"

The governor, Kate Brown, held a press conference regarding the shutdowns, praising those were obeying them and giving them accolades for their choice to keep people safe. She said that what Lindsey Graham is doing is "dangerous and irresponsible." She said that no one should be using a pandemic as a publicity stunt. This is close to word for word, but the article can't be tracked down. She had deliberately and publicly slandered me and was clearly targeting me.

CHAPTER FOURTEEN

DAY TWO
(WEDNESDAY MAY 6TH, 2020)

I RECEIVED A letter from the city of Salem, who I leased my salon space from. This was obviously a letter determined to intimidate me. I was in for a rough week and it was just beginning. The letter was less of a direct threat and more of a statement. Basically, that I was violating my lease according to a portion of a paragraph that vaguely outlined my agreement to obey all laws in the state and city. This mandate was not a law and I knew it.

Later that day, I had to go live on social media at 2:00 pm and let the nation know that I was not being arrested. There were supporters on the sidewalk with American flags, megaphones and lots of boisterous patriotism. I had construction paper over all the windows so people couldn't see inside, and obviously so the media couldn't take our pictures and blast our "unsafe practices." As you can imagine, it's impossible to "social distance" doing someone's hair. Truth be told, my clients and customers did not support the fake mask agenda, and quickly removed theirs after coming inside. They told me not to wear mine either. Since then, we have not enforced masks in the salon once, even when the paper came down. While the supporters were outside rallying, the police showed up to ensure everything was peaceful and calm and legal. It quickly circulated social media that I was rumored to be getting arrested. I started getting texts and phone calls. It was quite humorous to me but apparently a lot of my friends and family were hysterical. I even remember my mother-in-law texting me later that week and I didn't have time to respond right away. I texted her back and wrote "This is Scott. I have her phone. Lindsey got arrested." She was not amused.

I got word that Oregon OSHA had attempted to come to my salon and conduct an investigation. In other words, they were going to come to my salon, investigate and find a way to issue me some kind of citation. Their report that I accessed later states that they had received direct word from the Governor's office to instigate this. The governor needed to make an example of me. Word had it that the OSHA investigators saw the mass crowds of supporters outside and assumed they would be met with some form of altercation, possibly violence. In my mind, the passion and gusto that these supporters had, I would not have put it past them to physically remove OSHA from my door. Or I could see them locking arms and creating a barrier and I would have been pleased with that. I don't condone or enjoy violence anywhere in my life but knowing that we were up against a corrupt governor with a ferocious agenda, even a vendetta against me, I would have enjoyed watching a government agency be escorted off my property gently.

Here is an interesting story that only came to me months after. This is how the miracle of God works and it is chilling!

The supporters had been outside my salon for nearly three days when I received a phone call from the Salem Police Department and Oregon OSHA representatives. The call was basically a courtesy, telling me that they had indeed secured a warrant to investigate my business. They intended to investigate physically but, again, were concerned about an altercation in doing so. The Salem Police Department was, on behalf of OSHA, respectfully asking me to call off the crowd in order to prevent potential violence, keep peace in the community and overall allow my business to operate smoothly and without incident. If I were to ask the crowd to disperse and stop protesting outside, OSHA promised that they would not come to my business, but instead conduct their investigation via conference call. At this point, I had retained an exceptionally good OSHA attorney, George Goodman, who was involved in every conversation I had with Oregon OSHA.

This referral to George came from one of my husband's very dear friends, something that I don't consider coincidence. He and I agreed that because of my unwavering respect for law enforcement and my desire to maintain a peaceful reopening, I would ask the people outside to leave, respectfully. I trusted George based on his experience and I wanted to do what felt right. Protecting myself wasn't my first priority; keeping the peace and being respectful was. I knew that my supporters wouldn't understand. It pained me to have to tell them. I wanted them there, I needed them. I was so grateful for them, but this was the right decision. I didn't want my re-opening to turn into a violent or dangerous circus and I certainly wanted to be respectful to my local police officers. It was a favor they were asking, and I was going to oblige.

For months after this, I regretted this decision. After all, OSHA did issue me a $14,000 citation four days later. After all the respect and consideration I was giving out to my community and these organizations, their response was to unjustly cite me. So, for 6 months I kept asking myself why in the world I cooperated. I often wondered what would have happened if I hadn't. Would violence have occurred, or would OSHA simply not have come back? Would they come back and find that they had no right to investigate and be forced to walk away? What if I hadn't cooperated at all and maybe I would never have been issued any citation?

That regret was drastically reversed when a client came in 6 months later to have her hair done and said, "I have the most amazing story for you."

It went like this: Rachael was a strong supporter who stood outside my salon those days, proud of my reopening and praying for my safety and protection inside that salon during this time. She told me that on that day a prayer chain was hard at work, praying for a resolution to something that I had no idea was even happening. Rachael was friends with a local police officer named Trevor and his mom Kathy. Kathy had called Rachael to discuss what was happening down at Glamour Salon. Both women believed so passionately in their right to peacefully protest and in what I was doing. Kathy told Rachael that she was going to come stand with everyone fully knowing that her son had already been told he was to arrest anyone downtown on the sidewalk outside the salon the next day. Kathy was determined that her son would have to choose to do what is right and lose his job or arrest his own mom and friend. Rachael agreed to go down and stand with her.

Trevor had previously been working in a particular section of Salem, however on this day he was instructed that he would be patrolling my block where Glamour Salon was. He was informed by his commanding officer that anyone standing outside my salon on the public sidewalk was to be arrested the next day. He was told that if they don't make the arrests, that his job would be at stake. Trevor was a husband, father and being the sole provider for their home he could not afford to lose his job. Imagine, being told to arrest your own mother and a friend or lose your job. Imagine being told to do it and knowing it was the wrong thing to do in every way. He knew what he believed in his heart was right. He did not want to arrest these people. But there really did seem to be no resolution for anyone.

The prayer chain was started and grew, and Rachael said that nearly 1,000 people were praying over this horrific predicament. They were praying for a miracle. They were praying for me, for my business, for Rachel and Kathy, for Trevor. How in the world could this situation be resolved without someone getting hurt? They were stuck between a rock and a hard place.

Then someone called Rachael and told her. "Lindsey is calling off the protestors. She's asking us to go home." And just like that, Rachael felt relief that the pressure to stand up for me was relieved. And likewise Trevor would not have to make any arrests (including his own mom) nor was he going to lose his job. Because the miraculous resolution that 1,000 people were praying for came in an unexpected form. No one thought for one second I would call off the people supporting me. It was an unexplainable blessing. Between Kathy, Trevor, Rachael and I, did not have communication. No one had any idea that God was hearing our pleas and within all of us had already worked this out for all our good. I had no idea God was using me for this purpose. And knowing that God had other things planned, and His grace was placed on so many people outside my saon, I have no regrets. God's will was being done right under my nose and I had no idea. Yikes. I get goose-bumps every time I think of this story.

> *"For in the day of trouble, you will keep me safe in my dwelling." (Psalm 27:5)*

This is sort of a blur, and the exact numbers are unclear, but at this point a few more stylists had decided to take their business, leave Glamour Salon and work in a private studio. I think that the media attention and the small amount of liberal harassment had gotten into their minds and messed with them. I will never be sure what they were thinking at this point, about me or the salon, or what we now stood for. I just know that during this time, I recall losing more stylists and that was quite damaging to my business model. I also never made any of this public because I was secretly ashamed of these women. I was ashamed that I was FAILING in my business because I had decided to open and stand up for myself and them. For trying to protect my business and my livelihood, I was actually ruining it. I did NOT want the cancel culture to know that and get any enjoyment out of my failures, so I hid the fact that I was losing stylists. I hid the fact that my choice to save my salon was not costing me my salon. I also could not understand for the life of me why anyone would turn their back on someone who was standing up for them. Meanwhile, other salon owners and stylists were praising me, thanking me and recognizing that I was the only person speaking for them and confronting our rights.

Some of these women that left me were in the salon, sneaking clients in from the beginning. So, clearly, they believed they had the right to work. Clearly, they were not afraid of the virus or spreading it. Furthermore, they must have believed just as I did, that it was essential that they earn money to survive. But yet, when it came time for me to publicly open, with cause and intent and without shame, they turned their back on what was right, in fear of retaliation or worse, their own reputation.

But again, it was not the time to worry about that. I was focused on my stand and what would happen to my salon if I had not opened. It was disheartening to watch these women I had worked so hard for turn their backs on me, but I also knew that I was standing up for something much bigger than their careers and if they wanted to walk away from something that could have given them pride, that was their downfall. I had to worry about the salon, keeping our doors open and showing other business owners that we were fighting for their rights too.

> *"Be strong and courageous, do not be afraid or tremble at them, for the Lord your God is the one who goes with you. He will not fail you or forsake you." (Deuteronomy 31:6)*

CHAPTER FIFTEEN

DAY THREE
(THURSDAY MAY 7TH, 2020)

THIS MUST HAVE been a super uneventful day, as I have no live videos to refer back to and there were no dramatic threats by any government agencies. Good for me, yay. We will chalk that up as a win. As I sit here in present time and try to recall this whirlwind of a week, I have to sort through my live videos and photos to keep track of the timeline of events. This chapter is boring, and at that time, I was probably pretty grateful just to be doing hair peacefully.

I did hand my phone to a colleague and said, "Delete all my friends on Facebook." I was getting weird crazy liberal stalkers who were sharing my personal information and pictures. I didn't know who I could trust anymore and I needed to start fresh. Imagine if you can, wondering which of your friends now thinks you are a murderer for opening your business. Who is telling everyone how much you pay on your mortgage so they can use that info against you? Who is taking screenshots of your social media to slander you and shame you? People are really nasty and people who had known me for years and seemed to like and respect me, suddenly turned completely vindictive based on their political beliefs and the narrative. I, to this day, don't understand how the line was drawn politically. When I opened, it became excessively clear that Democrats did not support me and were quick to call me names and attack me, while Republicans cheered me on and praised my actions. I get the controversy around my re-opening IF you believed the mainstream media and that I would kill people's grandmas.

So that only leaves me to believe that Democrats believed this narrative and Republicans didn't. I am still finding it hard to believe that there was such a clear line drawn at this time in our lives but there was. Leftists specifically sought me out to slander me publicly. While the local conservatives were eager to shake my hand, encourage me and applaud me. I had never been outward about my political beliefs, and no one should have made any assumptions. But it became abundantly clear that I was a conservative, simply for wanting to open my business.

What a weird political statement to make unknowingly. It had nothing to do with who I voted for or how I voted. I just wanted to earn my living and darn it I had the right to! Soon though, I would make it very clear which side of the line I stood on. I had to. One side was viciously attacking me so I became more and more supportive and bold about my political beliefs because of them. I keep saying it, liberals made me who I am today. They have no one to blame but themselves. The harder and stronger they retaliated against me, the more strength I endured and the more bold I became. If they were going to be so loud and harsh with their belief system, I was not going to tuck my tail between my legs and sulk. I was going to boldly pronounce what I believe. Maybe even louder. I never had felt that way until they targeted me the way they did.

Having friends and strangers use my private Facebook page to try to slander me made me physically ill and anxious. My husband and I worked so hard for years on end to build our life and a life for our kids. We saved for 5 years to buy a boat. We had just built a beautiful home on country acreage. We wanted to give our kids a beautiful home and life as a family, and we had earned it! We accomplished all these things by working very hard, making sacrifices, and making good financial decisions along the way. Everything we had, we earned through old fashioned hard work and dedication to our businesses. Someone I didn't know had acted like a supporter to get on my Facebook and then ran her mouth everywhere saying "She's loaded! Don't support her. She has a brand-new boat and a new SUV and a mansion!" Facts: The boat is 14 years old (we bought it used); the SUV is to haul my three kids around (and also the very first car I have EVER bought brand new and I'm 40 years old) and the mansion is 2500 square feet. It's laughable. But suddenly my private life was up for grabs and anyone who wanted could say whatever they wanted about me.

It didn't matter what was or wasn't true. I started learning this the hard way. I was still, in my opinion, a nobody, but liberals thought it was extremely important to talk about me and start rumors about me like high school children. All the while I am trying to ignore them, not retaliate, but continue to stand up for myself.

Under the stress and pressure of everything else I was handling, I had to consider that my life was going to be exposed and people were treating me like a public figure. I created a Facebook page that I could manage as a person, instead of trying to filter friends and fake friends. I called it Lindsey Graham-public figure. The cancel culture got a real kick out of that. They were all up in arms about me acting like I was a public figure. Ironically, they helped in making me a public figure by constantly sharing my story and using my name. I don't believe all press is good press, but they certainly were assisting in making sure my name was heard everywhere. I didn't think I was a public figure at all, but I knew I had to lock down my private life and this page did that for me.

Leftists used a forum called Reddit to basically make up stories and say anything they wanted under the guise of a generic or fake username. In these stories, my husband and I were bisexual swingers. My husband was gay. My third child wasn't my husband's. My boobs were fake. I lived in a swinger's commune. I was a multimillionaire. It went on and on and on. Actual falsified stories were being told about me from someone I don't know in a situation that never existed. Like, full, legit evenings that involve myself and my husband that we were not present for. To this day, it is shocking to me that anyone would have the audacity and creativity to create fabrications of a night that never happened, all for the sake of slandering me. I haven't wronged very many people in my life, so I can't ever be sure who I wronged that felt the need to so badly harm me. I just recently read another thread that I used GoFund-Me money to divorce my baby daddy. My husband and I have been married almost ten years and have three kids together. I do not know where people come up with this stuff. I used to avoid reading it to save my little hurt feelings. But now I read it as entertainment sometimes. It's great book material, right? Are you not entertained?

In case you need to know, Reddit is one of the worst ideas I have ever seen in my life. It's just gossip but for the internet, oh, and anonymous. You can really just log on and start talking about someone you may not even know. But you can say you know them. No one would know if you didn't! Say whatever you like, make it sound legit, and boom. It's on the internet, and it becomes not just gossip but to some people, the truth. Do you know what that does to people? I'm guessing Reddit is personally responsible for some suicides. Did you know that months after all of this, my dad googled me, and Reddit came up? He read everything. Now, I would guess that almost all of it is a lie, I haven't read everything about me on there. Why? Because Reddit is not reliable. Why even use it? But my dad actually had to ask me to tell him the truth if Scott and I were swingers. Can you imagine how that felt? Someone had created a story so believable that my own father had to ask about my husband and my sex life. I think it was an eye-opener for him also, as he realized how much public attention my story was getting. He started to understand what it must be like to have people say and think things about you that aren't even remotely true.

After all, he was reading these things about his own daughter and questioning them, from a complete stranger!! Being called a swinger isn't the worst thing I've been called, and it won't be the last. Someone online commented on my tattoos one time and said I must be a liberal. That was harsh and I'm still not healed. But if I had to guess, I'm sure some people's lives have been ruined by Reddit and they should honestly be put out of business.

Here's an interesting situation I encountered too, after my GoFundMe raised money for my legal battle. On Facebook, a girl I have never met tagged me privately in a post about one of her friends dying. Apparently her young friend, whom I also do not know left behind a small child and she was trying to collect GoFundMe money for her funeral expenses. So, I do not know the woman who died and I do not know the girl soliciting me for money and I do not know her friends. The thread was basically that I had made so much money on MY GoFundMe, that I should find it in my heart to donate to this unknown person. I am still a good person and thought that I should donate because this poor child was going to be left without a mom. Some of the snarky comments by this girls' friends were to the effect that I wouldn't donate (you know, because they all know me so well). They also insisted that I made so much money off other people, I am obligated to give some to whom they deemed necessary. I commented that I would donate when I had the chance. Mind you, I was in the middle of fighting the government, press conferences, news interviews, social media attacks and standing up for America's constitutional rights.

The next day when I hadn't donated yet, these little hussies started going on and on about what a liar I am and how they knew I wouldn't help. I made a couple smart comments back about how busy I was, and that I was sorry I didn't donate to a stranger on their timeline. Then I gave $100. Not a lot. But this chick could have died from a drug overdose for all I know. I did not KNOW her!! Or anyone even related to her. Can you guess what the thread was about after that? Yup. I had allllll this money donated to me and all I was giving was $100? They went on and on about what a horrible person I was and selfish and greedy, etc. It was right then and there I fell in love with the BLOCK button on Facebook. To think that someone feels entitled to tag me and call me out personally to donate to them, money that was donated to ME, for my legal fight. Then to chastise me for the amount. Nope. I don't play that way. From that moment on, anyone who felt the need to attack me, slander me, blast me or harass me got the BLOCK button. Here's why. They aren't looking for an educational conversation. They aren't even looking for resolution to anything. They just want to fight. And if you let them or entertain them, they will suck your energy and time dry. And, worse than that, they will do it repeatedly, day after day. What kind of human can psychologically endure daily harassment and hate without taking some kind of emotional hit? Not me. I mean, I was, but I didn't want to take it on a full-time basis. The human heart was meant to be loved, treated tenderly and told it has worth. I was being told the opposite by leftists every hour of every day. I know that would have done damage to me and eventually my well-being. I knew that I needed to block out the hate permanently and accept only the positive. Once blocked, you silence them forever. Sure, new ones can come and go, but it was satisfying to take away their voice and know that they couldn't keep hurting me.

Here's what you need to remember about leftists, liberals, cancel culture vultures. They somehow make a living doing this. They love it. They live for it. They have all the time in the world for it. If you've got someone creeping your social media, continually harassing you, they are going to get into your head, and they're also going to cause chaos in your feed. BLOCK them. Immediately. It's YOUR page, it's your life, it's your platform. They don't get to live there and they certainly don't get any right to attack you on your space. Let them get their couple jabs in, laugh, then hit the BLOCK button and know that after they create three more fake accounts and keep trying, they'll eventually give up and you never have to be annoyed by them again.

> *"Consider it pure joy my brothers, whenever you face trials of many kinds, because you know that the testing of your faith develops perseverance." (James 1:2)*

I did this blocking from the very beginning. I did not encourage conversation with cancel culture vultures on my page. I didn't want my supporters wasting their time arguing with them either. So, I would simply BLOCK. It was liberating!

Someone would post something like "Oh, I know you are going to just block me because you can't stand anyone disagreeing with you and your precious...." BLOCK. I wouldn't even finish reading what they were saying! They were now trying to attack me because I wouldn't allow them to attack me....ON MY PAGE! Oh my gosh, they were actually trying to be victims and say that I was censoring them and trampling their first amendment rights. I'm not making this up you guys. But here I am, one year later and I know that the hundreds of crazy liberals that made a life commitment out of trying to hurt my feelings can no longer reach me. Not because I just don't care anymore, but also because they've been blocked on all my social media. I don't allow toxic people in my life, and I don't allow them on my social media. I am not sorry. I don't owe them anything, especially not a voice on my platforms.

Even though this day at my salon was uneventful legally, it was the beginning of a cancel culture. The beginning of the realization that on social media, you can anonymously say anything you want about anyone, and the masses will simply read it and take it as real. It's scary actually. Little did I realize that my fight was not going to just be against my governor and government agencies. I was going to be fighting leftists for standing up for my beliefs, on a regular basis.

CHAPTER SIXTEEN

DAY FOUR
(FRIDAY, MAY 8TH, 2020)

OREGON OSHA CONDUCTED the phone investigation I had respect-fully agreed to have at 8:00 am this day. OSHA had conduct-ed their own investigation (illegally) by checking my salons website and contacting anyone who had worked at the salon. Three of these girls were the ones I had terminated due to bad behavior and unprofessional conduct. The entire salon could have verified that these girls left on terrible terms and spent their last few weeks creating drama and tension in the salon before I would no longer tolerate them.

In summary, OSHA interviewed girls who despised me and wanted to hurt me. I had just essentially fired them. I told them their contracts to work and lease at Glamour Salon were void and they were no longer allowed on the premises. Yes, that's how badly this went down. Another liberal stylist had left on her own bad terms because she did not agree with my stance of re-opening. This is a girl I had talked to repeatedly about her negative attitude and problem with gossiping. I had to inform her twice that she would have her contract termi-nated if she didn't stop gossiping about the other stylists and creating a negative atmosphere. Well, what do you know? I gave her too many chances, let her stay, and now she had the perfect opportunity to trash me to a government organization. (Later, this same stylist, even after knowing me for 5 years, would call me a racist for not wanting my salon burnt down by BLM), I needed to stop giving some of these women the benefit of the doubt. Only one stylist who was actively working at my salon was interviewed. One. The other four were "fired" or left on bad terms. The others did not respond to interviews, and I don't blame them. They shouldn't have to. In hindsight, did OSHA purposefully only interview the stylists that had no longer been associated with my salon in order to get negative feedback? Because if OSHA had called every stylist at my salon and no one responded, how could they have even had an authentic investigation? They had already promised to my attorney and the police that they would not enter my establishment. You got that part, right? They were going to conduct an investigation into my salon for being a hazardous workplace. But they were never going to enter the workplace. The irony of that escaped no one.

In the statements issued by one of these disgruntled stylists, she claimed as directly as possible that I micromanaged her (like I have time for that), and that I behaved like a boss. She claimed I told stylists when they could and could not work. This is not true because they had code access to the doors to work whenever they wanted! She claimed that I limited their computer access so they couldn't adjust their schedules. Also a lie. Every stylist had her own log in to manage everything about their schedule. In fact, please see below the document I was given before my interview. Julie, Hayley, Kandace and Chelsea were all stylists currently at the salon, and even though I was aware that some of them were not fully on board with my decision, they did not find it necessary to lie and slander me. Unlike the other four, who were bitter and angry that they were no longer part of my salon. I'm comfortable sharing the legal testimony of these girls, because everything they have stated to try to slander me is a direct and provable lie. This does nothing to tarnish my reputation as a business owner because I can legally dispute every wrong and untruthful statement in these documents. So can every other stylist that has ever worked with me.

I was flabbergasted to say the least. My mouth dropped as I read lie after lie from stylists who had been a part of my salon for 4 years. Interesting that I was such a horrible salon owner, but they continued to work there, right? Which is it? I'm a horrible person and yet you worked side by side with me for four years? And what was the motivation here? Even if you didn't agree with my decision to open, did they really want to see me fined, locked up, or put out of business? What a vindictive thing to do to a person who has repeatedly given you second and third chances, despite your own toxic behavior. There was absolutely no surprise at all that the three stylists who I "fired," were quick to tell completely different lies. They all had different stories to tell about what a horrible boss I was, even though they had all been working happily at the salon for 2-5 years, without a single issue in the past (on my part). As I read their lies, I realized I could easily dispute these for the record with actual physical proof and documents. I could prove that they were lying. I find it somewhat shocking that they would lie to a government official about things that they knew couldn't be proven and risk their own legal consequences. When this case moves forward, they will be asked to testify under oath. I can't wait to see the stories change once they realize they could perjure themselves.

> *"Then you will know the truth and the truth will set you free." (John 8:32)*

I spent about 2 hours on the phone with my OSHA attorney George Goodman and two OSHA representatives during the investigation. Let me just point out that in the history of OSHA, George is not aware of any investigation that has ever been done over the phone. Without entering the premises. He is also not aware of any investigation that has been concluded in 5 days. Most investigations take 6 months.

Go into this story with that information handy.

It was clear to myself and George that this interview was going to lead to a citation, no matter what I said. The questions were direct and I answered them directly and honestly, yet they didn't seem to want to accept my answers. It was like a reality show, where they would ask the question and when I didn't answer the way they wanted, they would ask it a different way. The answer was the same. It was easy really. I told the truth. They wanted to establish that my stylists were employees. They most certainly were not, in any way shape or form. Here's how I ran my salon: You pay your rent, you set your schedule, you decide what services you offer and how much they cost. You manage your social media; you advertise for yourself. You handle your unhappy clients. My policy was to leave my stylists alone unless they were breaking salon rules or endangering the salon's reputation. They were independent in every sense of the word. They could come and go as they pleased, using door codes to enter. They could cancel their day if they needed to. I would have no idea what any stylist was doing with her clientele at any given time unless I looked at her books. Does that sound like employees?

This was also for my benefit. I didn't WANT to micromanage anyone. If I wanted a full-time job, I would have a commission salon with employed stylists. I wanted a salon with stylists who would pay their rent and do their own thing. That is exactly what I had. There was not a single question OSHA asked me that I didn't have an honest answer to. There wasn't a single question that made me nervous. When the interview was over, I nodded my head and thought to myself, "Well, that went well. There is no way they can legally issue me a citation." Throughout the day, OSHA began contacting the stylists listed on my website to question them. In a message in our group, I told them "Just tell the truth." That's it. Once again, I knew I didn't need to tell anyone what to say, the reality was that if they did, OSHA couldn't find any reason to label them employees. I got ready for work and headed to the salon.

Ready for the kicker?

While at the salon, my babysitter called me and told me that a man from child protective services came to our home. He was following up on a claim against me and wanted to speak to me and my children. Molly was often our sitter; she loves our kids, and she is a really good person. We trust her wholeheartedly. She was very smart too; she asked for his card and sent him away, as he was trying to ask her intrusive and disturbing questions about our family. That was the last straw. I knew this was all part of some massive plan to target me, harass me, and threaten me enough to not only shut me down but shut me up. In my first press conference, I boldly told reporters that I had a right to provide for my family and work. The next morning, a false report was filed, directed at threatening my children. Imagine that. All you heard in any of my press conferences from there on was that CPS came to my home, but it's particularly important to understand exactly how they treated me and my kids during this process. Here are the intimate details.

Maddie sent me the business card info for Omar Ruiz, the CPS agent who was assigned my claim. This guy never should have seen my name. After this story went national, two whistleblowers released to my attorney and me the false report, as well as the visit summary. There are some alarming concerns with how CPS handles these claims, as you will soon see. First of all, the call came in the morning after I opened from a blocked number and an anonymous caller. Let me be clear here. Anyone, anywhere, can call CPS and make false allegations against anyone for any reason or no reason at all. They don't have to validate or prove these claims in any way. The phone call reporting me was very distinctly directed at me, and tried hard to validate my husband Scott's innocence. The call was dedicated to ensuring that I was the parent responsible for the allegations claimed. They included completely absurd and almost laughable scenarios. I want to break these down in an effort to display how common sense could have been used at any point by CPS agents to validate that this report was phony and falsified.

Before I do that, you absolutely must know that in the claim, you won't even believe this, the anonymous person said to the CPS agent on the phone, "I don't know Lindsey, I've just heard rumors." Yes. This statement was confirmed to be made verbatim to the CPS agent screening calls and yet this claim was pursued. In the report it is written, "Caller: anonymous, states she has known the family for years." Wait, read that again. First it was said that this person didn't know me. Then this person said that they've known my family for years. Hello? How is that not suspicious? The report also says "Provided vague details. Hearsay, rumors, etc. Caller has not directly witnessed what she is reporting."

The claim said my baby's diaper was always dirty and my baby always had a diaper rash. How would a person who didn't know me have access to my baby's genital areas? Furthermore, even someone I knew intimately would not be someone I would walk around flashing my baby's genitals to. Additionally, please keep in mind that my baby was now only 6 weeks old. Almost his entire existence had been at home in lockdown. Stay home, stay safe propaganda. Who was admitting that they were visiting my home and my baby's diaper enough to have this knowledge?

They also listed my baby's name as Gunner. That is not his name. When I informed the CPS agent of this, he seemed unconcerned that the person reporting my family isn't even close enough to us to know the kids' names! Hello? Red flag anyone?

The claim said my toilets were dirty and my home had black mold. "The condition of the home was described as unclean. The toilets are dirty and black. There are sippy cups with black mold in them." I had a housekeeper who came monthly to help me with my home, light cleaning, laundry etc, since I was a working mom. Anyone who knew me, would probably know that. So, how in the world would I, Scott or a paid housekeeper, not tend to my toilets? Our house was also brand new, we had just built it and moved in one year prior. This was public knowledge. How would a brand-new constructed home have black mold already?

The claim stated that I was an alcoholic but Scott was not. I was the dangerous parent who got drunk every night and left my children unattended. This one is interesting because I would have to be a very good drunk; being a successful business owner, mom, wife, friend to many, and not one person in my life informing me of my alcohol problems. I must have hidden it well to be successfully operating six businesses, managing three little kids and maintaining a good marriage with my hubby. I love me some good red wine, absolutely. Especially at the end of a hard workday. But what a terrible and expensive choice for an alcoholic. Maybe I am not an incredibly good one. A good one would be on a first name basis with the liquor store, and buy cheap vodka to keep the habit cheap. But what do I know? I'm an alcoholic. An alcoholic who managed to have three perfectly healthy babies without fetal alcohol syndrome.

There was more mumbo jumbo in there, all very entertaining and all very unprovable. The report used my maiden name, which was also very odd. Not my legal name of 9 years, Lindsey Graham. A good, even basic agent would recognize that if these intimate details of my life were not correct, there is no way this could be a credible report. Once again reminding you the person even admitted to not knowing me. But this report passed the first screener at CPS as valid, and was passed to a second screener, who not only agreed that it was valid, but put a RUSH on it! I can see the scene now in my head, as a cartoon. "Karen! We've got a baby with a diaper rash out in Silverton. I need your best agents out there STAT. Put a rush on this file. This baby's life depends on it!" He is sweating and frazzled with stress as he pushes through a claim that has no merit or warrant and goes back to his desk satisfied that he is changing the world, one moldy toilet at a time. In another home, a parent is starving, beating or abusing their child, but thank God someone checked my toilets for mold. Spoiler alert: they found none.

Upon receiving Omar's info, I called him and invited him to our home on Monday, May 11th. I was eager to put this behind me and show him what a joke this claim was. I also had never been contacted by CPS and I was not aware of my rights as a parent. Later, I would find that most of Omar's behavior was illegal. On Monday, Omar came to our door, very officially and yet he also seemed timid. He interviewed me privately without Scott and asked the dumbest questions. Did I drink alcohol? How often? What kind? Did I drink with my kids at home? Do I clean my home? Do my kids eat? What do they eat? How do I discipline? Do I change my baby's diaper often? Wowwwwwwww. Then he interviewed Scott privately. Same dumb questions, same dumb truthful answers.

Omar, buddy, look around. The house is clean, the parents are successful, hardworking entrepreneurs. The kids are happy, healthy and not a single report has ever been made by any sitter, day care, school, teacher or family member concerning their welfare. But Omar the ogre, made me walk him through our house, open toilet seats, show him our fridge, our pantry, and he actually did look into my baby's diaper, then acted all offended about not wanting to see too much of the baby's private parts. Sex Ed in 5th grade taught me that the private parts that make the poop and pee are in a diaper, but I don't think Omar got that class. He kept averting his eyes from the diaper being pulled down and exposing my child's genitals that he demanded I show. Yikes. Play stupid games, win stupid prizes.

The whole thing was nerve racking. I kept waiting for him to laugh and say, "I'm done here. Clearly there's no concerns in this home. Sorry for your trouble Mrs. Wilson, I mean Graham. Wait, this report says another name, I don't get it." Omar did not say this. Instead, he demanded to speak to Trigger, who was 6 years old. Mind you, I was NOT afraid of what Trigger would say. The truth will set you free. But Omar insisted that I was not allowed in the room with him. I said I would stay quiet. I said I wouldn't look at my son. I said I was uncomfortable with it. He would not have it. He went into my son's room alone, shut the door, and what was said, asked or done in that room, I will never know. Any parent, no matter your race, religion, political beliefs or values, can recognize that this was a complete and utter violation of our family and our home. To put a child through an interrogation about his mom and dad, alone, with a stranger is disgusting. To do this to an innocent child when there are absolutely no claims to validate this kind of behavior is disturbing.

If Omar were a good, attentive, smart agent, he would have walked out of our house hours ago and closed the case. Instead, Omar excused himself to make a suspicious phone call out in his car. He came back in, handed me an informative letter that outlines what happens when a child or children are removed from their home, and told me he would need to schedule an interview with my 3-year-old daughter, Oakley. As he closed the door behind him, I burst into tears and fell into Scott's arms. Why was he informing me that my children could be removed? I went to a dark place in my mind and pictured everything you see in movies; my daughter being taken out of my arms, ripped from me, crying for me, while a stranger takes her somewhere foreign and scary. While I cry in agony, reaching to take her back, I am also trying to remain calm so she won't be afraid. Trigger is crying uncontrollably while someone holds his hand and walks him away from his mommy. (He's a mama's boy.) And baby Ranger, who only knows my voice, my smell and my skin, is placed in a hard crib in a strange place and has no idea where his familiar life is. With some stranger attempting to take care of him when they know nothing about him. To say that this was a nightmare is an understatement. To look at myself in the mirror and know that this is happening because I am standing up for myself was heartbreaking. This was all my fault, because I'm taking a stand and the powers that be do not like it one bit.

How in the world could I continue with this battle while my children are being threatened? That was a sacrifice I was not willing to make, and whoever they are, they knew it. This was another one of those moments that quitting was not just an option, but a must. I would need to decide how to announce that I would close my business if my family could just be left alone.

It's crucial that you understand that by this time, I was sleepless, exhausted, emotionally drained and truly mentally beaten up. I was discovering what happens when you do something publicly. My right to work was controversial and the political line had been drawn. "Friends" were gossiping about me; enemies were elated at being able to trash me. Old coworkers were making up their own versions of me to help facilitate the agenda that I was a money hungry, self-centered, careless business owner. The lies started, the rumors, the hate and the slander all started building up and becoming something I dealt with on a regular basis. Cancel culture was calling, texting, messaging our businesses, leaving negative reviews, etc. I was dealing with the personal attacks to my character, while trying to run my business, while serving clients, while doing radio and news interviews, while fighting the government all by myself. Now, to have my children threatened, and for this battle to come into my home, I was done.

I called my attorney, Rick and told him what had happened. I couldn't believe that the situation had taken this drastic turn in my personal life. I was shocked that this was happening, and even more shocked that Rick was not. He said, "Lindsey, you just stated in your press conference that you are doing this to support your family. This should be no surprise that the Governor is now targeting your family. This is not a coincidence." I wasn't ready to admit defeat to anyone but myself at this point. And that quickly turned around. He went right to work, filing a tort claim against CPS, alleging a lawsuit immediately for their actions.

People who specialize in these types of cases came forward and offered me support, guidance and advice. Margo Logan is a well-known CPS parent advocate in Oregon. She was a huge asset to me in this time and continues to fight for parents. She was a wealth of knowledge and legalities and told me everything I needed to know to fight this. I learned quickly that what was being done to me was not only unjustified, but in many cases illegal. CPS agents are never allowed to interview children and disallow the parent to be present. Not only was my home and my privacy violated, but my rights.

This new information and encouragement gave me strength. People stood up for me again and I was taken to a point where my mentality changed once again. I knew that CPS could not actually remove my kids, and I now had legal backing to enforce this. We went on the offense, publicized their vindictiveness, and began legal proceedings against CPS. I had now resolved even harder to remain open, because the state and its agencies had pushed me to a point of ferociousness. The continued attacks gave me drive and motivation to prove them wrong. They wanted to intimidate me into closing, and I was not going to give them what they wanted. It would set my entire stand back weeks and our governor would know exactly what to do to shut anyone down again if they stood up to her. I was once again emboldened.

"No weapon forged against you will prevail, and you will refute every tongue that accuses you. This is the heritage of

the servants of the Lord, and this is their vindication from me, declares the Lord." (Isaiah 54:17)

While I was dealing with all this government harassment, more stylists were secretly moving their stuff out of my salon, breaking their lease and cutting ties with me. Apparently, me having the nerve to stand up for our salon, allow them to work, and defy illegal mandates was not highly regarded for these Benedict Arnold's. These are the women I was doing this for, them and myself. I was fighting for all stylists and all small businesses. When I really needed these women I had previously called friends, they couldn't have my back. In fact, not only did they not have my back, but left me in my most desperate time of need, in a time when I couldn't possibly take a moment to even absorb what was happening. Because of my controversial stand, I lost another handful of stylists who didn't want to be labeled murderers.

What baffled me the most was the idea that even if this was controversial, didn't they genuinely believe they had the right to work? Staying, and standing up for themselves was a moment of truth and if they believed in their rights, why did they abandon the one person sticking up for them? I was slowly watching my salon fall apart at the seams in almost every possible way. The stand I took was going to change me and ruin me. I could see it.

"When justice is done, it brings joy to the righteous, but terror to evildoers." (Proverbs 21:15)

CHAPTER SEVENTEEN

DAY TEN
(THURSDAY MAY 14TH, 2020)

ON THIS DAY, which was in the second week of being open against the lockdowns, I received official notice from my OSHA attorney that Oregon OSHA was issuing me a $14,000 citation, citing that I was operating an unsafe facility for employees. Even though I had at one point expected a $70,000 fine, after the phone call and interviews, I was living confidently that I would not receive any citation. The facts in the case do not substantiate a citation. I still did not have stylists that were employees. This was absurd and I really was flabbergasted.

My first instinct was to pay the citation, however; if I did, there was no reason that OSHA couldn't come back to my salon again at any time and start a new investigation and issue yet another citation. If I paid the citation, it was also expected that I close my business, since it was unsafe and all. If I fought the citation, it would mean more legal fees (much more), but as long as the citation is pending, I could stay open, and guess what? If you are in a pending litigation with OSHA, they cannot come onto your premises to investigate you if that litigation is open. No brainer. The end goal is to remain open. The citation was going to be thrown out eventually anyway, I may as well fight it, keep my business open, and avoid further harassment. For the record, as of now, the legal fees for this darn citation so far have passed $25,000 all on their own, and we haven't even gone to court yet, but the principal is there. By paying it, I would have admitted to deserving it. I would feel like that was my way of accepting it and complying. OSHA did not deserve my money and they did not deserve for this citation to be upheld and paid. I was going to fight it. I still am.

> "The troubles of my heart have multiplied; free me from my anguish. Look upon my affliction and my distress and take away all my sins. See how my enemies have increased and how fiercely they hate me! Guard my life and rescue me; let me not be put to shame, for I take refuge in you. May integrity and uprightness protect me because my hope is in you." (Psalm 25:17-21)

The hits kept coming. At the salon, some of the stylists received emails from the Oregon Health Licensing department. A copy of this letter is in the back of the book. They were being told that if they were working at Glamour Salon, they were to stop immediately or they could face the following penalties: $500 per day or $5,000 per violation. A court ordered closure. A revocation of their license. A class C misdemeanor charge. This letter was signed and authorized by multiple agents at the office, including Lillian Shirley, Sylvie Donaldson and Robert Bothwell. I received this threatening letter as well, along with a similar letter also threatening to revoke my facility license, which would mean that the salon could never operate again. You know they would never reinstate it for me after this.

When the stylists received these letters, they became terrified. They could not imagine losing their license to do hair, it would devastate them for life! Governor Kate Brown had just opened up another county that was 20 minutes down the freeway, and hair salon there could be open and working. It made sense to play it safe, and the stylists I had left found a salon that would let them rent by the day in Albany. They would take their stuff down there and operate without threat until I could reopen "legally". I didn't blame them one bit. Their careers were now being threatened. But I was calling these bluffs at every turn, and I knew they couldn't enforce this either. It was like they had copied and pasted a bunch of random threats and stuck it at the bottom of a letter with no date. I knew there was no law surrounding this lockdown and you couldn't hand out class C misdemeanors like Halloween candy. This was just another letter thrown together that tried really hard to look legal, but was not. I was standing my ground but I didn't think anything less of those stylists who couldn't.

The most ironic moment of this day, looking back now, was something my very good friend, Lissy had said. She was a stylist at my salon and has been a dear friend since 1997. She came to me after receiving her letter and telling me she was going to work in Albany until this was over. She started crying, her lip quivering and said "Lindsey, please come with us. You have been very strong and brave, but please don't do this. I can't sit here and watch you lose everything you've worked for." She told me she would be devastated to see everything I worked so hard for disappear. I cried a little, and smiled a little, and told her that I wouldn't. I told her that I would be ok. I still believed I could fight this, and it would all work out. They could not enforce these things and I knew it. I was going to stand strong and remain at the salon, even alone. I promised her that I would be ok and I watched the stylists pack for Albany. I did hold my ground, and they never did enforce any of those threats, but I lost everything anyway. It's weird to think about her saying that, and not knowing that in less than one year, I would still lose it all but for very different reasons.

"But whatever was to my profit I now consider loss compared to the surpassing greatness of knowing Christ Jesus my Lord for whose sake I have lost all things." (Philippians 3:7)

CHAPTER EIGHTEEN

DAY ELEVEN
(FRIDAY MAY 15TH, 2020)

MY ATTORNEY, RICK and my political advisor, Roger agreed that I needed to update the public about what I was enduring trying to keep my business open. To my knowledge, only two other people in America had attempted this publicly and they were getting the same type of treatment as I was. I had called a press conference for today and laid out the last 10 days of harassment, bullying, intimidation and vindictiveness. This was my life, I was living it, and experiencing all the emotions that came with it. But I never expected it to reach so many people.

I had posted on Facebook that morning:

"Getting as many morning snuggles in with my babies before this nightmare continues today... huge announcements at the press conference this morning at 10:30. Once again, please keep me and my family in your prayers throughout this journey. It all started because I needed to work..... now I've become a TARGET for the government and my entire life is under fire. I believe I did the right thing, deciding to open my store that provides for my family. And I believe God will provide the right path moving forward. And put the right people in my life to guide and sustain us. Just pray."

When I watch the video now, it is once again as though someone else was living that nightmare and I am an outsider watching it. I've even caught myself choking up watching as I explain when CPS interviewed my son without me. Imagine going from being a normal, average person, mom and wife, to being a political figure and crying on national television. It is still as if that were someone else's life.

My press conference went viral and it became national news. People were appalled at the amount of harassment I was enduring and disgusted that my children were being targeted. Americans were furious and the support came in droves. This is when I started getting national media attention and more exclusive podcast and news interviews. I was thrilled to be supported by Glenn Beck, Dana Loesch, Lars Larson, PragerU and David J Harris Jr. My story was accelerated and gaining me support from political figures I respected and admired. It furthered my belief that I was doing the right thing and standing for something. The people I considered the good guys had my back. That only encouraged me more.

"I have summoned you by name; you are mine. When you pass through the waters, I will be with you; and when you pass through the rivers, they will not sweep over you. When you walk through fire, you will not be burned; the flames will not set you ablaze." (Isaiah 43:2)

After I announced to the public the horrific event surrounding Child Protective Services, Lissy spoke at the press conference. She was "ashamed of our governor, ashamed of Oregon." She boldly professed her disgust at what was happening to the citizens of Oregon, and me specifically. She was so brave and powerful in her conviction and I was proud to call her friend more than ever in that moment. But after the press conference, I walked back into the salon to find her hysterical and in tears, shaking. She was so caught up in the moment of being able to stand up and say how she felt, she didn't think of the consequences. On our website is each stylist's picture, phone number and contact info. She was now terrified that because she had spoken up, her information would be accessed and the government would now come after her. She knew I was busy but she begged me between sobs, to delete her from the website so her children wouldn't be at risk.

Are you guys crying yet? This is the America that WE were living in. The idea that if you spoke up, you were going to become a target for the government to terrorize, just to shut you up or shut you down. I couldn't believe what I was witnessing, watching my friend of 20 years break down in fear, terrified of losing her kids just for standing up for me publicly. I felt guilt. What I was doing was affecting the people who stood by me. What I was doing could have consequences on people I loved. The government was succeeding in breaking me down mentally. I was starting to question AGAIN what I was doing, what I was losing because of it, and who was going to get hurt along the way.

After my press conference, I was invited for the first time to join Fox National news for an interview. My story was reaching people, and even still, I had no idea how outraged the public was becoming over this tyranny. I was so lost in my own story, I still wasn't completely aware of how radical my fight was becoming and how powerful it would be.

CHAPTER NINETEEN

DAY FOURTEEN
(MAY 18TH, 2020)

DICTATOR GOVERNOR Kate Brown, in all her mightiness had stated last week that Marion County could open today. So now, all salons in my area were able to be open and operate. Things calmed down. A lot of local stylists messaged or texted me to say, "Thank you." They believed that Kate Brown felt forced to open salons because I clearly wasn't going to back down, and soon, their bluff would be called if I weren't arrested or some other dramatic penalty. Other stylists said that we would have been open weeks ago if I hadn't made a big scene. That she had punished us by opening other counties before us. Even now, 18 months later, there are stylists who said that if I hadn't stood up to her salons would have gotten shut down again. In Oregon, other small businesses were locked down over and over. Salons were not.

Kate Brown has locked down Oregon twice after the initial surge. She continued to shut down certain business and place impossible restrictions on them. Oregon is the number one state in America that has the most covid restrictions 18 months later. A massive number of businesses in Oregon have closed or will close permanently soon. Her reign has been a dictatorship and has harmed and killed small business and many families. There were petitions to recall her twice and somehow, neither have worked. The conservative citizens of Oregon are devastated and continue to feel her wrath even now.

CHAPTER TWENTY

DOWNTOWN SALEM'S BLM RIOTS
(MAY 30TH, 2020)

AS NEARLY EVERYONE in America remembers, the Black Lives Matter movement fired up again in late May due to the death of George Floyd, and protests were planned almost daily in liberal cities like Salem, Portland and Eugene. With these protests typically come antifa, and as you know now, they were causing quite an ordeal in Oregon regularly. When I say ordeal, I mean burning buildings, attacking innocent bystanders, tearing down statues, breaking windows, looting, stealing, terrorizing neighborhoods, destroying businesses, and vandalizing all kinds of property. Riots, according to everyone who can think critically. Peaceful protests to leftists.

The protests scheduled for weeks at a time were alarming to everyone in the area and social media was scattered with threats of antifa in downtown Salem by the capitol with busloads allegedly driving in. My salon was just 3 blocks from the capital. I was forwarded posts and messages by multiple local people that stated direct threats to my salon. One even asked if someone could "kick Lindsey Graham's ass" and another said to "burn down Glamour Salon first."

It's fair to say that I did not want my beautiful salon burned down. I also did not want to get beat up. I just spent my life savings building it, and there were hundreds of thousands of dollars in equipment and product in that space, including the other stylists. I was at home with my kids and husband when this information started filtering in and I made a dramatic decision. I was not going to let protestors kill my business, not after everything I just did to keep it alive. I made a public call to arms and asked anyone with a right to bear arms to come downtown and protect our precious city. Nearly 300 men and women showed up and the entire downtown was covered with people and business owners ready to protect their livelihood. The first one on the scene was our very first customer since re-opening, Brad. Turns out his military experience is extensive, and he started rallying the troops and directing, using his skills to keep people organized and calm. Brad was at my salon hours upon end, checking in on me and keeping the salon safe. He was a Godsend truly. I would trust him with my children's lives.

Some businesses had already boarded up their windows. Some small business owners brought friends. The people downtown were clearly a combination of people who answered my call, and people who wanted to protect their city and their shops. It was a dramatic scene and one that I won't soon forget. Everyone was calm and rational, but ready for anything, as we waited for the peaceful protest to eventually turn into a violent riot, as they have always done in the past. After the peaceful protest, as expected, there was a rowdy group that stuck around, disregarding the police, causing problems, assaulting officers, throwing liquids and glass at officers and breaking the windows of businesses. We all found out later that some of those police officers involved were injured and rioters were being arrested. It was not peaceful.

I was glad that we were protected, and I am thankful for those patriots that came to our side. I was told later by other businesses and by the Salem police department that Salem might have turned out like Portland, had I not made a call to arms. Portland is still burning, a year and a half later.

The result of this call to arms took a turn I never could have seen coming. Probably because I have a brain and I use common sense on a regular basis. I also don't connect dots

that aren't there. Believe it or not, because I didn't allow protestors to burn down my building, I became, drum roll please,
you know it.

RACIST!!!!!!

The ultimate insult to all Republicans and conservatives
now. The insult that spreads like wildfire and has no intention
of being true, but darn it, it makes headlines. I was labeled a
white supremacist for a few ridiculous reasons. First, that
there were "far right" groups in attendance, groups that are
themselves inappropriately labeled racist. Groups that consist
of a variety of ethnicities, including leaders who are black. But
because they have right-leaning, conservative and traditional
values, leftists have declared the entire organization racist. Because they were on the public sidewalk, the narrative was that
they were my close friends, so I must be a white supremacist
also. These groups are far from racist. They have been labeled
this way because of liberal cancel culture and the mainstream
media bias. The second reason was even more ridiculous.

According to social media and people who don't know how
to research actual situations, there was a man driving around
downtown blasting "F*ck the Police." It's a song that I personally would never recognize because I don't listen to that kind
of crap. There was a patriot going live on social media in front
of my salon, and while he is recording, you hear someone yell
in the background "Kill the minorities." ("Kill the minorities"
is a chunk of lyrics from that dumb song.) Wow, yes, that is an
alarming statement and filled with hate. If someone around
my salon yelled that, I would be disowning them immediately, asking them to leave my salon and issuing a statement. But
with clarity of mind, as I watched this video go viral, with my
name attached to it, I knew in my mind that the details were
hazy, and I'm not dumb enough to make a blanket assumption
that it was, without a doubt, a patriot yelling that in front of my
salon. Keeping in mind also, that most patriots are NOT racist,
that's usually the leftists. I actually looked at Scott and said
"Dude, that could be anyone yelling that. It could literally be a
car driving by." And guess what it was?

A car driving by. The next day, AFTER my name had been
blasted all over social media by the cancel culture, a local man

posted the videos of a Mexican man cruising around downtown blasting this song, "F*ck the Police" and as he drove by
Glamour Salon, yelled the lyrics out the window. The lyrics
being "Police think they have the authority to kill all minorities." Literally, video evidence that this entire propaganda was
a lie and the people calling for my beheading didn't care one
bit. And just like that, I was cancelled. This video was taken as
fact and no one bothered to investigate its authenticity or re-
liability. The narrative was once again: Lindsey Graham hired
white supremacists to guard her salon, and this is what they
were yelling.

It was quickly and falsely spread that I intentionally summoned and paid white supremacists to protect my salon.
There aren't enough eye roll emojis in the world for this story.
Now, let me just say for the record that I don't knowingly asso-
ciate with white supremacists. Never have. I don't personally
know anyone that is racist. I think we all know that I am NOT
racist, and you probably never thought I was. I can tell you for
a fact that it doesn't really matter what the truth is. What matters is that liberals can direct any volume of slander against
a conservative, and it becomes "true." They can rally troops
to aid their agenda and use this platform and mob mentality
to ruin someone's business and livelihood. I was dramatically, overnight, the worst human being in the world, according
to Oregon liberals. I was a danger to the community. I was a
white supremacist bringing racist far right groups and militia
into this peaceful protest.

The following days were a nonstop barrage of complete
and utter harassment.

The next two or three nights, BLM continued to riot and
"peacefully protest" downtown, where chemicals were being
thrown at police, fires were being started and glass was being
broken into crowds as bombs, sometimes filled with urine. Salem Police had issued a curfew in an attempt to rid the streets
of these liberal thugs causing chaos and violence in our downtown community. The patriots guarding businesses and downtown apartments were being told by an officer that a curfew
was in effect and if they planned to remain downtown, they
needed to be indoors, in order to respect the curfew or they

would have to act against them as well. If they didn't take action, obviously they would look like they're playing favorites. This was all said by a Salem officer to a group of armed men, who happened to be standing directly outside my salon. The video also went viral, with the narrative being that, of course, the officer WAS playing favorites by telling them to go indoors. Leftists threw such a tantrum that the police chief had to issue a public statement within a few days regarding the matter. This series of events occurred so swiftly that I could barely keep up with what was happening downtown, even though after a few days, it wasn't even about my salon anymore. It was about protecting the entire downtown community.

I was getting tons of Facebook messages calling me vile names on Glamour Salon's Facebook page. I was getting hundreds of Facebook messages calling me vile names on my personal Facebook. I was getting hundreds of Facebook messages calling me vile names on all four tanning salon Facebook pages. I was getting hundreds of messages calling me vile names on Glamour Salon's Instagram. I was getting hundreds of messages calling me vile names on my personal Instagram. I was getting hundreds of messages calling me vile names on all four tanning salon Instagram pages. I was getting emails at Glamour Salon. I was getting emails personally. I was getting emails at all four tanning salons. I was getting text messages.

I had a client named Christy that I had served for almost 10 years, message me to say that "My daughter and I will no longer be coming to your salon. You are a disgrace and a disappointment." I was getting phone calls at Glamour Salon. I was getting phone calls at all four tanning salons. I was getting one-star reviews on Glamour Salon. I was getting one-star reviews on all four tanning salons. My photo was being circulated and made into racist memes on Facebook. My face was being circulated and made into racist memes on Instagram. Someone created an Instagram account just to share articles about me and slander me. I checked it out for a hot minute, and I don't know where the information was coming from, but it was hilarious. Almost every single accusation was untrue. What a waste of time, spreading lies about someone you don't know and then getting, what, mad? About things that don't even affect you. (It only had like 14 followers, but STILL!!!) I also checked out the girls that were following the page. And, well, nothing to say there. Let's just say, it wasn't anyone who I felt would ever make an impact on my life, or even their own. Ok, that's enough. Don't be mean, Lindsey.

My children's childcare providers Lori and Shawn were a married couple, a white woman and a black man. I dropped my kids off every school day with them, and they were sweet, wonderful people. I was so devasted by what Lori might read online that one morning, I pulled her aside, started bawling, and told her that I wasn't a white supremacist. I thought that she might read something, and that she and Shawn would be concerned about my family's beliefs. I really thought that she might think we were racists! She shook her head in awe and told me that they would never believe that, and that they loved our kids. She was emotional with me, watching me in pain, as I felt the need to defend myself to her. Shawn would never hear of such a thing. She seemed appalled that the community was spreading such a hurtful lie when it clearly had no merit. How did it come to this? That I had to justify who I was to people who already knew in my heart who I was? How did these people get me to feel like I had to tiptoe around people I already had a relationship with?

They weren't even close to finished with me. Liberal cancel culture was logging into my salon's system, and they were making fake hair appointments for every artist working, all day long so that a real client could not book, and we would be booked all day with clients who weren't coming. People were driving by the salon and yelling obscenities at the salon, flipping me off regularly.

Someone or multiple people had joined forces and were going on to google.com and changing the category of my business. They were changing us from "hair salon" to "public bathroom." They did this repeatedly day after day. I would get notifications in my email that I had to approve this change. It was exhausting and discouraging. These things, when they happened, were so painful and demeaning. While this was happening to me, I was in devastation. I had a strong face for the public but my heart was aching. Attempting to bring back these emotions is difficult, because now that God has brought me through the storm, I see what He was doing with my faith and my strength.

Someone started a change.org petition to have my business license revoked. (Insert eye roll). I am a pretty smart person. I guess most of these people are not. It should be common knowledge that you cannot decide impulsively to start a petition about anything you want, then get enough signatures that it becomes real life. Seriously. Otherwise, wouldn't we all have a lot of things go our way if we could just convince 10,000 people to agree and sign an online petition? Shoot, I would abolish abortion today. I'd have a petition to remove all leftists from red states. But this petition circulated all of Oregon and farther, and when I last checked, over 14,000 people had signed it.

So I watched in horror, as the community I was a huge part of, signed a petition saying they no longer wanted me in their state doing business, or even existing. It was incredibly destructive to my mental health and wellbeing. It was one of the lowest points in my life. I don't think I can really explain how devastating this was to me. It was heartbreaking. I was previously loved by people in this community, and I did nothing to deserve this treatment. How could people be so simple-minded to believe that I should be satisfied with my business being vandalized and destroyed in the name of some organization?

But vindication came, when the change.org petition went absolutely nowhere, and those who donated to the campaign to ruin me discovered that their money was simply taken by the organization. I read with a smile as the signors reprimanded the guy who started the campaign and accused him of stealing their money and tricking them. They slandered him, attacked him and in turn, cancelled him. His name was public information. He thought he was doing everyone a favor. They donated to the site to shut me down and their money went nowhere. It was a bit redeeming. I thought to myself "How does it feel to have the mob turn on you buddy? To be accused of stealing people's donations and scamming them? Not particularly good. I feel no sorrow for you."

One night, someone sprayed obscenities on my salon windows for all of Salem to see. I woke up to find that the words "Nazi" and "BLM" had been sprayed onto my front windows. No other business had this happen to them. When the news caught wind of it and called me for a statement, they aired a small segment that afternoon. Hateful leftists in Salem stated that I did it myself, that I vandalized my own business to get the attention. The idiocrasy was never ending.

Here is a small glimpse, a portion of the hateful emails and texts and messages I received almost nonstop for 3-4 days. Almost all ANONYMOUS of course. Leftists do not have the courage or tenacity to speak hate and violence using their real identities. They hide behind their computers.

"Why are you abusing your kids you little c*nt"

"I will no longer be coming to your salon due to your association with white supremacists."

"No one wants your racist a** here."

"Fu*k you and your racist salon."

"You are a greedy, selfish bit*h"

"I hope you lose everything and go bankrupt. You're a piece of sh*t"

That's just scratching the surface! That's also about 1% of the messages I received over the course of my fight. I am receiving hateful messages to this day. The difference is that now I laugh at them. But during this time, I was terrified for my family and my own life. Clearly, these people knew where to find me at any given day. At Glamour Salon, a salon that was all over the news, and one google search away from an address and directions. If anyone wanted to really "get rid of me," they could. So many people in Salem knew me, I was worried that someone would find my home address as well. Easily. It got to the point where I had pulled all my curtains shut and made sure my firearm was near me and accessible. I had nightmares that someone would wait until we went to sleep and break into our house and hurt my kids. I ran multiple scenarios through my head of what these psychopaths would or could do. I considered having all our kids sleep in our bedroom. I never told my husband this, but I would wake up out of a nightmare and go check on the kids, check the doors and make sure the house was secure multiple times a night. I never told anyone how scared I really was. I thought that they would think I was being ridiculous. I also thought that if something did happen, I brought it on myself, and people would blame me. I also did not WANT anyone to know how scared I was. I was supposed to be this brave person and being scared to the point of almost paranoia was not brave. I kept these feelings and fears to myself and continued to put on a brave front and push forward.

Good news...after four months of this hate and threats, I discovered something pretty incredible.

These leftist haters, (cancel culture vultures I call them now) never once had the nerve or courage to walk into my salon and tell me anything to my face. Not once. Not ONCE did anyone come into my salon and call me a racist to my face. Not once did anyone walk into my salon and cuss me out or threaten me to my face. The only place they had any courage was behind their phones and computers. They never had any intention of confronting me personally. They didn't have the nerve. They never did. They were the epitome of keyboard warriors. I can always live with the fact that I will always have more courage than them, in any situation in life.

One girl walked by the salon almost daily and regularly flipped me off. But the one time I went outside to talk to her, she started running across the crosswalk, yelling racial slurs behind her. She ran right into the comedy club across the street from my salon, where she worked, and I let the local police know that she was threatening and harassing me. I watched the police officers knock on her door, and it looked like they gave her a little talking to, while her arms were flailing and she desperately tried to excuse her behavior. Want to hear the best part? The next time that little stinker walked by the salon, her head was hung, and she never even looked over. She was ashamed and it was beautiful. I call that a win. As soon as you stand up to them, they become the little babies that they are and they cannot fight for themselves in real life. I no longer play defense. I play offense. I play it well.

This cancel culture lasted about 72 hours before they found someone else to attack. But those 72 hours changed my life entirely. After this attack, I no longer felt safe in my home, in town, at work, or even around in the community. I didn't feel safe walking through downtown to get my coffee or a quick bite to eat. I would basically now go home, go to work, and not go out to socialize unless it was to a friend's home where I knew everyone. I never did social distance or mask up, so being social was still a part of my life. Or was. I truly felt that Oregon was no longer going to be home for me or my husband.

This was my first experience with cancel culture and it did not feel good. I had no idea what the cancel culture was, or that it affected real people like myself. I 100% thought that if I just explained the situation firsthand, that people would hear me, hear my heart and realize that in no way, was this something it was being made out to be. I was filled with emotion; I was heartbroken, and I was completely devasted by the turn of events surrounding that week. My first instinct was to do damage control. I went LIVE on social media, cautiously reiterating that I didn't knowingly call racists to my salon. Of course, I wouldn't do that. Please forgive me that it happened (if it did) and know my heart. And if white supremacists DID come, to stay away. I don't endorse that. Mind you, in no way was I proclaiming that ANY of the people who came to guard my salon were indeed racists or white supremacists.

I have no clue, and knowing the cancel culture now, and knowing some of these people more intimately and personally, I would back them. What I know now is that likely none were to be found, but again, the truth doesn't matter. There are so many far right, right leaning and conservative groups that have been falsely labeled as such. Some men and women from those groups came downtown and publicly protected all of downtown Salem. For them, I am thankful, and it needs to be stated on record, that I am truly sorry for how they were treated. By the community, by the public and by me. In my horrific attempt to redeem my reputation, those patriots thought I was turning my backs on them and throwing them out. That was never my intention, and it pains me to know that after everything, they felt betrayed and disregarded. I went live on social media, with this victim mentality, that racists came to my salon, and I had no clue, and I'm so sorry and blah blah blah. This is the cancel culture. I was weak and wrong. I cringe when I watch that video. I curled up in a ball and bowed to their hatred and demands and apologized for what? What racist hate organization stood downtown? And what exactly did they do? No one got hurt, no one yelled racial slurs, no one touched a single protestor. And yet, every person on the sidewalk was attacked by cancel culture.

Get this: one of my friends and clients, Rena, was fired from her job because a picture surfaced of her standing on the sidewalk outside my salon, a public sidewalk, during the protests, and her co-workers called her a white supremacist. They refused to work with her. What would have happened, I wonder, if she had just said she was actually part of the protest? I'm sure that would have been perfectly fine. She suffered as a result of standing up for me, and expressing her rights, and simply helping a friend in need. Cancel culture is the real pandemic in America.

For what it's worth now, anyone who stood outside Glamour Salon that night, and ensured that my business was protected from riots, looting and damage, I thank you. I never should have given in to the cancel culture that didn't really care if you or I were white supremacy, that just wanted a fight. They wanted to cancel us. It worked. I should have had your back and I'm sorry I didn't. I think most of you know that I wasn't trying to turn on you. I was weak, and I had no clue what was happening to me. I'll never make that mistake again. I promise you.

This catalytic event is what sealed my life and my salon's fate. My assistant walked out on me, leaving only a Facebook message saying she "felt threatened at the salon" because of who I was having guard it. Her mom was later seen bragging about how proud she was that her daughter "left this racist, bigot woman." Two or three more stylists magically had other opportunities present themselves. My receptionist that was finally back to work, gave me her notice, stating that "she can't support the people I have guarding the salon." When I politely informed her of her ignorance and how irrational it is to base your life decisions on what you read on Instagram, she walked out. She still believed that one of my patriots had yelled "kill minorities," even though it was now pretty widespread that the video was debunked. She walked out on me without looking back because she caved to the cancel culture. I used to be a tolerant person. I no longer am. I shook my head, in utter disappointment that this girl who had worked for me for years would have no inkling to stand up for me and give me the benefit of the doubt, even after hearing the solid truth!

People were abandoning me left and right. All of them knowing who I was and what I had stood for. All of them, for the last years, thanking me for the salon I created and the empowerment I advocated for. At the time it was so hurtful and so hard to understand. I have always said that they just couldn't be strong and that was ok. But it is not ok. I am saddened that I took a stand for every single one of these women, and when the dust settled, they scurried away in fear. They jumped ship the first chance they got, when something got even a little hard for them. They never once thought about the massive sacrifice and emotional turmoil I was enduring. Here I was, enduring relentless bullying by every state agency, my personal life being slandered, lies being told about me, my family being threatened, and their first instinct is to peace out and leave me high and dry, knowing full well what it would do to me emotionally and long term.

Eventually, through everything and after the dust settled, I said goodbye to 23 out of 25 stylists at my salon. Glamour Salon was doomed, but not by the government.

I went through my leases one day, long after everyone had left and I was now cleaning out my desk permanently. My stylists had all walked away from their signed commitments. Most of them has just renewed their lease at my salon. Knowing that I would never go after them legally, they knew they could leave and not suffer any consequences. I added up the loss I had just suffered. An entire year of leases, now completely void. I had lost my salon's entire source of income. I had lost almost $200k in revenue that was supposed to pay for my salon's lease, utilities and expenses. If I were to try to keep my salon open, I would go bankrupt. In an effort to save these women their own loss of income, save our small businesses in Oregon, save my salon and everything I had worked for my whole life, I had essentially cost myself everything. I was getting new clients who supported my cause, but I had lost all my liberal clients who now referred to me as a white supremacist. My business, my entire career was slipping through my fingers and yet, I still did nothing wrong to deserve it.

A liberal with a fake account sent me a Facebook message with a meme she created with my picture. The picture was of me wearing my MAGA hat, smiling. The meme said, "I don't always play Patriot Barbie, but when I do I steal people's money and...." I forgot the rest. It was of course, something really dumb and intended to just break my little heart. It was supposed to be the ultimate insult. I was supposed to be offended. But PATRIOT BARBIE??? I mean, I am a raging patriot. I love my country!! And Barbie, a doll recognized for being glamorous and feminine? Uh, ok!!! To show cancel culture I was sick of their crap, and to get this liberal back at her own game, I renamed my Facebook public page Lindsey Graham-Patriot Barbie. I shared the meme and I laughed about the insult which resonated as a compliment to pretty much everyone.

My supporters loved not only the name, but the concept of shoving insults back in leftist's faces instead of curling up into a ball in despair. I was now the Patriot Barbie. I ran with it. This cancel culture was eating me up, but within it, I was finding strength, or rather, God was strengthening me. Little did I know that this really was the beginning of Patriot Barbie. As time went on, and I hurdled every political obstacle thrown at me I was owning this alter ego. The liberals had created their own nemesis. And little did they know, that once I was completely cancelled, there would be nothing holding me back.

We also rejoice in our sufferings, because we know that suffering produces perseverance; perseverance, character; character, hope. And hope does not disappoint us, because God has poured out His love into our hearts by the Holy

Spirit whom He has given us." (Romans 5:3-5)

Americans watched me stand up for my rights and my family and do so boldly in the public eye. While they maintained that I was this brave, strong woman, the face they saw on tv was real, but there were emotions I was burying deep down in my heart. I was trying so hard to be this brave soldier for everyone, I didn't want them to know that the rest of my business was falling apart. The entire time this was unfolding, my stylists were slowly abandoning me. One by one, they were moving on to a situation that didn't involve being called a racist, or a fascist or a murderer. While the news was reporting my fight with the government, I really was still fighting for my business. I just didn't tell anyone that I was losing my fight.

Only two friends, Lissy and Phyllis, stood with Glamour Salon to the end. Lissy stood tall and loudly denounced everything being done to me. Lissy has been my friend since 1997, since high school. She knows me to the core, and she knew that I was enduring the fight of my life, all the while being walked out on by people who claimed to support me. She spoke at one of my press conferences, she fought for me online, she took on the rumors and lies and defended me every chance she could. That woman is an angel and she stuck it out through everything until the day I closed. She will always be the friend that stood by me during the storm that changed my life, and I will never forget that. In my opinion, her ability to stay with me through all that, she showed was just as brave as I had to be. Phyllis knew my heart, prayed with me, for me and kept hoping that everything would be ok. That was not the case. Both these women endured trial by fire just for continuing to work at Glamour Salon and both deserve my heartfelt thanks.

"You intended to harm me, but God intended it for good."
(Genesis 50:20)

CHAPTER TWENTY-ONE

CANCELLED
(JULY, 2020)

LUCKILY, WHAT KEPT us surviving just a bit longer were some stylists who had come forward and WANTED to work at my salon because of my stand, more than a handful thankfully. But that was not God's plan. God had bigger plans for me, but I wasn't paying attention. He was taking away my salon because He had something better for me. He let me hang on as long as I could, but His plan was always to close that chapter of my life. I just wasn't ready to accept that yet. Glamour was staying afloat, barely. Behind the scenes, my family was making life altering decisions. In the middle of a life changing decision, we had finally stopped to ask ourselves if we were no longer "home" in Oregon.

My dad had moved to Arizona years ago and he was never coming back to Oregon. He was in love with the weather, the people, and his new active way of life. Scott's mom was gearing up for the same move in just a few months. She had decided she wanted to retire somewhere hot and more active as well. It was going to be extremely sad to see both grandparents leave. Scott's dad had died suddenly a few years ago, right when we were building Glamour's forever space. Our kids' only grandparents were about to live in another state. We would soon have no support system. Things were looking pretty bleak for us in Oregon. We had just built this beautiful house, but it no longer felt like home. I felt vulnerable and targeted. I was concerned for our safety and I was no longer seeing the future for our businesses.

The cancel culture went after Scott's new gym, claiming he was also a white supremacist since he was married to me. Woodburn was a primarily Hispanic community, and Hispanics in Oregon, at least the millennial "woke" ones, jumped on the oppression train and decided that we must also be racist against Mexicans. Weird, because we chose to build a beautiful new gym in that community specifically. Not sure why racists would place themselves in the middle of people they despise, unless they weren't actually racist! Mercy me, what a concept.

We had to sell our portion of the gym ownership to our partner and publicly announce that we were no longer part of the company, so that the gym could survive. How humiliating. We tried hard to write a public announcement that in no way would entertain the idea that we were actually white supremacists, but also didn't take any jabs at the idiots in the community that actually believed we were and how obscene that was. It was also a public announcement essentially that they had won and we were pushed out of town. All very humbling. All a huge disaster. Scott and I were watching our entire life's work crumble around us and wondering when the hits would stop coming. We had no clue how we were going to recover from this, or why it was happening to us, but we both had very strong faith. It never occurred to me once that God wouldn't take care of us.

I sat in my car at one point, after losing pretty much all my stylists, hearing Scott tell me we had to sell the gym, and watching social media blow up about what kind of person everyone now assumed I was for absolutely no reason. I was crying uncontrollably and just letting the pain of everything soak in, the complete and utter devastation manifesting into a future that was no longer secure for us. I prayed and I told God that I trusted him, that I knew He would never let this happen without a plan and a reason. I told him it sucked and I was in pain, and I didn't understand His plan for me. But I knew our family would be okay. I prayed that He would try to reveal His plan sooner than later so I wouldn't have to suffer long.

"May the Lord answer you when you are in distress." *(Psalm 20:1)*

It is hard for me to admit what I was going through. The mob that did this to me is craaaaaaazy, and they are weirdly obsessed with me and everything I do. They are going to read this and find joy in the fact that they truly did break my heart and caused me immense pain. But I have to admit it so that it's understood what God brought me back from. That this was one of the hardest things I have lived through. I came through it because my God is mighty, and I came through stronger, braver and more resolute in my beliefs. It used to be a big deal for me to have a reputation in my community. I always cared what everyone thought about me. It stressed me out if I found out that someone was saying unkind things about me or untrue things. I cared what people thought of me.

Well, I am definitely cured from that now! I realize that anything can be said about me, regardless of having truth or merit, so I stopped reading the comments and I stopped caring when I heard a rumor that was being passed around. It rolls right off my back. I am talking about actual anxiety that came with any kind of emotional distress involving friends or family. I no longer have this anxiety. I can raise my eyebrows, smile and let whatever is being said about me continue on, knowing that the truth is out there, but they are not interested in finding out. I am honored to have been persecuted for what I stood for because I believe that it was always God's plan for me and I followed it through, with His strength.

"Blessed are those who are persecuted because of righteousness for theirs is the kingdom of heaven." *(Matthew 5:10)*

As Scott's mom stood in our kitchen, listening to the events unfolding in our lives, the slander and hate being thrown at us, the complete and total devastation of our life's work, she said "Maybe you guys need to move to Arizona." Scott and I looked at each other, and it was decided. This was a conversation that was never had and never even considered. But in that moment, I believe God just told us "Yes." By the end of the day, I told Scott, "You know I'm serious right? Let's go." There was nothing left for us in Oregon. Nothing that would improve our businesses, nothing that would eradicate the vicious rumors and hate, nothing that would better our children and certainly nothing holding us back. This was a turning point, in which the entire future of our family was suddenly on a completely different path than we had planned for the last 10 years.

Everything we knew, and our kids knew, was going to change. We didn't even know what we would do for work or for income in Arizona, but we knew we had to leave. My emotional well-being was at stake and our family's safety was becoming a concern. We began making plans immediately and a weight was lifted. I could endure the hate, the harassment and the attacks, because I knew I would no longer have to live with these people. What they thought of me would no longer matter. It was so freeing. As the hate continued to pour in and the Governor continued to lock citizens down again, we imagined how we would feel if we were not moving, and it was bleak. Everything in us was reiterating that for our family's safety and future, we were right to leave. I started laughing at the obsessive behavior of the cancel culture vultures and thinking to myself, "You are nobody. You mean nothing to me. And soon, you will no longer affect my life." All the while, these nasty and sad people continued to track my movements and attempt to create more hostility toward me.

Throughout this battle, I could not help but thank God for the trials I was enduring, knowing He would make them good. People I loved continued to tell me that God was going to bless me for everything I had endured. I knew they were right. God never lets us go through anything without a beautiful plan. This fight had hurt me so badly, that I couldn't imagine how good He was going to make it, in return for my faithfulness.

"Now my heart is troubled, and what shall I say? Father,

save me from this hour? No, it was for this very reason I
came to this hour. Father, glorify your name." (John 12:27)

After telling my close friends that I was moving, it became more real or more painful. I had built my entire life in Oregon. My best friends were all here and we regularly had events together. I was not going to be able to see them nearly as much as I was used to. I kept telling myself that I would make new friends quickly, but nothing would compare to the friendships I had built with these women. This is my core group of women who support and love me unconditionally. I love them more than I can explain. These women have seen me at my worst, my most humiliating and my most humbling. These are the women that call you out when you're wrong and are fiercely loyal when you're not. They have had my back more times than I can count and I consider them family.

Before I left for Oregon, we had a going-away dinner where we laughed, cried and reminisced about our good times and prayed that I could fly up and make them work still. During this dinner, I wanted to make abundantly clear that my faith had taken on a huge role in my life now. I have never been "preachy," and my friends would likely be shocked to know how deep my faith in God is. I never want to annoy people by always sounding religious and I certainly don't want anyone feeling like I judge them. Especially my friends. During this dinner, I smirked and told them I needed to get serious for a moment. (I'm rarely serious.) I told them I felt that Jesus was coming back soon, and we were in end times. I directly asked them if they were all "right with God." It was important for me and always will be to know that I am going to spend eternity with these women. They are beautiful souls, good hearted and incredibly generous and thoughtful. But we only get to heaven through salvation, and I needed to know my best friends were saved. After confirming this, we were back to laughing again, when the waitress came up to the table. Being the direct person that I am, I also asked her if she was going to heaven. She started smiling, and told me about her children, and making sure they were saved. She confidently told me that she also believed we were in end times and that her family was going to heaven.

As she told this story, I watched my friend Jenny's eyes start to well up. Something was happening inside her; I could feel it. The Holy Spirit was about to do something in her. I told them both to move to another table with me, where Jenny confessed that her heart was harboring pain and resentment for the loss of her mom and brother. She had distanced herself from God and was still angry with Him for taking her family. She was ready to let that go and forgive, in the middle of the restaurant. The waitress, Jenny and I bowed our heads and right there, in front of everyone, we prayed.

Jenny cried, I cried and the waitress was shocked. God was moving in the most unexpected way, at the most random time. Jenny's life was changed. She went home with a new energy and said that she could immediately feel God around her and back in her life. He was already speaking to her and showing her signs of His presence. She sent me a text that night, telling me how different she already felt and how she finally felt peace again. Allowing myself to be blessed and give myself to God, has allowed me to experience these moments with my close friends, and be a vessel for God to work.

"Listen to my prayer oh God, do not ignore my plea; my thoughts trouble me and I am distraught at the voice of the enemy, at the stares of the wicked; for they bring down suffering upon me and revile me in their anger. My heart is in anguish within me; the terrors of death assail me. Fear and trembling have beset me; horror has overwhelmed me. I said "Oh, that I had the wings of a dove! I would fly away and be at rest-I would flee far away and stay in the desert; I would hurry to my place of shelter, far from the tempest and storm." (Psalm 55:1-8)

CHAPTER TWENTY-TWO

EMBRACING MY JOURNEY

IN THE MIDST of all this pain and chaos, were some highlights. A director named Jeff Roldan contacted me from California. He was doing a documentary on the lockdowns, and how it was affecting small business owners, schools, parents and families. He flew up to Salem and came to our house and the salon for the interviews and filming. Jeff was so down to earth, so compassionate and so concerned about my story and my wellbeing. He was someone I felt I could trust to say anything to, and he would take it exactly as I meant it, not twist it to meet another narrative. He was a concerned citizen who was documenting how horrific this lockdown has been on Americans in all situations. Jeff's producer, Rick Jordan, flew in as well for the filming, and once again, was such a genuine guy, I felt completely at ease. These men were horrified as my story unfolded.

While at the salon, a guy on a bicycle rode by the window and was screaming something at me, calling me a "murderer" and flipping me off. I smiled and waved as usual. He went and found an old pizza box from the garbage and wrote on the back "You're no one's hero. You're a murderer. Watch your back." Rick and Jeff were shocked that not only was this happening, but that I was so used to it now. No one should be ac-climated to this kind of hate, but I was.

"The wicked plot against the righteous and gnash their teeth at them; but the Lord laughs at the wicked, for He knows their day is coming." (Psalm 37:12)

The documentary, Liberty Lockdown, was released in 2021 and was a huge hit amongst the California patriots. There were viewing parties and private screenings. The movie has yet to hit its peak, as social media continues to silence conservatives and censor anything that doesn't fit the narrative. Liberty Lockdown is a movie that I believe will hit its peak and expose so many of the corrupt moments in the nation that mainstream media did not air. The stories compiled in this movie are absolutely shocking, and it is also a major tear-jerk-er. Spoiler alert: a mom gets arrested for letting her kids play on a playground. It is unreal.

For a private screening, I flew to California to meet some of the other people in the movie. It was so inspiring. Alan Holstetter was a man in Huntington Beach who bravely stood up against the lockdowns. Their terrible governor, Democrat Gavin Newson, had the city put a chain link fence around the beautiful public parks at the beach. The beach, a place where, even if you believed all the social distance nonsense and mask mandate and fake science, you could still safely visit. Alan and other patriotic citizens rallied in the area, and started removing the fence. After all, it is THEIR tax dollars that paid for it, and fencing off a public park was complete and utter dictatorship. Alan held his ground. While being threatened with jail time and arrest, he held on to the chain link fence and peacefully resisted. Alan, who is also a former law enforcement officer was arrested that day for his peaceful protest and faces multiple charges in California for standing up for himself and other citizens. He is my hero!

While in Huntington Beach for this private screening, I was also invited to speak at a Trump re-election rally on the pier. It was something I never imagined doing but was extremely excited. I had been through hell these last few months, and speaking publicly about it, to people who were like minded, sounded like the pick-me-up I needed. Trump rallies will go down in history. The people are happy, excited, patriotic and energetic. They are almost always HUGE in numbers. President Trump set new records with caravan rallies and voter turnout. The rally was everything I hoped it would be. It was on Halloween day, and we were encouraged to dress up. I put on a Captain America jumpsuit, red knee-high boots, red glitter lipstick, a Trump flag as my cape, and a MAGA hat. I was "Patriot Barbie" in her first public speaking event. I was completely in my element. I got to stand with Peggy Hall, the healthy American, Leigh Dundas, the firecracker attorney, and MAGA hulk, the social media icon. I had my speech all written out but after watching everyone speak with fire and passion, I realized I could not read off a piece of paper. I put it away. Then I freaked out and got it back out. Then I put it away again and prayed that God would guide my words and my heart. And instead, I did a speech from the heart. It was recorded and is available on YouTube. It was fun to watch later, because I really was speaking from the heart with my passion and I forgot everything that I said.

This rally made me want to be more public and open about my story, and our rights and everything that I was originally fighting for. Public speaking was always something I was good at, but never had a purpose for. I feel like now I do. Perhaps this is where God wants me?

CHAPTER TWENTY-THREE

OUR FLEE FROM OREGON
(AUGUST 2020)

SCOTT AND I started checking out properties in Arizona near our family and found that we could start over very easily there by simply selling our newly built custom house, buying a home there for half the price and putting away money to start a new business venture. God had His hand in all of it. The way that things worked out, the way He lined up the dominos to fall as they did was all in God's perfect timing.

I saw a home online that was gorgeous, and way too expensive but I laughed and clicked CONTACT REALTOR. I left a message and was called back by a woman named Ashley. Remember, I love to empower other women, so I was stoked to get a chick. I called the number back and another agent at the office answered. I told them I was returning a call to Ashley about a home, they transferred me to Wesley. Wesley? No, I want my girl, Ashley (I've never spoken one word to her ha-ha). I told Wesley I must have dialed the wrong number; I was working with someone already. He gently told me that it was a realty group, and they are all agents in the office, that he would be happy to help. (He was not being shady. This was true. The agent's share commission and Ashley was out of the office anyway.) God gave me Wesley. He knew we needed Wesley. Christopher was a Christian, Republican, Trump loving patriot like myself, and that dude worked his butt off for us. Thank you, Jesus.

Wesley had a wife who was a hairstylist, but soon to be realtor. They had three kids, all our kid's ages! They became our first friends in Arizona and we are so thankful for them. Maybe Ashley was cool too, but it didn't matter now. Now, we had Wesley and Jaqcuelyn. Yes! Every week, Wesley would send us the homes on the market in our desired area and we would scour them for the perfect fit. Houses were flying off the market within 48 hours of being posted. We would have to fly down one weekend and dominate the open houses, make an offer and fly home, all the while having faith that God would sell our house in Oregon.

One weekend, we made an offer on a house that I fell in love with in a beautiful community. The sellers did not accept it. The market was hot in Arizona (hot, get it?) and our offer was contingent on our home selling in Oregon. I was set on this home, and I thought it was the one for us. But God made sure it wasn't. Our offer wasn't accepted, and as creative as I typically am, I could not see a way around this. We were not going to get it. In my car, with a smirk on my face (I talk to God a LOT in my car alone), I told God that I knew there must be a better house for us, if He wasn't letting us get this one. I told Him how exciting that was. I loved this house, so imagine how amazing the house will be that He wants to bless us with. My goodness, I can't wait to tell you about God's goodness, phew.

On a flight back to Portland, after making an offer on this home in Arizona, I met a fellow patriot that was more connected to me than I could imagine. I was wearing my red MAGA hat, loud and proud. The young man that sat behind me said "I like your hat." I turned around to say thank you, when he showed me that he too was wearing a TRUMP hat. We got to talking about Arizona, and Oregon, and just life in general and the crazy times we were living in. He suddenly recognized me and said "Wait, do you own Glamour salon?" Scott laughed, and I said yes. He said, "I came to your salon and stood outside when the rioters were targeting you!" It was such a beautiful moment. There were so many men and women that joined me that night in guarding our city's downtown and I'll never be able to personally say thank you to all of them. I can say thank you through this book, but I wish I could shake every single hand personally. Being able to meet a stranger who gave up nights to protect my business and personally thank him was awesome. And what a strange and divine way to meet him!

On another one of our flights to Arizona to shop for our new house, Scott and I were stopped by a couple named Sara and Cody. Sara had recognized me from the news and wanted to say hi. She asked what we were doing in Arizona, and we quietly told her we were shopping for homes. She got excited and said that they were also! There was starting to be a mass exodus out of Oregon, as conservatives were recognizing the horrific outcome of a liberal government left unchecked and the destruction that was being praised in left leaning cities. Sara and Cody were the first of thousands of people leaving Oregon for red states and freedom. Cody, however, has been considering a political run in Arizona, and has shown an interest in bringing me on board somehow. I have never considered myself a politician and would never, but it is starting to become clear that America doesn't need politicians. We need patriot citizens. We need people in office who care about our freedoms, our country's foundation, its citizen's rights, and God. It's yet to be seen how this awesome connection will play out in my life. Wait, is this where God wants me?

We got an offer on our house in Oregon and we accepted it. The pressure was on to find our home in Arizona. We looked every weekend and had an emergency plan to jump on a plane to look at one if needed. We planned a weekend to visit, and I told Scott I didn't even know why we were going still. There were no houses on the market that weekend that looked promising. Friday night, Wesley's program sent a home that Scott saw first. "Uhhhh babe.... check out this house." It was everything we wanted and more. It was the perfect price, great location, and to us just a dream. We called Wesley and said, "What's wrong with this house?" He laughed and said that the homes in that area really were in that price range. We were getting on a plane the next morning and I said, "Book us to view it the minute we land." We landed at 10:00 am. The first available showing was at 12:00. The whole morning had already been filled with showings. When we arrived, the house had been shown 9 times and had almost as many offers. The homeowner had to work from home and she was up in her office. As I was walking through the house, freaking out about how amazing it was, Wesley kept telling me to quiet down. I could not contain my excitement. This was our blessing. I knew this would be our home.

We went to lunch with Wesley directly after, and I said, "How much do we need to offer to get this house?" Houses were going OVER asking price and cash only. With the sale of our home, we had just enough to get this one without having to apply for a loan. Another blessing. Applying for a mortgage loan when you are moving states and basically unemployed for the last year was going to be nearly impossible.

Wesley gave us his idea, and we agreed. He took a drink of his beer and nodded. I slapped the table and said, "Well go get your laptop!' It was a Patriot Barbie moment. She can be kind of bossy.

He did. He submitted our offer, called the realtor and came back to the table, smirking and noticeably confident that we just bought our home. The owners had verbally agreed to accept out offer. It was another moment God had complete control over. Turns out, there were more showings after us, and someone else made a higher offer even. But the family felt that they should honor our offer since they already accepted it verbally, and ethically, the home was ours. What divine intervention! What morals! A family refusing more money because they wanted to honor their word.

We flew back to Oregon with joy in our hearts and a peaceful feeling only provided by the knowledge that God really was providing for us in a time where we could not provide for ourselves. Our entire life was being up ended.

Scott and I planned to come down one weekend and make some updates on the house before we moved in. He drove a moving truck down a couple days early and took a load and I flew down later to help. We wanted to make some small updates and get the house ready, so when we got down with the kids, we weren't moving into chaos or trying to work on the house with three little rascals running around! While we were working on the house we found out that Oregon was on fire. It was terrifying news to hear! The fires started in rural areas, and no doubt, being started, were consuming a lot of the state. Luckily, we were flying home the next day. Our friend that was watching the kids packed them up and took them to her house. Our house was creeping into a dangerous level!! With the kids safe and sound, we started to then worry about the danger our house was in. I couldn't begin to imagine what would entail if our house that was about to close were to burn down. It was frightening.

Scott and I flew back to Oregon to black skies and gloom. My heart was filled with disgust, as I imagined the devil himself residing here and his darkness consuming this state. It felt like an omen. With everything Oregon was starting to stand for, it was becoming a hell. Portland officials were allowing and condoning BLM and antifa to riot for months now and innocent people were suffering in that area endlessly, while our governor and mayor encouraged it. Kate Brown was still locking down and restricting businesses repeatedly. Innocent business owners had already been shut down for months, and now had their windows boarded up permanently, so that they wouldn't also be robbed blind, or their business lit on fire. Now, the state was on fire. More people were suffering and losing what they had left. The devastation in Oregon was almost too much to comprehend. And our "leaders" were not only unconcerned, but unsympathetic. Residents who had once supported Kate Brown, now watched their state fall apart, in ashes literally, as she continued to collect her paycheck and benefits while bankrupting most small business owners without remorse. Watch any press conference. She has an evil smirk on her face as she announces her next restriction and brags about how she is protecting her citizens.

In our flee to Arizona, I needed some kind of plan to continue to earn an income. I couldn't just walk completely away from the 15-year clientele I had built. My plan for the move, was to fly back to Glamour Salon every 4 weeks and for one week, do all my clients. I would do that every month as long as I could. That was realistically going to be my only income.

Glamour Salon was no longer my focus business. I did not have enough stylists to continue to pay the rent on this new, huge location, and especially not enough to cover additional overhead or profit. I was actively looking for a buyer. If someone could be present and work on it, recruit new artists, it could be amazing. But my heart was no longer in it. My one week of work in Oregon was going to have to carry us for a while and the salon overhead while we started over in Arizona.

After we landed back in Oregon, got the kiddos and went to check on the smoke damage to our home, we continued to pack and prepare for the big move in a few weeks. My one-week schedule was starting September 14th, so we were going to stick around until September 18th to make the move. Leaving earlier would mean I would have to turn around and fly back again to work AND we still had another load to move with all our furniture. I worked at the salon September 9th, but by 10:00 am on September 10th, I felt strongly that we needed to be out of Oregon. I don't know what the reason was, but I called Scott, and without hesitation or question, I said "Put the boat on the truck, fill it with the kids' clothes and stuff, whatever we need to live with, fill it. Pick me up at the salon at 7:00 tonight. We're moving. We're leaving this state tonight." That man did not doubt me for a second. He did what I asked, and even though it was going to make my schedule a bit more difficult in the next week, I had an overwhelming feeling of terror.

I felt strongly that we were "running for our lives." I kept looking behind us as we charged down the freeway, watching the black skies slowly fade. I kept checking on my kids. I stayed up while Scott drove through the night, watching our progress, and feeling safer with every mile we distanced ourselves. When we crossed out of Oregon, I had peace. I felt free. I felt safe. I don't know what unknown threat was lurking in Oregon for my family, but I know that sometimes God clearly speaks to me through emotion and feelings. I trust that whatever made me want to flee Oregon was left far behind us, and I may never know what God was saving us from.

"Even though I walk through the valley of the shadow of death, I will fear no evil, for you are with me." (Psalm 23:4)

CHAPTER TWENTY-FOUR

STARTING OVER
(SEPTEMBER 2020)

OUR MOVE TO Arizona turned out to be one of the greatest blessings of our life. I was immediately a desert girl. I love the sun, the cacti, the gorgeous sunset and the amazing weather. Our family has started being more active, spending more time together, going on hikes, enjoying new events and having slumber parties in the back yard. We felt at home instantly, and most importantly, we felt safe. Our businesses had always consumed so much of our time. Even the time we did spend as a family would often get interrupted by emergencies, issues at the job, employees not showing up to work. We were slaves to our jobs. God has freed us from that. He has taken us to a new adventure that lets us be a family, spend real time together, and enjoy our work! He blessed us just as I had faith that He would.

One of the decisions we had made about this move was to try our hand at fix and flip properties. We had both wanted to do it for years but were too busy with our other businesses to try. We had all our money wrapped up in those businesses and our new home. Now that we were forced to start over, that was going to be our new business venture. Failure was not an option. I did not want another salon; I was done being stabbed in the back and managing women who were never there for me if it didn't suit them. I also didn't want another business that could be cancelled. Scott didn't want to open another gym; he was just done investing into businesses that needed lots of managing and employees. We wanted the freedom that God was blessing us with. Two of his gym employees in Oregon walked out on him, claiming his wife was a white supremacist and they couldn't support that. We had both been through the ringer with employees and drama in our industries and we wanted to be free from that. We also saw this as an opportunity to start something new and different. We felt God was giving us a do-over.

We had to reinvent our entire life, but we believed that with God in our corner, He would provide. We were a few months into living in Arizona, and not sure where to start making contacts. It was a full-time job, researching people who would connect us and not take advantage of us, knowing we were amateurs. I was starting to get worried about this new venture as we realized we couldn't find the right properties, and the network was very tight.

When I moved to Arizona, I felt that I could be louder with my opinions and beliefs. I felt that the community who turned on me was now a shadow I was leaving behind and could no longer scare me into submission. My businesses were gone, there was nothing to "cancel." I did not care what the liberal leftists in Salem, Oregon thought or said about me. It no longer affected me, it only affected themselves. They could continue to obsess and fawn over me and everything I did. I wouldn't see it, hear it, or acknowledge it. I became more excited about my alter ego, The Patriot Barbie, and what opportunities we might have together. Public speaking? Politics? A podcast? A conservative newscaster? I am still waiting to hear from God on that next step. But as I dove into the scene in Arizona, God continually placed people in my life to guide me and the connections have been alarming and exciting.

I had decided for some unknown reason that it was important for me to go the Trump 'Stop the Steal' rally in Washington DC. Something inside me told me that I needed to. (If you'd like to hear it for the record, YES, I believe that there was cheating, and that Joe Biden did not get elected President. Yes, I believe President Trump rightfully won. Yes, I voted for him. Apparently, I should have stolen ballots and voted for him multiple times, like the opponents did. Yeah, I said it. I'm such a conspiracy theorist.)

I had to rearrange my entire client schedule to do so, and my poor husband had to manage our home without me, but I pulled it off. I booked a flight to leave on January 5th, and get in late at night, just in time to get to my room and sleep. I would wake up the 6th, go to the rally, see our President speak, and march for freedom to our nation's capital. I would get back on a plane the next morning and be home before dinner. I was taking this trip alone but I was determined. I knew people I could meet up with when I got there, and something was calling me to go.

I dressed in full patriotic gear for the flight, flag leggings, a Patriot Barbie tank top, and red glitter lipstick. A gentleman who looked very normal (not raging patriotic like myself) complimented my attire while we went through security and said he was also going to the rally. I thought I might get harassed in my little get-up, but I only got compliments. (I've now learned that leftists are very loud on social media behind a keyboard but have no courage in real life to attack everyday citizens, the way they do online.)

I boarded the Southwest plane, which is open seating, and gladly took the emergency exit row for two reasons:

A: I am the perfect candidate for that row, I used to be a flight attendant for Southwest, so I know how to quickly and effectively escort passengers to safety in an emergency.

B: Everyone knows the emergency exit row seats have more leg room.

Which is why, when everyone kept walking past my row, I started to wonder if I forgot my deodorant. I turned to the flight attendant and asked her "Isn't is weird that no one is sitting here? She agreed that normally, it's everyone's first choice. It was weird, but not if you're a believer. See, God needed Mark to sit there. And he did.

Mark was the gentleman who complimented my outfit earlier in security. After we got through the normal chit chat about how jacked up our country is, we started getting to know each other. I told Mark my story and how my family was starting all over in Arizona, trying to start investing in real estate and flipping homes. I told him it was hard because we didn't know anyone and had no connections yet. God is so good. Are you ready for this?

Mark had been flipping homes in Arizona for over 20 years and now his children do it. Mark was a licensed realtor. Mark was successful at it and had moved on to land sales. Mark handed me his card and told me that when we got back, he would sit down and give me all his contacts for flipping. Are you serious? What are the odds? Sometimes, I think God gets a kick out of watching His handiwork. It brings me to tears writing this, knowing that all I have to do is ask. In faith. His plan is just so shockingly incredible.

> *"Therefore I tell you, whatever you ask for in prayer, believe that you have received it, and it will be yours." (Mark 11:24)*

As promised, Mark, his wife, Scott and I went to lunch, and Mark gave us the A-Z in home flipping. He gave us his contacts. One of those contacts was the connection we needed to get our first flip home. For months, Scott and I were floundering about, treading water, trying to find a way to start our new business in Arizona, knowing very few people and barely connected. Had God not placed Mark on that airplane next to me, I wonder how long we would have been able to keep treading. God had our lives in His hand, and He was placing the people we needed right where we needed them to start our new life, make friends, make connections and pursue His will.

If you think that story is wild, you better keep reading, because God hasn't shocked you quite enough.

After buying our home in Arizona, we were quietly packing our things to move, not wanting the media to get ahold of our choice and blast it to the cancel culture. I wanted to make sure my family was safe before I let anyone officially know we had left.

I received an email from a woman named Lisa, who had

been following my story and wanted to offer her support and love. She was a flight attendant from Phoenix and told me that if she should ever overnight in Portland, she wanted to take me to get drink. Something (always Gods' quiet voice I swear) told me to write this woman back. I don't always have time to write everyone back, although I do try. I told this woman that I was going to be in Arizona soon and would love to connect with her.

After conversation, I trusted her enough to tell her about our move. This woman was strong, affectionate and so supportive and loving. She invited me to an event at her home, stating I was her personal guest, and to ignore any event fees I saw. Turns out, she was throwing a fundraiser for Martha McSally, a conservative political runner in the US Senate race. At this specific event, we were surrounded by likeminded, conservative people, and were able to start making incredible connections. I was honored to have been invited personally by the host. I was even more honored that when I arrived, she ran from her bedroom, shouted my name and gave me a huge hug, as if we had been friends for years. Before moving here to Arizona, I had some abandonment issues from losing my mom. When I was treated a certain way by an older woman, I would almost immediately begin to place her in a motherly role for myself. I don't tell her this, and I don't think it was healthy. But for the longest time, I had no mom to look up to, to lean on, to confide in.

When I am shown love and affection by older women, I immediately connect to them as if I were the daughter they didn't know about. I was always looking for that strong woman that can act as my role model, and confidant. No one will ever replace my mom and no one will ever take on my mom's role. But I cannot help but be immediately attached and trusting to women who take me under their wing and speak to me and about me with pride and encouragement. After moving to Arizona and spending lots of quality time with Scott's mom, she has been someone I could not live without. She is fun, outgoing, outspoken, thoughtful and supportive. I always say she is my biggest fan. She beams with pride when talking about my fight and what I now stand for. I thank God for her!

While attending this fabulous event with amazing people, I made a lot of new friends and connections. One important connection was Brandie, a fun, outgoing and honest woman who hosted a women's Christ centered study at her home once a month called Power Soul. She leads the group in an intimate, down to earth setting, with food and drinks served and great community. The women in attendance are fun, bright and enjoyable to be around. I was thrilled to attend Power Soul and gain new friends. I knew that Brandie and I would be great for each other on all levels too!

On social media, I started campaigning conservatives to vet their local businesses, and direct their money and business to other conservative businesses. I felt it was important for us as Republicans to make a statement with our money and direct it to companies and business owners who would in turn donate their money to organizations who value what we value. Brandie loved my post and referred me to do business with Christine, a patriot, strong woman, who was also a realtor in Arizona. Brandie tagged Christine, who jumped on the post and said she would love to get connected with me! She invited me to an event at her home in Scottsdale, where realtors, brokers and investors would be, to network and enjoy a business social. After inviting me, Christine also said that she remembers meeting me (Patriot Barbie) in Nashville!

I told Scott that I felt awkward, this woman was inviting me to her home for an event, and I don't think she realizes I'm not who she thinks I am. I haven't been to Nashville in forever! I don't know who else gets called Patriot Barbie, but I was not someone she met in Nashville. I messaged her to try to straighten it out but she didn't respond. We went to the event, and she rushed to hug me and meet my husband! I said "Christine, I feel terrible. I don't know who else goes by Patriot Barbie, but I don't think we met in Nashville girl."

"Yes, we did. In the airport, on our connecting flight to Washington DC. (The Trump Rally.)

Full circle.

Are you guys letting this sink in?

On my trip to Washington DC, I met Mark and Christine. I met the people I needed to meet to jump start my real estate career to the next level almost immediately. In complete shock, it all came together. I now recall rushing to a bar in the airport to try to get food ordered before our connecting flight left to DC and this Asian woman was sitting next to me, doing the same thing. I gave her a Patriot Barbie sticker, and we convinced the live singer to play something patriotic. The whole bar sang along as I took a video of that awesome moment. I didn't even get this woman's name, but it was Christine. And I was now standing in her gorgeous home, with a film crew surrounding us and ready to meet Tarek El Moussa, from the Flip or Flop reality show, and his girlfriend Heather Rae Young, from the Selling Sunset reality tv show. As well as all their partners, and big-time investors. In attendance was our friend Brandie, who was now hosting her Power Soul Experience group in Christine's home, because it was getting so big in attendance. Brandie also now hosts a radio show, sponsored by Christine's businesses. Brandie, that night, heard my story and surrounded by strong Christian women, felt called by the Lord to lift up my story. She invited me to speak on her radio show about my trials and God's goodness. She has asked to interview me at Power Soul, to inspire other women to stand up in boldness for their convictions.

Once again, the grace of God has shocked me, and His ability to bring together everyone for His good, in His timing. Even as God is bringing people to me for support, empowerment and community, He is also using the evil to bring us together as well.

CHAPTER TWENTY-FIVE

FIGHTING CANCEL CUTURE...STILL

SHORTLY AFTER THIS wild event, I was sent a harassing email by a reporter in Salem, Whitney Woodworth of the Statesman Journal, called the "Statesman Urinal" by conservatives, if that tells you anything. Yes, they are a left leaning, liberal media outlet. Shocking. Their narrative is almost always directed at terrorizing conservatives and slandering right side politicians and figures. You know, typical media stuff. Whitney herself has twisted nearly every story about my stand into some sort of unflattering, accusatory article. It goes without saying that if she wants a comment from me for any article, I wouldn't give her the time of day. I have no interest in furthering the career of someone who has purposely set out to try to harm me and my reputation.

Whitney sent me this email, asking these outrageous questions that are more like an interrogation, than a simple media interview. Questions about my Patriot Barbie website, questions about my husband's prior bankruptcy, questions about the house we registered our new business at, very alarming and disturbing questions about our personal backgrounds and prior business relationships. Here it is:

Good afternoon,

In a joint project with the Arizona Republic, we are reporting on the closure of Glamour Salon and opening of Dream Built Homes. Our previous attempts to ask questions on this issue have not been returned. Please respond to the following questions by the end of day Monday, March 8.

1. What is the reason for the closure of Glamour Salon?
2. When will the salon close? How many employees will be out of work?
3. How many months did you operate rent free? Was your decision to close related to renewed rent demands?
4. Are all of your Oregon businesses closed?
5. What are the names of the businesses, when did they close and what was the reason for the closure?
6. You said your husband ran successful businesses before COVID. What can you say about his business record?
7. How do you explain his bankruptcy and business closures in 2015?
8. Didn't he also get foreclosed on in 2017?
9. How long have you and your husband been involved in real estate?
10. How many states are you and your husband licensed as a real estate agents?
11. How many states are you and your husband licensed as brokers?
12. Can you provide your license numbers and the dates you and Scott passed the state exam?
13. What is your relationship to the owners of the house where the business is registered at?
14. Why did you register your company at that address?
15. What kind of business is Dream Built?

16. Are any of the principles for Dream Built licensed as real estate agents?
17. If you and your husband aren't licensed realtors, how can you legally advertise your husband as a real estate agent on your website? Isn't that misleading?
18. If not, do you work with any licensed real estate agents? If so, who?
19. Are any licensed as contractors?
20. What drew you to the real estate industry? Do you have any background in real estate?
21. What transactions and projects has Dream Built been involved in? Please provide us a list with a list.
22. Most of the photos on your website appear to be your former home. Are there any other homes in your portfolio? Where are they?
23. Why does your website use stock art to suggest these are projects you've been involved in?
24. In the lawsuit against Brown, you cite a complaint to CPS involving your family. What did the complaint allege?
25. How was the complaint resolved/what was the outcome?
26. In an interview, you mentioned Antifa was targeting and tracking you. What did this entail? Did you report it to Marion County/Salem police or any other law enforcement?
27. Can you provide evidence that you have been tracked by these groups or their agents?
28. What is your business connection to Jake Linesh? Has he been involved in any other of your businesses? Is Hales a licensed contractor in Arizona? Can you provide his contract number?
29. If not, isn't it misleading to advertise him as an Arizona contractor?
30. How much money did your Patriot Barbie website generate?

31. Did you use proceeds from your website to buy homes in Arizona or elsewhere?
32. Can you provide an accounting of all the donations you received and how the money was used?
33. How many GoFundMe sites have raised money for you? Please provide links to those sites.
34. How did you manage to pay for your home construction project and buy a new home when you publicly said you were struggling to survive?
35. Is the Glamour Institute for Freedom involved in any other lawsuits besides your own?
36. How much has been raised through the Glamour Institute for Freedom?
37. What activities has the institute funded?
38. Do you think it's fair for you to solicit donations from Oregonians then to leave the state that has supported you?
39. You said you moved to a red state. Is this Arizona?
40. Do you have an Arizona driver's license?
41. Why did you pick Arizona?
42. Is there anything you'd like to say to supporters?

Thank you for your time,

Whitney Woodworth
Reporter

This email, coming from a supposed professional, is really creepy and I was thinking "why is this crazy chick tracking me to Arizona and stalking me? Why does it seem like she recruited another journalist to check into my family's background and credit report? Why does she feel the need to continue reporting on me when I don't even live in her city anymore? This is such a blatant and violating act, and ethically, as a reporter, shameful. Does she think I'm some big scam artist that she is going to expose??" Everything Scott and I have done to make this move successful has been on the record, by the books and legal. She teamed up with a reporter named Robert Anglen, from an the Arizona Republic paper, to "expose me." It was violating, yes, but honestly, mostly laughable. Right at that moment in time, Biden was signing dozens of executive orders like chiclets in a box, the covid vaccine agenda was being pushed and people were experiencing side effects, child trafficking was being exposed daily and the borders were being opened. In Oregon itself, Kate Brown put herself first in line to get the vaccine, schools still weren't open, there were still restrictions on businesses, and BLM was still rioting in Portland. There were so many credible and authentic news stories she could be writing about, much more interesting than Patriot Barbie. But they decided to run an article about my new credible business, and my move, and my website, all with the narrative that I stole GoFundMe money to buy homes in Arizona and I'm a fraud and a grifter.

The best part was that without any comments from me, nearly everything they wrote was so blatantly assumptive that the article received very little attention and almost no merit. It will likely go down in the archives as junk mail. In the article, they stated that I was not a licensed real estate agent, when in fact, that day, my license was approved. So, the article was false and slanderous at least. They scrambled to update the article online, and after they did, it was even more of a joke, because if the entire article is supposed to be an expose, and you can't even get the facts right, how can these assumptions be credible at all?

Within hours of this article circulating, my peace was confirmed. I had no anxiety over it like I would have in the past. I knew that God would protect me, and that people seeking truth would see right through this and shake their head. It was so blatantly an attempt to isolate and target me in a state I now called home. I had just officially announced my move and clearly reiterated that we felt safe in Arizona and what does Whitney Woodworth do? She tracks me down, stalks me and harasses me in my safe place. I'm guessing she isn't a mother, and possibly a sociopath. What kind of woman targets a wife and mom who is desperate to find a safe haven for her family, and goes after her? Not only does this reflect on her empathy as a human and woman but her poor ethics as a biased journalist.

"What then, shall we say in response to this? If God is for us, who can be against us?" (Romans 8:31)

Well, little wayward Whitney didn't realize that God is so much bigger than her and that His peace was surrounding and protecting me. No one so much as blinked at that article. But what did happen was patriots across Arizona, were reaching out to support me, welcome me and encourage me here. Whatever Whitney and Robert set out to do, it failed, and once again, God turned it to my favor and brought someone else into my life at the perfect time.

Shortly after this article aired, a woman named Dani contacted me. She explained in an email that it was clear what the media was trying to do to me, that the majority of Americans could now see through media attempts to slander conservatives and that she wanted to help. Turns out, this brave woman had also been cancelled by her community, her business name slandered and ruined and was rebuilding from the ground up. She owns a public relations company that specifically handles people like me, who are in the media, spotlight and news, but don't know how to navigate everything that comes their way. That's me alright.

We went to breakfast, told our stories, and I was refreshed by how real and honest she was. She was open and vulnerable about her life, situation and how she is handling it. She has been through so much of what I have, with harassment, lies and cancel culture, and has also come through with more faith and a stronger resolve. I felt immediately that she was someone I should stay networked with. It not only gave us both more power to withstand the negativity and hate but empowered us both as women. Announcing to the cancel culture that they themselves brought together two strong women was satisfying to say the least. I had already been writing my book, and Dani had published a book about cancel culture. It was divine that we should be connected, and I felt the motions of my life shift. Life was continuing to change for me, and this was just the beginning.

About 4 months into fleeing Oregon for Arizona, I received

a message on my Facebook page from a supporter. *Greg was from Oregon and had been following my story since reopening. He had been messaging me throughout, offering praise, prayers and supportive words. We had only communicated vaguely. We were chatting back and forth when Greg told me that he had horses, and he and his wife would love to take me and my husband on a horseback ride on the beach, just a friendly way to give us a break, and something to do to relax. It was such a genuine and sincere offer. I had not officially announced my move to Arizona, and I wasn't quite ready to break it to Greg that I no longer lived in Oregon to take him up on his offer. The back story with me and horses is not good. So bad, in fact, that my bucket list is quite short, but one of the few items on it, was to "ride a horse successfully."

Here's what that means.

My entire life, I have had the absolute worst experiences with any horse I encounter. In fact, I have never once had an experience with any horse that wasn't terrifying. I have been kicked, bit, charged at and stomped on. I've had arena horses throw me off. I've had trail horses run full speed, trying to decapitate me on tree limbs. I've had a horse at a church camp get in a fight with another horse, while my saddle started slipping and I fell underneath the horse. Are you seeing a pattern here? Horses sense fear. So after just a few of these incidents, clearly I was full of fear, and it was a vicious cycle where I was never going to be able to have a friendship with any horse as long as I feared it. And because of my history, I was afraid. So my bucket list item was to be able to conquer that fear, ride a horse, control the animal and have absolutely nothing go wrong.

Greg messaged me again a month later and told me the offer still stands. He and his wife were determined to treat us to a horseback ride, and Greg did not know my history. I felt that moment of divinity once again when Greg reached out to offer me this. I thought the opportunity to tackle this bucket list item was amazing. This time, however, Greg was sad to inform me, that they would not be in Oregon for a few months to accommodate. They were in Arizona!! Alright, this was my chance. I told Greg that my family had privately moved to Arizona and found out that he was only a few hours away. As the story goes, I loaded up my two older kids, ages 4 and 7, and told them we were going on an adventure! Greg and Anna put my kids and I up in a spare room for the night, treated us to dinner and karaoke, and took us all horseback riding. The kids were amazed and terrified all at the same time.

I went live on Facebook and told my story of horses and their vendetta for me. I wanted to capture the moment I got on a horse after 25 years of being absolutely terrified of them. For me, it was going to be this empowering moment, where I conquered a fear that I had tucked away my entire adult life. I never had a need to tackle this fear because horses weren't a part of my life. I wanted to know that the person I had become (Patriot Barbie) could do it because that chick is crazy bold. Guess what? I did (she did). I rode Turk for 2 hours out in the gorgeous Arizona desert. I showed Turk who was boss, and I did it with confidence. I was not afraid. Ok I was, but I knew I could handle it and I knew I could take control when I needed to if this horse decided to take me on.

By the end of the ride, I was talking to Turk like an old friend, scolding him when he needed it and shaking my head at him when he thought he could run without my permission. I was absolutely 100% in control of an animal I previously was scared to death of. Seriously, if a horse snorted at me through a fence, I would wince and squeal. Pathetic. I was positive that if I pet a horse on his nose, he would bite my entire hand off. Terrified. Now, in my new life, I was strong. I was brave. I really could conquer anything. Forget fighting the entire government of Oregon, I rode a horse darn it!! This Patriot Barbie chick was really changing things for me.

In December of 2020 my attorney Rick filed my official lawsuit against the state of Oregon and Governor Kate Brown. The legalities are extensive, but the concept is essentially that my rights were taken from me, and almost all Oregon small business owners, without due process. We were never given the chance to prove to the state that we could operate during Covid safely. I must reiterate that I don't believe the state, or any government has the right to take away our right to work, earn a living or operate a business. The government does not exist to determine when we, as humans, can and cannot make our own decisions or take our own risks. Even with due process, no business owner should have to prove they can operate safely. They can be open for business, and customers can use their common sense and education to decide for themselves if a facility is safe and they may enter at their own risk. Oregon OSHA, Oregon Health Authority, Child Protective Services and Governor Kate Brown acted as dictators and overstepped their authority.

It's important to me that we win this lawsuit because it sets precedent. A win will determine that the governor did not have the authority to weaponize these organizations against her own citizens and to threaten them for noncompliance. This would be a win for the entire state of Oregon, and its small business owners. It would protect them from further restrictions, mandates and lockdowns. It is a lawsuit for We the People. It is a lawsuit that will be years in the making and we are only in year one.

As of right now, the state has moved to make this a federal court case and is attempting to throw out many of the motions. Most will stick, including a retaliation charge and I will continue to move forward with the case. The $70,000 GoFundMe money has long been spent paying two attorneys in my charge to press forward. I am determined to continue but am now at another roadblock. My attorney has worked hard on this case, getting it to court and now with an assigned judge. He has been offered a great opportunity,that takes him out of private practice. To move forward with my lawsuit, I am searching diligently for an attorney that is willing to take the lead and move forward. I am faithful that God will provide the person He calls for the job. If I drop it, or back down, justice will not be served for anyone. I'm fighting for all small business owners! To follow the updates on my case, I encourage you to visit my website www.patriotbarbie.com. The entire lawsuit document has been uploaded and I plan to update this page as needed!

CHAPTER TWENTY-SIX

CLOSING GLAMOUR SALON
(APRIL 2ND, 2021)

GLAMOUR SALON WAS functioning without me in Oregon for a few months just fine. I missed the stylists, and they missed me, but things were feeling different. I thought it was maybe time to let someone else run the show. I was ready to be done with that chapter of my life, as long as it was in good hands. Now that I was living in another state, it's not that I couldn't do it, it's that I was ready to let go. I was jaded as a salon owner, and I was tired of getting hurt every time a stylist turned their back on me. I had decided to sell the salon to someone who would want to reinvest into building it into greatness again. I thought I had found the right person for the job and after many months of discussion, and mounds of paperwork, we began the process of her buying the salon from me and working to build it back up to the monumental business it once was. She seemed like the perfect woman for the job. I gave her every document, every report, and every detail I could about running the salon exactly how I did, to keep it successful.

She had already signed the legal paperwork needed to take over the lease, and I spent two extra days in Oregon, away from my family, training her on my systems. I ran her through my daily routines, my online system functions, gave her all my ordering contacts and wholesale vendors. I basically gave her all the inside information on how to run my salon. I gave her the details I had spent nearly 12 years perfecting. The day before we were to sign legal documents, and I had spent $2,500 on an attorney, she called and bailed. I had wasted hours and days and tears and excitement on knowing my salon was in good hands. Only to be stabbed in the back one last time. Not only did she back out on the deal, but she also moved out of the salon and never spoke a word to me again. It was the final straw. It was truly the final nail in the coffin. When she walked out, it was the breaking point of having a successful salon and knowing that it was only going to continue to fall apart. What I realize now, is that it was God pushing me out of the salon and onto my next adventure.

I was not ready to let go, and He was forcing my hand. It was the LAST time I was willing to be slapped in the face. I no longer wanted a life where the people I support and promote and encourage can turn on me and walk away without an ounce of remorse. I wanted out of the salon industry. I wanted to be in control of my business, not dependent. God wanted me to be free. He had other plans.

On April 2nd, 2021, after the sale fell through, I closed Glamour Salon forever. I had done my clients for the week. I had been commuting every 4 weeks to my salon, managing it remotely and working tirelessly to get all my appointments done in that small time so I could get home to my family. After everything I had done and the cancel culture attacks, I had to analyze my business and it was not pretty. Eventually it was no longer feasible. The salon was made for 25 people, and I was only leasing space to 6. With the rent, overhead and business expenses, the salon was soon going to be losing money. I had lost all motivation to recruit new artists and rebuild. I had spent the last 15 years building my salon. I didn't have the heart to start all over again. If I still lived in Oregon and was still willing to sacrifice for another few years, trying to grow my business back up, I could have held on. But I had been through the hardest 6 months of my life, and I didn't have the energy to start all over...again. It was a sinking ship, and I need to escape before I drowned. I told the stylists the bad news.

That on my next trip in March, I was going to close the salon, sell what I could, and take the furniture back in a moving truck for my real estate/staging business. The feeling of ultimate failure once again came over me. After all the hard work and years of sacrifice building this incredible business, I had nothing to show. It felt like the last 15 years had been such a waste. I had put my heart into my salon, and it seemed like I was always investing into it. When all was said and done, to watch it just evaporate was confusing. Why was I losing everything when I know I stood for what was right? Should I have just shut up and obeyed like the other businesses? What would my life be like if I had simply complied and waited for permission to re-open? I know the answer. I know in my heart that I would have lost my salon anyway. I would have lost stylists who could no longer afford to lease due to shutdowns. I would have lost clients due to their loss of income. I would have gone into debt trying to repay all the money I owed on lease, even though we were unable to work. I would have had to sacrifice and labor yet again to try to get my salon back up to its potential. I know that had I stayed silent, I still would have lost it all but I would not have had the experience I so gladly welcome now, of being courageous, being cancelled and ultimately being blessed.

Glamour Salon was no longer a success. That part of my life was now over. I shared tears and joy and laughs with clients who had been in my chair and part of my journey for over 12 years. That week, I gave them poster board and markers, to write whatever message they wanted. We hung them on the huge windows in the salon for all the city to see. I was being silenced in the media and censored. But this was my salon, and I had every right to put my beliefs and my clients' final words on our windows. There were some nasty remarks towards our nasty governor. There were patriotic sayings. There were scriptures. They were words of encouragement and love. There were Trump signs. We got to have our say, in a liberal city that got to say whatever hateful thing they wanted without repercussion. It was liberating and freeing. I could say these things now, boldly. I could no longer be cancelled. I could be called a racist, but I already have. I could be called a fascist, but

I already have. There were no longer consequences for me for speaking out and I was enjoying it immensely. I made quite a few of my own signs. Hee hee hee. There were signs from all perspectives. They read:

> "God is good. He has a plan for you. He knows you. He loves you."

> "Those who judge never understand. Those who understand never judge."

> "Kate can't shut down new beginnings. Well wishes and good luck Lindsey and the Glamour women."

> "Oregon kills another amazing business. Good luck Lindsey in a much better state."

> "One nation under God. United we stand, divided we fall."

> "Mask free since June 2020. ZERO Covid cases."

> "When tyranny becomes law, rebellion becomes duty —Thomas Jefferson"

> "I support you Lindsey. Lies do not become truth just because they are accepted by the majority."

> "I would rather be hated for who I am, than loved for who I am not."

> "We don't have to agree on anything to be kind."

Don't be deceived. Closing Glamour Salon felt immensely like a defeat in the moment that it happened. I had built it from nothing. I had gone from 3 stylists to 10, to none, then back up to 25. My heart was in that salon and the success that it had become. The salon represented someone that I was, who I had been known for, almost my entire adult life. I was closing a noticeably big chapter of my life, and not by choice. By force. It felt shameful. I felt like I had failed everyone. Especially myself. I found myself asking over and over if I had done the right thing. I know that I did and I know my business would not have survived the shutdowns Kate Brown continues to impose on her people. As I reflect on everything it cost me to stand up for my rights, I would not change a thing. I know that I would have lost everything anyway in her tyrannical restrictions. But I also know that I now stand for something and God has used my entire life story to prepare me for this moment, whatever it may be.

CHAPTER TWENTY-SEVEN

OUR NEW LIFE
(APRIL 2ND, 2021)

MY HUSBAND AND, I and our three little munchkins live in the Phoenix area. We live in a house we instantly felt was "home." We are definitely hot weather people and are in love with the desert air. My kids have taken up the outdoors more so than ever. We've started hiking on weekends and it's a pool day every weekend. With our new career, I can be with my kids more so than I ever would have in Oregon at the rate we were going. We love our new roles in our life and in our family. I am able to focus on being a voice for conservative women, an advocate for women empowerment, and a testimony for God's grace and glory. I have time to be Patriot Barbie, the alter ego I have embraced. Long story short, after all is said and done, if I could go back and do it all over again, I would. I would do everything exactly the same. It was God's plan, not mine. Just to be where we are now.

If I could have the chance, have my salon back, knowing the lockdowns would never happen, that everything would be just as it was before March 2020, back to being a successful salon owner, blissfully ignorant to politics, and my life would have just carried on as usual, I still would not take it. I am at a place now where I have to admit that God used me. He used me to fulfill a purpose that I still am not aware of. He is using me to carry out a divine plan. He allowed my life and my path to veer off into a place that no one would have asked for. I could have made different choices that would have ended this all a different way. But I would not do that. I would let God do this all over again because the blessings now are already good, and I know that God is not done with me.

We sold our custom "forever" home in Oregon and bought a beautiful home in Arizona. We had moved in only one year before the lockdowns. Now, in a shocking turn of events, here we were, listing it for sale. With the equity, we were able to take out a loan on our house and invest. In our dreams, Scott and I have always wanted to flip homes. God made that dream come true. For those of you who don't watch HGTV, you purchase a run-down home in a wholesale market or one that is grossly underpriced. It needs renovations, repairs or updating. You do these things to the home, redesign it, update it, etc. Then you resell the house for its new value, and the goal of course is to profit, after deducting all your expenses and remodel costs. In our new business venture, Scott finds the properties that can affordably be flipped, because he is definitely a numbers guy. He's great at math and thinking logically. We originally had planned that he would get his realtor license as well. I would make all the design decisions. From changing the layout to paint colors. I am the creative, artistic one. Both roles are a perfect fit for both of us.

Our move to Arizona allowed us to pursue this dream, something we probably never could have done in Oregon. The market in Arizona is booming, as conservatives and probably democrats flee blue states for freedom. We were one year into the "pandemic" and blue states were still enforcing and even creating new restrictions. California was still being locked down, while Oregon is now requiring vaccine passports. People are moving to Arizona en masse. While there were usually 30,000 homes on the market in most areas at any given time, there were only 5,000 in the late part of 2020, and into 2021. We would have no problem selling homes. As you recall, once we had our wholesale connection thanks to a patriot friend, we were able to find wholesale homes with no problem.

We altered our plan just a bit. I was now only a part time hairstylist, commuting up to Oregon once a month for a few days, and by the time you read this, I will be completely retired from the hair industry. I could use a fresh start and a new career. I decided that I should get my realtor license, so that when it came time to list our flip home, I could have that role. What I really wanted was to serve clients, show homes and host open houses. So, at the age of 40, I was diving into a whole new career. It was exhausting to consider, and I had plenty of moments where I wondered how it all went so differently than anyone could have predicted. I had been a highly successful stylist for 15 years. I was a great stylist and had a wonderful reputation. That was all gone and I felt forced to start fresh.

Knowing that nothing would change that, I had to think positively and move forward with the same kind of drive I had for doing hair. In less than a month, I had put in all my real estate school hours, while getting settled in our new home, managing the household, tending to the three kids, and trying to get us started in our real estate investing plan. We had been living in Arizona for nearly 5 months and had not gotten started in flipping. We were both getting nervous about our new path and if we would be successful. I underestimated how easy it would be to make connections and get to know people in a new state. I had been established in Oregon almost my entire life and I suppose I took for granted how much investment I had in my community there.

Studying had always come easy to me in high school. Hair school was easy because I had loved it and was extremely passionate. Real estate was NOT something you could get into without knowing your stuff. I breezed through the school lesson, but I did not retain the information as easily as I thought I would. I was also still trying to settle into life here, missing my friends, getting into new routines, finding healthcare and schooling for my kids, and juggling the household, all while trying to start flipping houses!

The information was thick. You can't guess your way through the exams. I failed the school exam twice and then realized I need to get more serious about studying. For two days, I crammed, studied, quizzed myself and went back through the entire book. When I finally felt brave enough to test again, I passed with flying colors. With this new confidence, I immediately wanted to test with the state before I forgot any crucial information. As you can probably imagine by now, God had my back. I logged in to schedule a state exam. I was leaving for a birthday trip a few days later and I wanted to take it and pass it before I let all that studying slip away on vacation. There was one exam slot available. One. At 6 am the next morning. I snatched it up and told Scott he had kid duty. I walked out of the exam with a passing grade!! (Not until after having a decently hostile debate with the desk clerk about their mask policy.)

I thought I was in the clear! I was excited to get home and apply with the state. I had my hours, a passing grade on the school exam, and a passing grade on the state exam. Just needed to fill out the proper paperwork and get official. Panic set in when I got to a form that was asking if I had any prior "Disciplinary action taken against any license issued" with any state licensing agencies in any state. I read the question over and over, trying to find any wording that would prevent me from having to divulge my Oregon drama. There was no way around it. I would have to submit my Oregon OSHA citation to the board to be previewed, before my license could be approved. It was a huge blow, and unlike hours before, when I thought I would simply be granted my license, I was now extremely anxious that the citation would prevent me from getting my real estate license. It was a big deal, in my opinion, that a state had issued me a $14,000 citation for defying a government mandate.

We all know the citation is bull, but if the wrong person saw it and their politics carried more weight than it should, this could be bad. I left for my birthday vacation and prayed that I could relax and have fun, and not worry about this. The website said that it could be two weeks before receiving a response on an approval. Two days later, on my birthday, at 11 pm, I checked my email and had received notice that my license was approved! I was now officially a real estate agent in Arizona. The relief was overwhelming, and I was determined to hustle hard when we got home, after our much-needed trip away.

Scott and I have begun flipping homes on a regular basis. We are great at it! (Mostly him. I am really enjoying the time God has given me with my children.) We purchase cute little homes in Sun City, a senior community that looks like the neighborhood from Mr. Rogers. You drive through beautiful, well-kept homes with lush green lawns. The streets are lined with orange trees, and sweet little seniors walking their tiny pups. You may have to stop for the golf carts crossing here and there or gaze at the massive bocce·ball court as you drive by, but Sun City is the epitome of perfect retirement community. The first day of flipping, we were met with curious neighbors looking to see what the neighborhood happenings were. As time goes on, we are getting into a good routine, trying to manage the family, the flips, my trips to Oregon, and my new role as Patriot Barbie. We discovered that our dream really was a dream. Scott is incredible with numbers, working out the deals, finding the flips, and researching discount suppliers. I absolutely love designing the homes. I spend plenty of time going through design apps looking up what I want my inspiration to be and my overall look. Then more time finding something that looks close to the inspiration without being a copycat.

After our first house was finished, I was addicted to the feedback from other realtors about the look, the design and the staging. Everyone had raved about our work, my staging and our beautiful design. I had brought all my salon furniture down in a rental truck from Oregon and purchased a few couches and rugs. I could fully furnish and stage a small home to list, with the little things I had acquired and all the salon furniture. The first flips went so smoothly that we both knew that not only were we good at it, but that we were going to be successful. God did have a plan, and it was better than we had ever expected.

Delight yourself in the Lord, and He will give you the desires of your heart." (Psalm 37:4)

Shortly after moving to Arizona, I had found a great patriot friend and neighbor. She is a fierce woman of faith, protective of her family, and passionate about God and country. She has been a huge blessing to me. The kind of friend and neighbor that suddenly rings your doorbell for a glass of wine because your car is parked at home. And it's welcome every time. She also brings chocolate, so that's helpful. She invited us to her church, reiterating that masks are not required. Remember, Scott and I were both raised in church and we both had great faith. We both have relationships with God, but neither of us had made any effort throughout our marriage to find a church home. We always made the excuse that Sunday was our only day to sleep in. The kids were tough to get up and get ready. We couldn't find one we liked. We became the family that went on Easter and Christmas. Even though I don't believe that you need church to be saved, I do believe that when you find the right church, you have a community encouraging you and uplifting you as well as keeping you accountable.

We decided that the way things were going in the world, it was probably time to get our kids raised in a church and dedicate our lives to teaching our kids about God. "Get right with God" was my new mantra. When all is said and done in America, and it has hit the fan, God is still on His throne, and our kids' salvation was now the most important thing in the world for us. I also knew that after the year we had, God had blessed us and securing my faith and my walk with God was extremely crucial. My faith that was skimming the surface of my life, had now roared its head, and proven to be the one thing that kept my family and myself from insanity. It didn't matter how I felt, because after attending one service, we knew that this was our new way of life. We were going to be faithful and serve.

We were going to make God a priority. After all, He made us a priority. To ignore everything He had blessed us with would be an insult. God had brought us through the fire. The pastor spoke from the heart, he spoke with conviction, and we felt immediately that his message was from God. He spoke brazenly about end times, and what our country was going through. His message resonated with us, and we found ourselves nodding the entire sermon. God is calling His people to rise up and speak up.

> *But mark this. There will be terrible times in the last days. People will be lovers of themselves, lovers of money, boastful, proud, abusive, disobedient to their parents, ungrateful, unholy, without love, unforgiving, slanderous, without self-control, brutal, not lovers of the good, treacherous, rash, conceited, lovers of pleasure, rather than lovers of God.." (2 Timothy 3:3)*

After 10 years of marriage, we were finally attending church regularly. God gave us a new life, a new home, a new career, and now a church community that could reinforce our faith. We have finally enrolled our kids in a private faith-based school, where they learn about Christ's love and sacrifice, not the demoralizing curriculum of public-school systems. We can trust the information that our babies are being taught, so that they too can be pillars for God and speak truth in a world full of lies. God has blessed our kids with innocent faith and strong minds. After the year we had, we both wanted to get to a place where we could grow stronger in our faith and be truly thankful for the trial God had brought us through. When I reflect on the blessings God has brought our family for the trials we had endured, I wonder if nothing else really matters, except that God brought us back to Him. We've both had our faith restored, our hearts really in tune with what God has done for us. We both have a new reality that God will always provide for us. After the last year of torment and hate, we finally looked to God for healing and help. When we needed it most, we sought God, and He was there, unfailing.

> *"You will seek me and find me, when you seek me with your whole heart." (Jeremiah 29:13)*

Within weeks of attending church we had instantly made new friends with some of the other couples our age. They had kids who could play with our kids, and the same beliefs and personalities. God just kept on providing. There were things we didn't even realize we needed in life that God gave us. We continue to watch our lives thrive in a time where everything we once knew had changed suddenly and drastically.

Securing our faith and hearing God's word through our pastor, has been a miracle. Without sounding too "conspiracy theory," (and I don't care if you think I am anyway), we are in times that look a lot like what God says are near the end. We are facing a world that has no faith, no love, no empathy, no morals, no love or care for God. We live in a world where wrong is applauded and right is condemned. As the nation rallies for partial birth abortion and gender reassignment, Christians are advocating for protecting lives and honoring God and are being slandered for it. What has become of a nation when God is offensive, and sin is applauded? As God is more and more removed daily, we see more hate, more division, less morals and less tolerance for those who speak up for their beliefs. We are in a holy war and I am not ashamed to know or say what side I am on. The morals and beliefs that God has instilled into me are nonnegotiable. I don't apologize for what I stand for. The cancel culture and media would be thrilled to label me a conspiracy theorist, a radical, a far right. I'm ok with that.

> *"Because the sovereign Lord helps me, I will not be disgraced. Therefore, have I set my face like flint, and I know I will not be put to shame." (Isaiah 50:7)*

What people of this world want to call me is only a problem for them. My worth lies in what God has called me to do. He has called me to speak up and speak loudly for His purpose. I will continue to fight the dictatorship that government entities are trying to enforce. I will fight for unborn babies. I will fight for children. I will fight for the other humans in this world that see the evil being praised and condemn it. I will fight for my children's future. I will fight for those who can't fight for themselves.

It has been a huge accomplishment for me to take time out of my life, away from my kids and family, away from pursuing bigger things for my career, to write this story. It was supposed to be the last year of my life, fighting government and fighting for my family's rights. But as I wrote, God led me down my darker path, revealing to me throughout this process, that without everything I had previously endured, I would never have been the woman I am today. The woman who could stand up for her fellow Americans and stand convicted of what is not only my beliefs, but what God tells me is right and true. As strong and fearless as I have felt the last year of my life, guess what? I'm still scared. What will people do with this story? What will people do to try to use my pain and choices against me in the future? What am I thinking, putting everything out there to be damned, slandered, harassed and shamed? My past is disgusting to me. My choices were horrendous. Everything I confess to in this book leaves me vulnerable. It brings to the surface things I have hidden for years, except to close friends and people I felt needed witnessing. No one wants to go public and admit to the things I have. It's embarrassing.

But God has told me; it's for His glory. If one person can read a book about a life of bad choices, pain, heartache, recovery, forgiveness and blessings and give their life to God, then this book is a best-seller in my opinion. I am building the kingdom of heaven people! God is using my sin to bring people to Him and that is worth every torment I get. It's worth all the shame and slander on this earth. I DON'T CARE!!! I no longer care what the people of this world think of me. Considering how the people of this world are starting to behave and believe, they aren't the best judge of character anyway. Just saying.

> *"I have told you these things so that in me, you may have peace. In this world you will have trouble. But take heart. I have overcome the world." (John 16:33)*

Guys, I did what God had me do and I stand by it. It cost me everything. And it was the greatest accomplishment of my life. If I could give anyone any advice moving forward in this crazy world, it would be to listen. Hear what God wants you to do and even if it sounds terrible, scary, crazy and unachievable, do it. Risk it all for the glory. We all know that God rewards those who obey him!!

Here's why I think God is using me. I'm sooooo not perfect. In fact, I'm so far from perfect that when people see me, or hear me, I think they probably don't assume I'm a Christian. I don't look like the stereotypical Christian. I'm covered in tattoos. I care too much about my appearance. I get Botox. I don't always use the most appropriate language. I enjoy wine. I am flawed. I am human. Sometimes I can be hurtful, selfish, and self-absorbed. In no way would anyone in their right mind assume that I have a passionate love and relationship with God. But that's exactly what it is. It's not religion. Sure, I go to church, I pray, worship and take communion. I listen to my pastor speak intently. Those things qualify as religion. But what I have is a direct connection and relationship with God. The dude made me, so He knows how I am and who I am. I talk to Him the way I talk to everyone else. There's no need for me to try to be someone we both know I am not.

With this kind of relationship, I can ask God to convict me of my sins. To let me know what He wants from me and what behavior needs to stop. That's between Him and I. Just like your life is between you and Him. More than we need to stop judging each other and convicting each other, we need to trust God with our own lives and trust God that He is taking care of others as well. There are some things that religion does not allow, but what matters is that you and God have communication about it, and you trust that He will let you know what He wants for your life. I go to church and worship and pray, because God and I both know that I need that to stay close to Him. When I encourage people to grow close to God, it's not about rules and religion. It's about giving your life to Him and then what happens after that, is between you and Him. No one else.

"When you and your children return to the Lord, your God and obey Him with all your heart and with all your soul according to everything I command you today, then the Lord your God will restore your fortunes and have compassion on you.." (Deuteronomy 30:2)

CHAPTER TWENTY-EIGHT

THE MORAL OF THE STORY

WHAT YOU'VE HEARD is a story about how a woman who was previously a mom, wife, hairstylist and business owner, took on the government, and in return, lost nearly everything. Only to be blessed tenfold. Everything you've read. Everything I've done. Everything I can do, is through Jesus Christ. God has been a part of my life and in my heart since I was born. My parents dedicated me to Jesus, and I accepted Him into my life at a young age. Having a personal relationship with God has changed who I am and secured my life as His child. Without my faith and without God, I believe wholeheartedly that my story would not end the way that it has. Shoot, it's not even over yet, but I know one thing. He has nothing but good for me. That is something I will never need to doubt or question. I have decided, after all is said and done, that I don't even know what I want anymore.

All the things I had placed my foundation on, everything I was happy and content with physically has been taken from me. You think that is bad, but it's not. God has shown me bigger and better things; blessed our family and changed what I always thought was the best thing for me. Moving forward, people ask me, "What do you want do with your life now?" I don't know and I honestly have more faith in trusting God to tell me what He wants me to do, because I know that His plans will always be better than what I think is best.

> *Do not throw away your confidence, it will be richly rewarded. You need to persevere, so that when you have done the will of God, you will receive what He has promised."* (Hebrews 10:35-36)

I am so excited to see where He leads me next. Even as I consider politics, talk shows, podcasts, or a political run, I know that God knows His plan. And I can trust His direction. Some of those options sounds terrible, and if God led me to that choice, I might frown and question Him. I would do it begrudgingly, with disdain. But also knowing that He would bring joy from it if it were His will for me. That kind of trust and faith, which I learned this past year, is alarmingly peaceful. No matter what comes my way or what direction my family is headed, I trust God wholeheartedly. This nation is clearly under attack. There is no doubt that our country is catering to the sinful, immoral and corrupt beliefs of people who do not honor or trust God. I have faith that if our nation were to finally hit rock bottom, as I did, and turned their face toward God, He would heal us. This needs to be the focus of every American, every patriot and every believer.

> *"If my people, who are called by my name, shall humble themselves and pray and seek His face and turn from their wicked ways, then will I hear from heaven and will forgive their sin and will heal their land."* (2 Chronicles 7:14)

My life as a bold, outspoken patriot is just beginning. I've found my courage; God has blessed me with resolve and endurance. My legal battles with the state and government have only just begun. But one thing I have found in this journey is freedom. Yes, freedom, believe that. Not America's freedom, or anything the government offers, but my own personal freedom. I have the right to my beliefs, my convictions and to have a voice for them. I have the right to fight for them. I have freedom in knowing that God is bigger than government.

I have freedom in knowing that God has more control than government ever will, and they cannot take what they don't own. (Thanks, Bree, for that nugget of truth.) I have freedom in knowing exactly who I am and knowing that I can now be that person unapologetically. I have the freedom of being persecuted for my beliefs and God will make it my blessing.

You will have to follow me on social media to stay updated about my legal fight and lawsuits. It will be something I fight for, probably the rest of my life, for my children's sake. It will be ongoing for years and I will not back down.

On a flight back to Oregon recently, something came over me and I needed to convey a message to all the leftists in Oregon that wanted so badly to cancel me and run me out. I needed them to know that they did not win. When I first opened against the mandate, and after my call to arms, leftists continued to demand I apologize to my community for being a threat and a nuisance. I finally wrote out my overdue "apology" and posted it.

A HEARTFELT APOLOGY TO SALEM LIBERALS

"Since reopening my business last year against Governer Brown's tyrannical lockdown targeted at small businesses and families, Salem leftists have DEMANDED I apologize for my actions, calling me a murderer, a threat to the community and insisting that I was endangering the lives of others. One year has passed with NO Covid cases or symptoms linked to my business and yet no apology has been given for your ignorance. Instead, here is the apology you are so desperate for and I hope it resonates everything I continue to stand up for. One year has passed since I opened my salon against Governor Kate Brown's mandate. It has been the greatest year of my life. I'm sorry that you wish I could say differently. During the reopening of my salon, the entire nation had my back. I received thousands of emails, texts, messages and letters from all over America, wishing me well. Cards telling me how brave I am. Americans thanking me for standing up. While my own liberal community spewed hate and division. I realized how strong I was and you helped me with that. I was in the fight of my life against Kate Brown and YOU and I stood my ground. You chose to harm me instead of supporting me. You chose to encourage others to torment and threaten me to close. I'm sorry that you wished I had caved. When I opened my salon and stood up for my rights and yours, I did so safely. You called me a murderer. You wished death on me and my kids. You had hate in your heart and fueled it with fear. There has never been a covid case traced to my business. When you realize that your rights have been stripped and you can no longer stand up for yourself and your family, perhaps you will understand why I did. I'm sorry that you were manipulated by fear and instead of being brave yourself, directed your fear onto me.

You tried everything in your power to destroy me, demean me and terrorize me and my family and my associates. You tirelessly attacked us for bringing light to a corrupt shut down and for exercising our right to work. You so desperately needed to be vindicated that your belief superseded everyone else's beliefs. You were wrong. I'm sorry that it wasn't true.

After months of listening to and reading your hate, lies, slander, name calling and attacks, I made the hard decision to leave your state and pursue greener pastures. It has been the best decision of my life. God took your harm and He turned it to His good. I will never apologize for the glorious plan God had for me. I will never apologize for taking my family to safety. I'm sorry that you think YOU had the capability to torment me and that I would endure it. I'm sorry that you thought your hate for me would have lasting effects on my life. I'm sorry that you were never important to me and all you did was make me stronger.

God had a plan for our family. He had a plan for our fight. He had a plan for all of these and you simply played the role He intended you to. You were a vessel for God to take my family to better and bigger places, where He can bless us and redeem us.

I'm sorry that you were not aware of how great my God is. I'm sorry that you cannot comprehend what it's like to have faith that can move mountains.

After 15 years as a successful business owner in Salem, I am taking my skills, training and entrepreneurship to another state. You have contributed to taking millions of tax dollars away from your own city, your children, your livelihood and your neighbors. Because you are so uninformed and intolerant and you don't even know why, you are only harming yourself. I'm sorry that you don't recognize this and have only caused yourself devastation and destruction. I'm sorry that your behavior so far has not reaped you any rewards.

To all the liberal cancel culture advocates in Oregon, I thank you. For fulfilling a beautiful plan for my family. For playing a part in the blessings God had for me and a fresh start in a place I now call home and am happy. I am not sorry for opening my business. I am not sorry for having my fellow Americans protect it when you tried to threaten it. I am not sorry for standing strong while you tried to destroy me. I am not sorry for having the courage to leave you behind and start a new life. I am not sorry that you thought I would stick around and take your abuse and threats. I will never apologize that my God made your harm a blessing.

I'm sorry that you didn't realize right away that your efforts were in vain. That I was a child of God, and the harm you were bringing me would be counted as blessing shortly after. I'm sorry that you don't know this kind of love and grace. For that I am so so very sorry."

I will no longer apologize for my beliefs. God has called me to a higher purpose. I was not put through the last year of trials to sit back and let cancel culture ruin me or take my joy. I did not endure the hardship of a lifetime to crawl under a rock and wallow. My God has allowed me to face my giants and conquer them. Now my giants look like ants when I compare them to the power of God. With Him, I can overcome anything and I am freaking ready to. The fight has been brought to my door and it has threatened my family. I will take it head on and I will fight for all Americans and Christians, as we face the attack of a lifetime against our culture, our values and our convictions.

The type of faith and strength to endure what I have, after losing almost everything, is not my own. It's God's gift to me. It's Him working inside me. It's Him blessing me. He has gifted me now with the ability to speak loudly and bravely for Him, for what He has allowed me to endure as part of His plan. The gift I have now is that I've been completely cancelled for my beliefs.

There I nothing stopping me from being His disciple, His voice, His testimony. There is nothing anyone can do to harm me for speaking up and speaking truth. God used the entire year of 2020 to refine me and redefine me. I didn't have a purpose in Him until He called me to become the person I am today. I know that He isn't finished with me, but I am now aware that He is present and working on me and I can now be open to that calling and follow it. When everything was taken from me, I was able to be given a fresh start and allow God to bless me as He intended. Even as I wrote this book, I found my journey with God being redefined. When I started writing, I was angry, hostile, bitter and resentful to the people in my life that have wronged me. I have felt blessed by what happened as a result, but that didn't take away my deeper feelings. God was working in me, as I told my story to reveal what I needed. What I needed was to truly recognize that those people who harmed me, played the role that they needed to in order for God to work His plan accordingly and take me to the place He meant for me. Every single bad thing that happened to me or was done to me, HAD TO HAPPEN, for my new chapter to begin. Every stylist had to turn their back on me and leave. Every leftist had to attack me and threaten me. I had to lose my salon completely, or God knows I would have kept pushing and trying and resisting to keep it alive. Every single moment in the last year had to go just as it did, for Him to be able to bless my family as He has. With that mentality, I can have no regrets. I would do nothing different.

Even as I began writing this book and searching for the right words from the Bible to insert, I found God had already provided. I sat down to write, opened the Bible I've owned since high school and started looking at the Scriptures I was sent on social media. I had asked supporters to remember my story and tell me what Scripture came to their mind. Some of the same ones kept popping up, and some new ones that I had never heard. Many were given that I never would have associated with my own life or this journey. I felt blessed to have been given the opportunity to affect others' lives in a way that they associated these beautiful Scriptures with my fight. I had compiled a list of the Scriptures I was sent. I began reading my Bible to see where they would fit into my book.

I flipped to the back of my Bible where, 15 years ago, in a study, I had started writing Scriptures about persecution and trials. I found that I had nearly 10 scriptures written out in the back of my Bible that directly related to my life for the past year.

I got goosebumps as I read words that in no way had applied to my life previously, but were now exactly what I needed to hear and feel from God.

Who could have predicted that one day, God would call me to write a book about something life altering? And that when I would begin writing, I would find that He had been preparing me my whole life for it? And that I would find my own guidance in my own Bible, written over a decade ago for no reason. And that when I asked my friends and supporters to help me with Scripture, they would name the exact ones? How could I not recognize in that exact moment that God has been working tirelessly throughout my life to get me to this place and time? He has placed everyone in my life for a reason and allowed everything to happen to me for a purpose. He has been carrying me through my own muck to keep me from ruining the divine plan He has had for me. Despite my own flawed human efforts and behavior, He has been silently present and active in my life, ensuring that whatever bad I create,

He can make good. As I sat at the table reading these Scriptures and crying in peace, I knew that He was allowing me to write this book, so that I could address my own inner issues. When I sat down and wrote the things I have been through, I was able to speak freely and let everything pent up flow out of me. I could write every detail about the people that have wronged me and hurt me. It felt good to release that energy and put it all out there.

When I went back to read what I had written, I saw a hurt, angry, bitter woman, who needed the people who hurt her to know what they had done. That isn't who I want to be. I saw what a scorned and jaded person could be, holding on to resentment. I read my own stories and asked God to let me let go. Let me forgive those who have hurt me and turned their backs on me. Free me from a life of resentment and anger. The people who have wronged me did so for His purpose. I had to experience the loss of so many people and so many earthly things, to let Him give me the blessings I never even knew I wanted. I forgive the women that I have stood by who walked away from me. I forgive the hurtful things that have been said about me. I forgive the hateful people who have done things to harm me. I know that's what God wants for me. And honestly, who can be mad that people did what they did, if it's served God's purpose? I am exactly where He wants me, in the role that He wants me. Anything that it cost me to get here was worth it.

Just as I read Ryan Stephenson's story, and found myself relating to him, I ask that you look at your own life and reflect. As I read his journey of faith, I found myself continually asking God to reveal to me His plan. I asked God to be present, to be clear and to be direct. I begged that my path would be crystal clear. I was ready and willing to obey, I just needed to know what I would be obeying. Of course, He did. He very directly told me to write this book.

I ask that you look for signs of God's goodness in your life. Events and occurrences that you may have previously considered negative may have a new meaning, as your faith is not only restored but solidified. There are very distinct reasons God has allowed certain things to happen in your life. You may have pain, anger, burdens and unsettled emotions. But God knows your purpose and He is waiting for you to acknowledge that He has promised to make all things good. When you stop asking yourself "Why?" and tell yourself that there already is a why, God will hear your faithfulness, and show you why. Instead of asking why God would allow something terrible to happen to you, know that His purpose is already being fulfilled and remind yourself that out of anything bad God will always make good. Then start looking for His miracles. They are always there but if you aren't looking, you are losing what He has for you. When you dive into your ultimate faith in Him, He will start placing the right people, the right opportunities and the right moments in front of you, as an offering.

If you want to live the rest of your life with this kind of faith, strength, confidence and blessings, please know that you can, when you ask Jesus into your heart and let him take control of your life and your life's plan. It's that simple.

If you don't know Jesus, and you want to, I've included a salvation prayer below. You read it, you mean it, and you pray it, and you are His.

Pray this prayer and you will be forever changed, I promise. When you do, I would love to hear your story. Knowing I have saved one person with my story is all I need to know!

You will always have God's mighty hand to guide and hold you. You will also have a place in heaven with your new Christian brothers and sisters!!!

Jesus said to him, I am the Way and the Truth and the Life; no one comes to the Father except by (through) Me. (John 14:6)

Dear Jesus,

I accept you as my Lord and Savior. I ask that you come into my heart today and forever. I ask that you be a guiding light for my life and that you protect me with your righteous right hand.

I ask to be born again and be surrounded by your abounding and unconditional love. Forgive me for all my sins and breathe into me new life and a new start in you.

Amen

See you in Heaven friend!!

Find friends with faith. Find an honest and truthful church home. Get a fantastic Bible and pray daily. Worship Him in song. Talk to God at all times and ask Him for guidance and He will never steer you wrong. Buckle up buttercup, you're about to get blessed.

Thank you to the people who either contributed to my fight financially through donations or sent me a heartfelt and encouraging letter or card during the hardest part of my fight. You may think that you didn't make a difference, but you did. I read every card, saved every memento and listened as you emboldened me with your words and praise. YOU helped me more than you will ever know, and I thank you so much. Thank you to everyone who donated to my GoFundMe. Thank you to everyone who sent me a supportive message, text, comment, phone call or email. Thank you to those of you who continue to fight with me and for me. I cannot even begin to capture every person that reached out. I cannot load phone call records. I cannot find every email. I cannot research every Facebook or Instagram comment. I can't even track my GoFundMe donors.

If you played any role at all, even a negative one in this journey, I thank you. You, my friend, were a vessel in God's plan for my life. You fulfilled a purpose, whether you know it or not. You were exactly where you needed to be and said exactly what you needed to in that moment. I am thankful for each and every person my path has crossed in this lifetime. I am blessed for you and your purpose in my life.

LINDSEY GRAHAM became a nationally recognized figure for her defiance of small business lockdowns in May of 2020. During the media hyped hysteria of Covid-19, Lindsey and her husband owned 6 small businesses in the state of Oregon. Lockdowns were going to bankrupt their family. In an effort to preserve everything they had worked for, Lindsey reopened her Salem salon against Governor Kate Brown's "stay home orders." This turning point in her life created a movement and an icon.

Branded "The Patriot Barbie" by cancel culture leftists, Lindsey has embraced her alter ego and is a public speaker, activist and political advocate for the Republican party, conservatives and Christians across the nation. Her husband and three small children were forced to leave Oregon and start their lives over in a new home with new careers. Throughout this ordeal, Lindsey has boldly spoken of her faith in God and how He has blessed her family in their fight for freedom. Now in Arizona, Lindsey and her husband Scott are property investors, while Lindsey is a licensed realtor in the Phoenix area.

She has retired from the salon industry and now speaks at rallies, events, political fundraisers and manages her Patriot Barbie apparel line. Lindsey has become the bold and unapologetic face for Christians, conservatives, pro-lifers, military and police officers. Where this stand will take her next, she is waiting for God's calling.

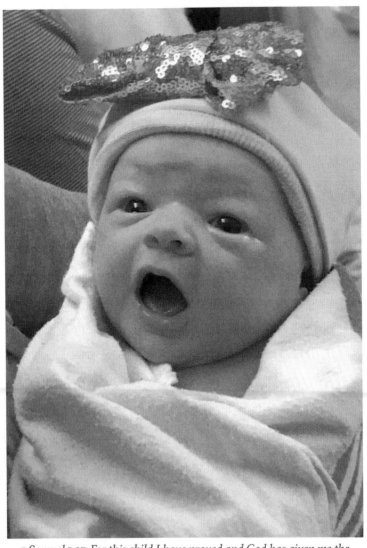

1 Samuel 1 27. For this child I have prayed and God has given me the desires of my heart. My sweet little girl, Oakley

6 weeks into lockdowns, I had a family and a newborn to provide for. I was done being told I couldn't support them

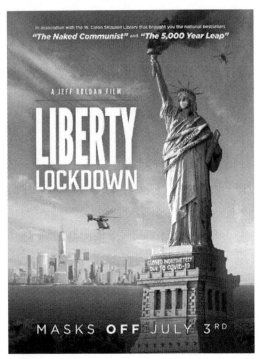

A documentary my story was featured in. Censored of course by main stream outlets, this documentary is alarming and emotional.

After embracing Patriot Barbie, I had a logo designed for my social media and apparel line

The stone in your hand might be small but the God who is with you is bigger than the giant in front of you. It is not about your stone but it is about your God.

A meme sent to me in the heart of my fight, which I have never forgotten. It's given me strength.

A memorable picture of Scott and his dad before losing him in 2018.

A proud conservative and strong Christian, Maga Hulk is an inspiration and has a gift for encouraging and inspiring.

A proud supporter that had driven three hours to attend a rally. He stopped by to meet the salon owner that was fighting Kate Brown. I finally met him one year later at a speaking event.

A stranger saw my outfit during a photo shoot and pulled her car over to get my signature for a Republican! Us patriots have to stick together.

After being cancelled in Oregon, God blessed me with a new career. I am now a licensed realtor in Arizona.

After years of development, I finally launched my own hair extension company, Beauty Couture in 2017, at the height of my salon status.

Capitol Coffee, in Salem brought the entire salon lunch and drinks while we were standing up to lockdowns.

Me

Cleaning the salon before re-opening. Leftists would later attack me for having my mask below my chin, despite the fact that we were not open, and the photographer was 6 feet away.

CPS agent Omar Ruiz handed me his card when he came in to illegally interview my family and child, without me present.

Getting into demolition of my new location. Raised with a strong work ethic, I always had my hands in everything I could for my businesses.

Interviewing with Brandie Barclay, the founder of PowerSoul at FaithTalk Radio.

Guarding my salon from rioters and community members who threatened to harm me and my business.

Making new friends at the Stop the Steal Rally in Washington DC January 6, 2021.

Hugging patriot friends in a mask free salon, against orders.

Cramming in real estate hours online, with baby sleeping soundly on my chest. Starting over in Arizona, with three kids, a big move and no connections, is one of the scariest things I've ever embarked on.

I had packed up my salon to close forever. I said goodbye to 15 years of hard work, and prayed that God woul heal my broken heart.

My life. Seriously. Yours too.

Meeting and speaking with Peggy Hall, the Healthy American.
She is a force to be reckoned with, and so adorable.

Meeting Tito Ortiz in Huntington Beach at my first
Patriot Barbie appearance October 2020.

My first appearance on Fox News, after OSHA fined me $14,000 without evidence, proof, or a legal investigation.

My first new friend, right off the plane in Washington DC at the Trump Rally. He wanted a picture with the Patriot Barbie!

My mom and I, months before she died, sharing a girlie shot in a dive bar. She was fun, outgoing and would have probably been one of my best friends.

Kristy Boley, another brave business owner in Oregon, defied lockdowns as well. She was fined, threatened and eventually forced to sell her business to escape.

My press conference on May 14, 2020. I hold back emotions as I tell the nation that my family was being threatened.

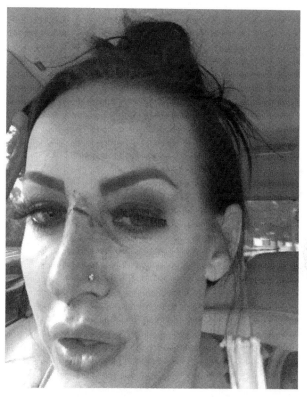

On my way to the emergency room, after a remodeling accident in the salon. While removing some shelving in my new location, I broke my nose.

Patriot Barbie rides a horse! After 25 years fearing horses, God finally gave me the courage to tackle my fear.

On the way to the Open Oregon Rally, three days before I re-opened Glamour Salon against the mandate.

Proud patriots stood outside Glamour Salon, after BLM and antifa threatened to burn it down.

Re-opening Day, May 5, 2020 and the crowd of supporters outside the salon.

Russ Taylor, myself, Alan Holstetter, Jeff Roldan and Morton Irvine Smith, friends involved in the production of Liberty Lockdown.

Scott and my oceanfront wedding in Washington in 2011.

*Shortly after our move, my mother in law and her fiance moved
10 minutes away. We were so proud and happy to be in Arizona and
felt safe and free, as a family.*

Some of the families that came out to support my choice to re-open my business.

Speaking at my first Trump rally in Huntington Beach on October 31, 2020.

*Stacy Ann, KSLM Radio, supporting me daily and praying for my family.
I appreciate you.*

*That crazy God moment when I met Christine, and had no idea that she
was someone God wanted in my life, months later!*

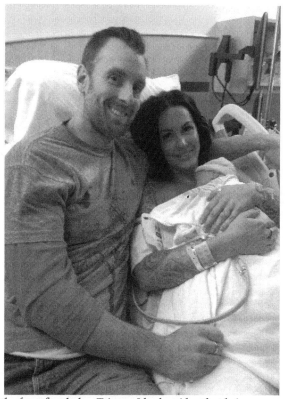

The birth of our first baby, Trigger. I had no idea that being a mom would bring me such joy and the most important role of my life. Having a baby changed how I felt about working so hard .

The crowd of supporters outside Glamour Salon, the day that I re-opened May 5, 2020.

The Grand Opening of Glamour Salon, May 5, 2009. I was a young entrepreneur, excited and scared.

The picture used all over the media to slander me, and eventually start a petition to remove my business license.

The pretty princess events that my salon would host for the community in Salem, Oregon. We would invite, pamper and encourage the girls in the community.

The support and love of these women on the day I opened, and every day since, has been a blessing.

This is me, opening my doors publicly on May 5, 2020, and allowing my first customer back in, Brad. Brad would later be a patriot who defended my salon against attacks and vandalism.

Two of my favorite Patriots, who continued to rally for me for days.

Working for a national hair extension company, and published in a magazine, I had finally felt my career take off. My hard work was finally paying off.

The devastating view of tearing apart my salon when I finally had to permanently close.

Lease Violation Notice Glamour Salon 05.05.2020

CITY OF **Salem**
AT YOUR SERVICE

May 5, 2020

Lindsey Graham
Glamour! LLC
2030 Belinda Court SE
Salem, OR 97306
VIA Email: glamoursalem@gmail.com

Dear Lindsey:

It has come to the City's attention that you plan to open and operate your business in the leasehold space located at 195 Liberty Street SE in light of the Governor of Oregon's Executive Order 20-12. The City has granted a forbearance on your retail lease payments through June 20, 2020.

While we understand and appreciate the challenges and hardships to you, your staff, and your business brought about by the Covid-19 crisis, please note that operating your business while Executive Order 20-12 is in effect would be a violation of your lease. Section 6 of the lease states the following:

> The Premises are to be used only for salon/tanning and related purposes, and for no other purpose without the prior written consent of Lessor. No act shall be done in or about the Premises that is unlawful or that will increase the existing rate of insurance on the Building or increase the operating expenses for the Premises above and beyond that reasonable and customarily anticipated. Lessee shall not commit or allow to be committed any waste upon the Premises. **Lessee shall at all times comply with any and all laws, regulations or ordinances of any and all governmental authorities relating to the use and occupancy of the Premises and Building** and shall observe such reasonable rules and regulations as may be adopted and made available to Lessee by Lessor from time to time for the safety, care, cleanliness of the Premises or the Building, for the preservation of good order on the Premises or the Building, or the efficient maintenance and operation of the Premises or the Building.

Any violation of terms stated in Section 6 would result in default as described in Section 22 of the lease. Thank you and please contact me if you have any concerns of questions regarding this matter.

Sincerely,

City of Salem

CUMMINS GOODMAN DENLEY & VICKERS PC

ATTORNEYS AT LAW

100 S. COLLEGE STREET · PO BOX 609 · NEWBERG, OREGON 97132-0609
PHONE: 503-476-8200 · FAX: 503-476-8201 · www.cumminsgoodman.com

JAMES S. ANDERSON ⁺*
MATTHEW D. BAKER
BRIAN F. CHURCH
ELLIOTT C. CUMMINS *
MATTHEW F. DENLEY ·**
GEORGE W. GOODMAN
ANDREW H. GRAHAM
CHRISTINA N. JOSEPH
ROBERT B. NICHOLS
KOI BI E. TREBBIEN
DAMON L. VICKERS ⁺**‡
DOUGLAS E. WATSON

September 11, 2020

⁺Also admitted to practice in Washington
**Also admitted to practice in District of Columbia
‡Also admitted to practice in Idaho
*Also admitted to practice in Massachusetts and Georgia
*Retired

VIA EMAIL: glamoursalem@gmail.com;
lindseygraham7@gmail.com

Lindsey Graham
Glamour Salon
195 Liberty St. SE
Salem, OR 97301

RE: The Matter of the Possible Violation of the Oregon Safe Employment
       Act/Glamour! LLC

Inspection No.	:	317727431(13)
Optional Report No.	:	C0196-001-20
Date Issued	:	5/15/20
Our File No.	:	A-8820

Dear Lindsey:

INITIAL FILE REVIEW

This letter confirms completion of the review of the available materials concerning the above-captioned OR-OSHA citation. This matter concerns the appeal of an OR-OSHA citation issued to Glamour! LLC ("Glamour") on May 15, 2020. The single-item citation resulted from a May 4, 2020, complaint inspection of the Glamour! Salon located at 195 Liberty Street SE in Salem, Oregon. The citation alleges one "Willful" violation of ORS 654.022. That statute requires that employers obey and comply with every requirement of every order, decision, direction, standard, rule or regulation made or prescribed by the Department of Consumer and Business Services in connection with the matters specified in ORS 654.001 to 654.295, 654.412 to 654.423 and 654.750 to 654.780, or in any way relating to or affecting safety and health in employments or places of employment, or to protect the life, safety and health of employees in such employments or places of employment, and did not do everything necessary or proper in order to secure compliance with and observance of every such order, decision, direction, standard, rule or regulation. The allegation, of course, is that the salon violated the terms of the statute. The following is a summary of OR-OSHA's inspection file and other materials you have provided this office.

According to documents contained in the inspection file, OR-OSHA received an anonymous complaint about Glamour on or about April 9, 2020. The complaint alleged that Glamour was still operating and not adhering to the Governor's non-essential business closure order. It further alleged Glamour had taped paper over the windows to conceal activity, and that clients were entering through the back door. OR-OSHA notified you of the complaint via a letter, and requested a written response. You responded via email on April 23, 2020. In your response, you denied the allegations in their entirety. Your letter noted that you had recently fired "multiple employees" who had in turn threatened to report you to OSHA.

Although there are some indications in the file that OR-OSHA received around 20 complaints regarding Glamour between April 9, 2020, and May 7, 2020, only three of those complaints are mentioned in the inspection file as the basis for the inspection. Two other anonymous complaints in the inspection file are dated May 5, and May 6, 2020. They each essentially allege Glamour was operating in violation of the COVID-19 restrictions imposed by the Governor's Executive Orders.

On May 4, 2020, at approximately 1:50 p.m., the Safety and Health Enforcement Manager for OR-OSHA's Salem Office, Aaron Colmone, knocked on the door of Glamour. He held his ID up to the window. HCO Colmone is also a Safety and Health Compliance Officer for OR-OSHA. The file indicates you answered the door and allowed HCO Colmone into the salon. HCO Colmone allegedly advised he was there to investigate a complaint about Glamour, as well as a news story about the salon being open, or preparing to open, for business. Notes in the file indicate HCO Colmone explained "the penalties and what could happen" if Glamour did indeed open for business while the closure orders were in effect. The inspection file indicates you informed HCO Colmone that if he returned the following day after you opened the business, he would be refused entry and he should seek a warrant.

Multiple media reports are in the inspection file. These include written articles, as well as audio, and video recordings. Media reports indicate Glamour had reopened for business as of May 5, 2020. The reports describe interviews with you which indicate OR-OSHA had threatened to return and assess citations and penalties if Glamour proceeded with its plan to open. The articles also described a growing crowd of people on the sidewalk outside of Glamour who had gathered to support your right to open the business.

Records in the file indicate that on May 6, 2020, HCO Colmone submitted to the Marion County Circuit Court an application for an inspection warrant based upon the April 9, 2020, complaint. That inspection warrant was granted. The file also reflects that HCO Colmone was warned by law enforcement authorities that "for safety reasons," he should not attempt to go to the Glamour site in person. HCO Colmone was instructed to go to the Salem Police Department, and to telephone you to request you come to the station to speak with him.

You retained this office on May 6, 2020. A conference call was scheduled with HCO Colmone for the evening of May 6, 2020. At that time, he conducted a full opening conference. I represented the company during that conference. He also planned to interview you. At the beginning of that telephone conference, HCO Colmone read the inspection warrant. You noted that the address for the inspection was incorrect. As such, HCO Colmone was advised we would not permit the inspection until he obtained a valid inspection warrant. HCO Colmone corrected the address on the application and was granted a new inspection warrant on May 7, 2020.

HCO Colmone conducted a full opening conference via telephone on May 8, 2020, at approximately 8:00 a.m. I again represented the company. Following the opening conference, HCO Colmone conducted an interview with you as part of the inspection. HCO Colmone inquired generally about Glamour, the decision to reopen notwithstanding the Governor's closure order, the individuals who worked at Glamour, and the services they performed. You advised that the other workers who cut hair and provided other services at Glamour were independent contractors, not your employees. You also noted that those workers had all signed leases with Glamour leasing space to perform their services at a particular work station located on the Glamour premises. You also pointed out that the independent contractors would have independent contractor licenses issued by the state. You advised that these independent contractors provided their own tools and supplies, booked their own clients, set their own schedules, came and went as they pleased, and did not report to you for anything. You went on to explain the following: full time lessees had a key code to allow them access to the building at any time. Payments by customers were made directly to the person who performed services. Each independent contractor could choose what forms of payment they would accept. Glamour did not accept payments for the independent contractors. Glamour provided essentially a work station and some storage, as well as access to an online booking system. You again emphasized that the persons who had performed services since the reopening were all independent contractors and not employees. You reported that since reopening, you and the following individuals had performed services at Glamour:

- Jaycie Kerr
- Sarah Hompas
- Melissa Standish
- Laila Schmidt

Following the interview, HCO Colmone requested a number of documents related to payroll/income, contracts, termination of contracts, appointment lists, and COVID-19 policies and procedures. Available responsive documents were provided.

The inspection file reflects a number of interviews conducted by HCO Colmone. The following individuals were interviewed as part of this inspection:

- Kendall Peters
- Jessica Parker
- Danna Ward
- Kayla Morrison
- Kelsey Hardin
- Julia Morandi
- Hannah Lund
- Stacy Birch

Interview notes indicate Kendall Peters was interviewed on May 8, 2020. Ms. Peters apparently told the HCO that you had two assistants (Jessica Parker and Katy Max) who were employees, and were working when the salon reopened. She advised that Glamour had written contracts with its service providers. The service providers were required to follow certain guidelines, including purchasing extensions only through your company. The notes appear to indicate that payments from new customers were split so that, in essence, a finder's fee, or broker commission, went to Glamour. Ms. Peters appeared to agree that at least some of the service providers were independent contractors. The notes indicated that when Ms. Peters put in her notice (presumably to terminate her lease contract) she was cut off from using the computer and was not given access to her client list. She also reported that she was kicked off the premises prior to the end of her 30 days' notice.

Jessica Parker was interviewed on May 8, 2020. Ms. Parker indicated she was both an employee and an independent contractor. She reported that two to three days per week she worked for you and another three days per week she acted as an independent contractor. The notes indicated that she was paid as an independent contractor even though some of her work was that of an employee. There is mention of "commissions" which were rung up through the salon, out of which she only received 50 percent, with Glamour keeping the other 50 percent. There are no details as to what kind of work she was doing as an employee. The notes appear to also indicate that she only received 50 percent of the payments made by new clients. Again, the context of this comment is unclear. It is unknown whether this allegation pertained only to the first payment from new clients, or to all ongoing payments. Ms. Parker indicated she considered the two of you to be really good friends until she put in her notice. Ms. Parker told the HCO you locked her out of the salon at that point, and refused to pay her for work previously performed. Ms. Parker acknowledged that service providers were charged for certain common items (coffee, wine for clients).

Danna Ward was also interviewed on May 8, 2020. Ms. Ward told the HCO she was an independent contractor. However, she also indicated that she needed to ask permission if she wanted to change the days she worked. (It was not clear whether she was a part time or full time lessee.) She said that new clients were rung up through Glamour's system, and that she would receive 50 percent of the charge paid by the new client. She reported that providers received commissions on hair extension products. She also reported that some common supplies were charged back to the service providers. She complained about not receiving an itemized list of those charges. Ms. Ward reported her last day was March 9, 2020. Ms. Ward reported she was locked out of the salon's computer system. Ms. Ward indicated the salon was using "Tan Republic girls" (i.e., employees of a sister company) to do receptionist work at Glamour.

Ms. Ward also exchanged emails with OR-OSHA during the inspection. The emails indicate that service providers were not permitted to work at other salons while leasing space at Glamour. She told OR-OSHA that she carried her own insurance, but that you allegedly had told her she did not need it as Glamour's insurance would cover service providers. She again acknowledged that she was an independent contractor. Ms. Ward also apparently provided OR-OSHA with some text messages. Those texts appear to be between you and Ms. Ward regarding a dispute, and you terminating her lease agreement with Glamour.

Kayla Morrison was interviewed on May 12, 2020. The notes from this interview are very brief. Ms. Morrison advised that she was unaware of any employees that worked at Glamour since January or February. She was paid directly and set her own prices. She only rented space. She set her own hours and received no base wages. She noted a requirement to give 30 days' notice to leave but indicated she could not be "fired."

Kelsey Hardin was also interviewed on May 12, 2020. She told the HCO she was an independent contractor. She rented space by the month. She provided her own products, tools and cleaners. She indicated she could work when she wanted and set her own prices. Ms. Hardin indicated contractors could be "fired" with 30 days' notice. She indicated that "we" are all friends but she did not want to "break the rules like you."

Notes from a May 12, 2020, interview with Julia Morandi are located in the file. Ms. Morandi indicated she was an independent contractor. She advised that service providers rented chairs. New client fees were split between the provider and Glamour. She indicated the service providers set their own schedules and provided their own supplies. She noted a Tan Republic person worked the front desk from 10:00 a.m. to 5:00 p.m. The notes indicated advertising cost was split 50/50, presumably between Glamour and the service providers. Contracts could be terminated by you. If you terminated a contract, according to Ms. Morandi, the provider would be kicked out of the "system."

Hannah Lund was briefly interviewed on May 12, 2020. The notes from her interview confirm Glamour had contracts with service providers. Service providers could make their own schedules and apparently were paid directly by clients. The cost for common supplies (coffee, wine) were split among the providers.

Stacy Birch was interviewed on May 13, 2020. The notes from her interview indicate that you controlled prices charged at the salon. She indicated that only you had copies of the lease contracts. She said that all clients were logged in through the Glamour system. Service providers were not permitted to ring up new clients, and would get in trouble if they did so. She also indicated that service providers did not collect payments. Ms. Birch told the HCO that Tan Republic employees worked at Glamour. She identified Katelynn Rayburn as a receptionist, meaning an employee, that had been actively working the week the salon reopened. Ms. Birch reported Ms. Rayburn was paid under the table for her work at Glamour. Ms. Birch reported that while you made it clear that service providers were independent contractors, you were nonetheless very controlling. She indicated Glamour used to charge a late fee per minute if providers worked after hours. She reported that providers could not sell products which competed with the products you sold. Providers were not permitted to sublet their chairs and were only permitted to sell hair extension products marketed by you. Ms. Birch also told the HCO that you "told everyone" that OR-OSHA was trying to make the service providers employees, and that they should "tell the truth" because they are independent contractors.

A "new client ledger" was produced to OR-OSHA by Glamour, and is in the inspection file. According to this ledger, you, Sarah Hompas, Elizabeth Ozuna, and Melissa Standish earned new client fees between May 6 and May 11, 2020.

A blank "Glamour Salon Tenant Contract Suite Agreement" is in the file. The agreement sets out the terms of a space lease at Glamour. It generally identifies the tenants as independent contractors. Tenants are noted to be responsible for:

- Taxes;
- Accounting;
- Liability insurance;
- Malpractice insurance;
- Certifications;
- Licensing;
- Health/dental insurance; and
- Equipment, supplies, tools, and necessary items to maintain a business.

Tenants are also required to maintain an independent contractor's license from the Oregon State Health Licensing Office. Tenants are prohibited from:

- Subletting their space;
- Bringing personal belongings into the salon that will be in public view without approval from Glamour;
- Displaying personal items in the salon;
- Selling products which Glamour has the exclusive right to sell; and
- Selling hair extension products other than Beauty Couture brand products.

Part time tenants were restricted to working only during hours the salon was otherwise open. Full time tenants had access to a key card to get into the salon after hours. The agreement also contained a dress code.

The agreement provides that Glamour has the right to terminate the agreement at any time for any reason. Glamour was responsible for payment of utilities. The cost of common supplies were to be split between all tenants. New clients recruited by Glamour marketing were to be rung into the salon's system. Glamour received a 50 percent commission on each new client. It seems this was to apply only to the first payment made by such clients, but this is not made clear.

A "Payroll Summary Report" is located in the file. It indicates that between November 1, 2019, and May 11, 2020, a number of individuals (who were likely Glamour employees) received paychecks (presumably from Glamour though it is unclear). No paychecks were issued after March 26, 2020.

A document entitled "Discretionary Penalty Rationale" dated May 14, 2020, is present in the file. It reflects that Glamour operated on May 5, 2020, in violation of Executive Order 20-12. It reflects that Glamour continued to operate during the inspection after being notified by OR-OSHA that doing so would subject it to a citation and penalty. The document reflects that the Administrator did not believe the minimum penalty of $8,900.00 would provide sufficient financial incentive for Glamour to take steps to avoid future violations. A penalty of $14,000.00 was approved by the Administrator, Michael Wood

A violation worksheet indicates that Glamour was operating as a hair salon and was providing services for which close personal contact is difficult or impossible to avoid in direct violation of Executive Order 20-12. Employee exposure was noted to be services provided by you, Sarah Hompas, Elizabeth Ozuna, and Melissa Standish. OR-OSHA considered each of you to be employees of Glamour. Specifically, OR-OSHA identified the services reflected on the "commissions ledger" which took place between May 6 and May 9, 2020, as the basis for the citation.

Also included in the file are the following documents:

- Proof of Insurance Coverage;
- Facebook post advertising a position in your "assistant program";
- Multiple anonymous complaint forms;
- Glamour COVID-19 protocols;
- A list of stylists contacted by OR-OSHA;
- A letter from the City of Salem notifying you that operating Glamour while Executive Order 20-12 was in place would be a violation of your lease;
- An article on the 20 Factor IRS Test for independent contractors in a salon;
- An "audit techniques guide" for beauty and barber shops;
- An internal OR-OSHA email identifying Ryan Andersen as a person at the Oregon Department of Revenue who could assist in reviewing Glamour's payroll documents; and
- A large number of media reports and Facebook posts concerning Glamour.

A telephonic closing conference was held on May 14, 2020. HCO Colmone advised he was recommending a single item citation alleging a willful violation of ORS 654.022 for operating in violation of Executive Order 20-12.

On May 14, 2020, Governor Brown issued Executive Order 20-25 rescinding Executive Order 20-12 and setting forth a phased system for reopening Oregon on a county by county basis. Phase One of the system permitted reopening of personal service businesses including Salons. On May 22, 2020, Marion County entered Phase One of the reopening plan.

On May 15, 2020, OR-OSHA issued the following citation to Glamour! LLC.:

Citation 1 Item 1: Willful violation of ORS 654.022

ORS 654.022: The employer did not obey and comply with every requirement of every order, decision, direction, standard, rule or regulation made or prescribed by the Department of Consumer and Business Services in connection with the matters specified in ORS 654.001 to 654.295, 654.412 to 654.423 and 654.750 to 654.780, or in any way relating to or affecting safety and health in employments or places of employment, or to protect the life, safety and health of employees in such employments or places of employment, and did not do everything necessary or proper in order to secure compliance with and observance of every such order, decision, direction, standard, rule or regulation:

The citation was timely appealed on May 18, 2020. An informal conference was requested as well as a tolling of the abatement period or in the alternative, an expedited Hearing on the reasonableness of the abatement period.

THINGS TO DO

1. Please advise as to whether the above summary is consistent with your understanding of the facts in this matter.

2. I suggest I speak with Sarah Hompas, Elizabeth Ozuna, and Melissa Standish about their relationship with Glamour and the services they provided between May 5, 2020, and May 22, 2020. If you agree, please advise as to the most convenient way to conduct these interviews.

3. Please provide a full ledger of all services provided within Glamour between March 24, 2020, and May 22, 2020, which identifies the provider of those services.

4. Please advise whether a receptionist worked at the salon at any time after the reopening and up until May 22, 2020. If so, please identify the people that did this work and advise if they are available at this time to speak with us about the work they performed, and how they were compensated.

5. I suggest my office attempt to interview Kendall Peters, Jessica Parker, Danna Ward, Kayla Morrison, Kelsey Hardin, Julia Morandi, Hannah Lund, and Stacy Birch regarding their interviews with OR-OSHA. If you agree, I will retain an investigator to conduct those initial interviews.

6. Please advise as to any other individuals who leased space at Glamour over the 12 months prior to the re-opening, or who would have knowledge of the relationship between the providers and Glamour. Please identify those who you believe will provide information helpful to establishing the independent contractor relationship, as well as, more importantly, those you believe will not be helpful in this regard. I recommend each of those individuals be interviewed. If you agree, please provide the list of individuals including their contact information.

7. There are indications in the file that Glamour's policy was that all service providers needed to be registered as independent contractors with the state. Did you take steps to verify this was done? If so, please identify what those were. If not, why not?

8. Did Glamour's liability insurance cover the independent contractors? If so, why?

9. A decision needs to be made on whether to participate in an informal conference. I will give you a call to discuss options and strategy in that regard.

10. Unless the case settles beforehand, I recommend taking a discovery deposition of HCO Aaron Colmone to nail down the exact nature of the violation being alleged, and the details supporting the agency's conclusion that you and the other service providers working after the salon re-opened were employees and not independent contractors. If you agree, this office will set up that deposition and coordinate the date with you so you can be present.

ANALYSIS

OR-OSHA has categorized the citation as "willful." To satisfy its burden of proof on any citation the Department must establish the following relative to each cited item: (1) that the cited standard applies under the facts of the case; (2) the existence of a violative condition or of violative conduct; (3) employee exposure to a hazard related to the violative condition or conduct; and (4) employer knowledge (actual or constructive) of the violative condition or conduct, and of the employee exposure to that hazard. If OR-OSHA fails to meet its burden in regard to any of these elements for each citation item, such item will be vacated. In addition, to prove that a violation was properly classified as "Willful," the Agency must show that the violation was "committed knowingly by an employer or supervisory employee who, having a free will or choice, intentionally or knowingly disobey[ed] or recklessly disregard[ed] the requirements of a statute, regulation, rule, standard, or order." OAR 437-001-0015(63)(b)(A). Willfulness has also been characterized as involving "intentional disregard of" or "plain indifference to" OSHA requirements. *Oregon Occupational Safety & Health Div. v. Roseburg Lumber Co.*, 151 Or. App. 236, 247 (1997). Mere carelessness or lack of diligence is not enough to establish willfulness. *Id.* Again, it is the agency's burden of proof on this issue.

and shall do everything necessary or proper in order to secure compliance with and observance of every such order, decision, direction, standard, rule or regulation."

On its face, this statute is limited to requiring an employer to comply with requirements of orders, standards, etc. "made or prescribed by the Department of Consumer and Business Services" ("DCBS"). However, the violative facts noted in the citation refer to not complying with an Executive Order issued by the Governor, not DCBS. The citation does not allege Glamour violated any rule, order, etc. made or prescribed by the DCBS. As such, an ALJ is very likely to find that Glamour did not violate the cited statute.

However, other statutes were arguably applicable to what Glamour chose to do. ORS 654.031 and ORS 654.010 both come to mind as potentially covering the facts in this case. If OR-OSHA recognizes its error, it will likely try to amend the citation to cite one or both of these two statutes. OR-OSHA can amend the citation, or issue a new one, within 180 days of the opening conference. One goal on our side should therefore be to not shine a light on the fact that OR-OSHA likely cited under the wrong statute until 180 days after the inspection opened on May 7, 2020. So we should try to maintain a low profile until at least the second week of November.

If an ALJ determines that Glamour did violate the cited statute, the next question is whether any employees were on site during the time of the violation. As previously discussed, that issue will come down to whether either you, or the service providers working after May 5, 2020, were employees or independent contractors.

If Glamour had no employees during the period of time it was violating the Executive Order, OR-OSHA had no statutory jurisdiction to conduct an inspection at all, no less to issue it a citation. In that event, the inspection warrant was based on an affidavit that contained inaccurate information, and will therefore be vacated. Once the warrant is found invalid, the citation automatically will be vacated.

The inquiry into whether the service providers working after May 5, 2020, were employees will be very fact-intensive. Each and every stylist, receptionist, cleaner, etc. who worked at Glamour after May 5, 2020, and before May 22, 2020, when Phase Two went into effect in Salem, will have to be evaluated to determine if they were an employee of Glamour. The written agreements between Glamour and the service providers, although relevant, will not be determinative on their own. The manner of compensation is also relevant, but the most important factor will focus on the amount of direction and control Glamour exercised over the specific work activities taking place on its premises. Again, relevant to this determination is identifying who provided tools and materials, whether choices in this regard were limited by Glamour, and the extent to which the service providers' methods of accomplishing work tasks were tied in any way to direction from Glamour. The interviews recommended above should provide helpful insight on these questions. It should also be noted that several of the stylists were apparently working under Glamour's facility license. Of the individuals identified who worked at Glamour while Executive Order 20-12 was in effect, only Jaycie Kerr is identified by the Oregon Cosmetology Board as holding a specific Independent Contractor License. We will need to follow up with you in this regard as noted above.

Many of the individuals identified as being interviewed by OR-OSHA appeared to be disgruntled ex-employees. However, for the most part, they did not identify a significant number of factors which would be considered as supporting a conclusion that they were employees and not independent contractors. Mostly, the negative interviews described personal issues and money disputes more than examples of control or other factors which would lead to the conclusion they were employees. Nonetheless, it will be important to interview those individuals with an axe to grind to nail down their statements as to important factors in the employee/independent contractor determination so that we will be adequately prepared to deal with that information at the Hearing.

Thank you for referring this matter to my attention. I will obviously be in better position to advise as to the likelihood of defeating this alleged violation once the above "things to do" have been accomplished, but based on the inspection file, we appear to have viable defenses. I look forward to speaking with you once you have the opportunity to review the above. In the meantime, please feel free to contact me, or if I am unavailable, my partner Jim Anderson, with any questions or concerns.

Very truly yours,

CUMMINS, GOODMAN
DENLEY & VICKERS, P.C.

/s/ George W. Goodman

Citation Notification

Oregon Department of Consumer and Business Services
Oregon Occupational Safety and Health Division (Oregon OSHA)
1340 Tandem Ave NE, Suite 160
Salem, OR 97309-0417
Phone: 503-378-3274

Citation and Notification of Penalty

To: Lindsey Nicole Graham, Member Glamour! LLC 100 S College St Newberg, OR 97132	**Inspection Number:** 317727431(13) **Inspection Date(s):** 05/04/2020-05/14/2020 **Issuance Date:** 05/15/2020 **Optional Rpt Num:** C0196-001-20 **Employer ID No:** 1805795-000

Inspection Site:
195 Liberty St SE
Salem, OR 97301

The violation(s) described in this Citation and Notification of Penalty is (are) alleged to have occurred on or about the day(s) the inspection was made unless otherwise indicated.

In the interest of assuring a safe and healthy workplace, the Oregon Occupational Safety and Health Division (Oregon OSHA) conducted an inspection at a workplace under your control. During this inspection, violations of the Oregon Safe Employment Act and occupational health and/or safety rules were found.

This citation lists the violations and a date by which they must be corrected. If you are not able to correct the violations by the correction date, you must apply for an extension of the correction date by following the instructions outlined later in this citation. Oregon laws require that under certain conditions violations of occupational safety and health rules carry a civil penalty. If penalties have been assessed on this citation, they have been computed in conformity with Oregon Administrative Rules, Chapter 437, Division 1. If you want to appeal this citation, file your request for hearing <u>within 30 calendar days</u> as outlined on the next page. If you choose not to appeal this citation, it becomes a final order 30 calendar days after receiving it. You must abate the violations referred to in this Citation by the dates listed, and pay the proposed penalties.

An effective Safety and Health program not only assures the correction of cited violations, it also requires actions to prevent violations from recurring. Through continued cooperation of employers, employees and Oregon OSHA, a safe and healthful workplace for all Oregon employees can be achieved.

Michael D. Wood, Administrator
Oregon OSHA

Posting - The law requires that a copy of this Citation and Notification of Penalty be posted immediately in a prominent place at or near the location of the violation(s) cited herein, or, if it is not practicable because of the nature of the employer's operations, where it will be readily observable by all affected employees. This Citation must remain posted until the violation(s) cited has (have) been abated, or for 3 working days (excluding weekends and holidays), whichever is longer.

Penalty PAYMENT - Penalties are due 20 days after the citation becomes final order (which is 30 days after receipt of this citation, unless appealed). Either make your check or money order payable to "Department of Consumer & Business Services (DCBS)", and mail to **DCBS, Fiscal Services Section, PO Box 14610, Salem OR 97309-0445**, or pay online at http://osha.oregon.gov/rules/enf/Pages/citations.aspx#req. <u>Please include the Inspection Number on the remittance and return a copy of the invoice with payment.</u> Oregon OSHA does not agree to any restrictions or conditions or endorsements put on any check or money order for less than the full amount due, and will cash the check or money order as if they do not exist.

Employer APPEAL Rights - To appeal a citation, you must clearly state in writing that you are requesting a hearing on the citation and specify the alleged violation(s) contested and the grounds upon which you consider the citation, proposed penalty(ies), or correction period to be unlawful. The request for an appeal must be filed within **30** calendar days of receipt of the citation. You can file an appeal in writing or on-line at http://osha.oregon.gov/rules/enf/Pages/citations.aspx#req. An appeal is considered filed on the date of the postmark, if mailed, or on the date of receipt if transmitted by other means. If mailed, the appeal letter should be sent to: **Oregon OSHA, PO Box 14480, Salem OR 97309-0405.**

A request for an informal conference alone is not an appeal of a citation, and any unresolved issues discussed at an informal conference will not be forwarded for appeal unless there is a timely request for hearing filed. **If you do not request a hearing within the required time frame, this citation will become a final order that is not subject to review by any agency or court.**

IMPORTANT NOTE: Appealing a serious violation or the reasonableness of the correction date does not automatically extend the correction date. You may apply for an extension of the correction date through Oregon OSHA or request an expedited hearing on the issue of the correction date with the Workers' Compensation Board Hearings Division (Oregon Revised Statute 654.078(6)).

Letter of Corrective Action - You are required to complete and mail the enclosed Letter of Corrective Action to the appropriate field office on or before the latest correction date on the citation. Please provide a detailed explanation and supporting documentation (if necessary), such as drawings or photographs of corrected violations, purchase or work orders, air sampling results, etc.

EXTENSION of Correction Date - To apply for an extension for correcting a violation, go online to submit a written request to http://osha.oregon.gov/rules/enf/Pages/citations.aspx#req, or submit a written request to the **office listed on the "Letter of Corrective Action"** and include:

(1)   Employer name and address.
(2)   The location of the place of employment.
(3)   The inspection number and optional report number.
(4)   The violation number for which the extension is sought.
(5)   The reason for the request.
(6)   All available interim steps being taken to safeguard employees against the cited hazard during the requested extended correction period.
(7)   The date by which you propose to complete the correction.
(8)   A statement that a copy of the request for extension has been posted as required by OAR 437-001-0275(2)(d) and (j) or for at least 10 days, whichever is longer; and, if appropriate, provided to the authorized representative of affected employees; and, certification of the date upon which the posting or service was made.

Your request must be postmarked or received by the Department no later than the correction date of the violation for which the extension is sought.

Employer Discrimination Unlawful - The law prohibits discrimination by an employer against an employee for filing a complaint or for exercising any rights under this Act. An employee who believes that he/she has been discriminated against may file a complaint with the Bureau of Labor & Industries (BOLI) no later than 90 days after the discrimination occurred.

Notice to Employees - The law gives an employee or his/her representative the opportunity to object to any abatement date set for a violation if he/she believes the date is unreasonable. The objection letter must be mailed to Oregon OSHA and postmarked within 30 calendar days of the receipt by the employer of this Citation and Notification of Penalty.

Adopting Federal Rules by Reference - Whenever federal rules have been adopted by reference, the federal rule number has been noted in the citation. If information is needed regarding the Oregon standard, contact the Oregon OSHA field office addressed at the top of the first page of this citation.

Posting on the Internet - Federal OSHA publishes information on all inspections and citation activity on the Internet under the provisions of the Electronic Freedom of Information Act. The information related to your inspection will be available not sooner than 30 calendar days after the Citation Issuance Date. You are encouraged to review the information concerning your establishment at www.osha.gov. If you have any dispute with the accuracy of the information displayed, please contact this office.

If you would like to discuss this citation, call the Oregon OSHA office in your area:

Portland	503-229-5910	Salem	503-378-3274	Medford	541-776-6030
Eugene	541-686-7562	Bend	541-388-6066		

Oregon OSHA
Oregon Department of Consumer and Business Services

Inspection Number: 317727431(13)
Inspection Date(s): 05/04/2020-05/14/2020
Issuance Date: 05/15/2020

Citation and Notification of Penalty

Optional Rpt Num: C0196-001-20

Company Name: Glamour! LLC
Inspection Site: 195 Liberty St SE Salem, OR 97301

Citation 1 Item 1 Type of Violation: **Willful**

ORS 654.022: The employer did not obey and comply with every requirement of every order, decision, direction, standard, rule or regulation made or prescribed by the Department of Consumer and Business Services in connection with the matters specified in ORS 654.001 to 654.295, 654.412 to 654.423 and 654.750 to 654.780, or in any way relating to or affecting safety and health in employments or places of employment, or to protect the life, safety and health of employees in such employments or places of employment, and did not do everything necessary or proper in order to secure compliance with and observance of every such order, decision, direction, standard, rule or regulation:

a) On May 5, 2020 and after; the employer did not obey and comply with, and do everything necessary or proper to comply with and observe, Section 2 of the Governor's Executive Order 20-12, issued March 23, 2020, that prohibited the operation of barber shops and hair salons to protect the life, safety, and health of all Oregonians, including, employees in places of employment, due to the serious public health threat posed by the novel infectious coronavirus (COVID-19). As a result, employees were potentially exposed to the serious public health threat of the infectious novel coronavirus (COVID-19) while cutting or styling hair in close proximity to clients in direct violation of Executive Order 20-12.

Date by Which Violation Must be Abated:	Immediately Upon Receipt
Proposed Penalty:	$14,000.00

Total Proposed Penalty: $14,000.00

Oregon Department of Consumer and Business Services

Oregon Occupational Safety and Health Division (Oregon OSHA)
1340 Tandem Ave NE, Suite 160
Salem, OR 97309-0417
Phone: 503-378-3274

LETTER OF CORRECTIVE ACTION

Lindsey Nicole Graham
Glamour! LLC
100 S College St
Newberg, OR 97132

Inspection Number: 317727431(13)
Inspection Date(s): 05/04/2020-05/14/2020
Issuance Date: 05/15/2020
Optional Rpt Num: C0196-001-20

Inspection
195 Liberty St SE
Salem, OR 97301

IMPORTANT

When completing this **Letter of Corrective Action** (LOCA), refer to the corresponding item(s) found in the enclosed Citation. Please date and complete each item; sign and **return to the field office address** located in the upper, left-hand corner of this LOCA. Failure to return this form by the latest Correction Required Date may result in additional citations and/or penalties.

The Letter of Corrective Action is to be used by the employer for notifying Oregon OSHA of the correction for each violation listed.

AN EMPLOYER WHO FALSIFIES THIS FORM MAY BE SUBJECT TO A PENALTY OF UP TO $2,500 (OAR 473-01-225(1)).

If additional space is required, please identify the item and continue on the reverse side of the notice or another sheet.

No action is required for those violations which are preprinted as complied.

If insufficient documentation is provided, a representative of the Department will contact you and it may result in a follow-up inspection to verify correction of the violation(s). Completion of this form however, does not preclude the Department from conducting a subsequent inspection to verify correction has taken place.

LETTER OF CORRECTIVE ACTION

Citation 1 Item 1 The employer did not obey and comply with every requirement of every order, decision, direction, standard, rule or regulation made or prescribed by the Department of Consumer and Business Services in connection with the matters specified in ORS 654.001 to 654.295, 654.412 to 654.423 and 654.750 to 654.780, or in any way relating to or affecting safety and health in employments or places of employment, or to protect the life, safety and health of employees in such employments or places of employment, and did not do everything necessary or proper in order to secure compliance with and observance of every such order, decision, direction, standard, rule or regulation.

Correction Required Date: _____05/21/2020_____   Date Corrected: _____

Describe Correction: _____

_____

_____

_____

_____

_____

_____

_____

Oregon Department of Consumer and Business Services
Oregon Occupational Safety and Health Division (Oregon OSHA)
1340 Tandem Ave NE, Suite 160
Salem, OR 97309-0417
Phone: 503-378-3274

LETTER OF CORRECTIVE ACTION

There are a total of 1 item(s) to be abated.

If you were cited for any safety committee violations, please answer if this contact with Oregon OSHA assisted you in making your safety committee more effective: Yes_____ or No_____

Comments:

I certify that the above violations have been abated/corrected as documented by the date abated and the corrective action taken.

Employer Signature: _____   Name: _____
                                                                              (Print)

Title: _____   Phone: _____   Date: _____

Oregon OSHA Reviewer's Signature: _____   Date: _____

Oregon Department of Consumer and Business Services

Oregon Occupational Safety and Health Division (Oregon OSHA)
1340 Tandem Ave NE, Suite 160, Salem, OR 97309-0417
Phone: 503-378-3274

INVOICE/DEBT COLLECTION NOTICE

Company Name: Glamour! LLC
Inspection Site: 195 Liberty St SE, Salem, OR 97301
Issuance Date: 05/15/2020

Summary of Penalties for Inspection Number   317727431

Citation 1, Willful	$14,000.00
Total Proposed Penalties	$14,000.00

PLEASE RETURN COPY OF THIS INVOICE WITH PAYMENT

Oregon Revised Statutes, Chapter 654, the Oregon Safe Employment Act. Subsection 654.086(3) states: "When an order assessing a civil penalty becomes final by operation of law or an appeal, unless the amount of penalty is paid within 20 days after the order becomes final*, it constitutes a judgment and be filed with the county clerk in any county of this state. The clerk shall thereupon record the name of the person incurring the penalty and the amount of the penalty in the judgment docket. The penalty provided in the order so docketed shall become a lien upon the title to any interest in property owned by the person against whom the order is entered, and execution upon a judgment of a court or record." *(Final order is defined as 30 days after receipt of the citation, unless it is appealed.)

To avoid additional charges, remit the total amount of the uncontested penalties summarized above. Please pay online at http://osha.oregon.gov/rules/enf/Pages/citations.aspx, call 503-947-7891 to pay by credit card over the telephone, or remit payment promptly to the mailing address shown below. Make your check or money order payable to: "Department Of Consumer & Business Services (DCBS)". **Please write Inspection Number 317727431(13)** on the remittance and include a copy of this invoice with your payment.

Mail your payments to: **DCBS**
                              Fiscal Services Section - Oregon OSHA
                              PO Box 14610
                              Salem, OR 97309-0445

Employer ID #:	1805795-000				
Company Name:	Glamour! LLC				
Opt Rpt Num:	C0196-001-20	Region ID #:	1054113	Fiscal use only	51101 0345

OSHA Threat

800 NE Oregon Street, Suite 930
Portland, OR 97232
Phone: 971-673-1229
Fax: 971-673-1299

Lindsay Graham
Glamour Salon
195 Liberty St. SE
Salem, OR 97301
GLAMOURSALEM@GMAIL.COM

RE: Letter Regarding Compliance with Executive Order 20-12

Dear Ms. Graham:

As you may know, Governor of Oregon has declared an emergency under ORS 401.165 et seq. due to the public health threat posed by the coronavirus disease 2019 (COVID-19). To reduce the spread of COVID-19, the Governor has implemented several community mitigation strategies including prohibiting the operation of certain businesses for which close personal contact is difficult or impossible to avoid, *including hair salons, esthetician practices, and tattoo/piercing parlors*, through Executive Order 20-12 (EO 20-12). A copy of EO 20-12 is attached.

It appears that your establishment may be operating in violation of EO 20-12 and you may be subject to the penalties described below. Disciplinary action may be taken against your cosmetology facility license (COS-FA-10205701) and your body art facility license (BAP-FA-10205702).

IF OPERATING, PLEASE COME INTO COMPLIANCE IMMEDIATELY BY DISCONTINUING OPERATIONS.

Potential Penalties for Violating EO 2012:
• **Civil Penalties:** You may be subject to a civil penalty up to $500 per day, per violation or $5,000 per violation. ORS 431A.010(1)(d); ORS 676.992; OAR 333-003-1010.
• **Court Order:** You may be ordered to close through an administrative or court order. ORS 431A.010(1)(c) and (j).
• **Licensing:** You may lose your licenses or face other disciplinary action. ORS 676.612; ORS CH. 690; OAR 331-020-0075; OAR 817-120-0005.

• **Criminal Penalties:** You may be charged with a Class C misdemeanor. ORS 401.990.
If you continue to operate, the Oregon Health Authority (OHA) may initiate steps to impose the penalties described above. For more information visit the Oregon Health Authority's website and COVID-19 webpage

Lillian Shirley

Lillian Shirley, BSN, MPH, MPA
Public Health Director
Oregon Health Authority, Public Health Division

Sylvie Donaldson

Sylvie Donaldson
Health Licensing Director
Oregon Health Authority, Public Health Division

CERTIFICATE OF SERVICE

I HEREBY CERTIFY that on the _____ day of May, 2020, I directed to be served the within COMPLIANCE WITH EXECUTIVE ORDER 20-12 upon the parties hereto, a full, true and correct copy thereof, by the method indicated below:

Lindsay Graham
Glamour Salon
195 Liberty St. SE
Salem, OR 97301
GLAMOURSALEM@GMAIL.COM

☒ by Regular Mail, postage prepaid
☒ by Certified Mail No. _____

☐ Via Fax
☒ Via E-mail

Lindsey Graham
7181 Elmers Ct NE
Silverton, OR 97381

☒ by Regular Mail, postage prepaid
☒ by Certified Mail No. _____

☐ Via Fax
☐ Via E-mail

☐ by Regular Mail, postage prepaid
☐ by Certified Mail No. _____

☐ Via Fax
☐ Via E-mail

_____
Robert Bothwell
HLO Regulatory Manager

Office of the Governor
State of Oregon

EXECUTIVE ORDER NO. 20-12

STAY HOME, SAVE LIVES: ORDERING OREGONIANS TO STAY AT HOME, CLOSING SPECIFIED RETAIL BUSINESSES, REQUIRING SOCIAL DISTANCING MEASURES FOR OTHER PUBLIC AND PRIVATE FACILITIES, AND IMPOSING REQUIREMENTS FOR OUTDOOR AREAS AND LICENSED CHILDCARE FACILITIES

On February 28, 2020, I appointed the State of Oregon's Coronavirus Response Team.

On February 29, 2020, the Department of Human Services issued strict guidelines, restricting visitation at congregated care facilities, including nursing homes.

On March 2, 2020, the State of Oregon Emergency Coordination Center was activated.

On March 8, 2020, I declared an emergency under ORS 401.165 *et seq*. due to the public health threat posed by the novel infectious coronavirus (COVID-19).

On March 12, 2020, I prohibited gatherings of 250 or more people, and announced a statewide closure of Oregon K-12 schools from March 16, 2020, through March 31, 2020.

On March 13, 2020, the President of the United States declared the COVID-19 outbreak a national emergency.

On March 16, 2020, the Department of Human Services imposed its most recent protective measures to restrict visitors to long-term care facilities and other residential facilities. The Oregon Health Authority has adopted similar measures at the Oregon State Hospital and other behavioral health settings and has limited admissions to the Oregon State Hospital. The Oregon Department of Corrections has suspended all visits to state prisons.

On March 17, 2020, I prohibited gatherings of 25 or more people, banned on-site consumption of food and drink at food establishments statewide, and extending school closures until April 28, 2020. I also encouraged all businesses not subject to the prohibitions to implement social distancing protocols.

On March 18, 2020, I suspended in-person instructional activities at higher education institutions through April 28, 2020.

EXECUTIVE ORDER NO. 20-12
PAGE TWO

On March 19, 2020, I ordered the postponement of non-urgent health care procedures, in order to conserve personal protective equipment and hospital beds for the state's COVID-19 emergency response efforts. I also directed the Oregon Health Authority to provide guidance regarding limitations and screening for visitors to hospitals and ambulatory surgical centers.

COVID-19 may cause respiratory disease leading to serious illness or death. The World Health Organization considers COVID-19 to be a global pandemic. COVID-19 spreads person-to-person through coughing, sneezing, and close personal contact, including touching a surface with the virus on it and then touching your mouth, nose, or eyes.

To reduce spread of COVID-19, the United States Centers for Disease Control and Prevention (CDC) has recommended community mitigation strategies to increase containment of the virus and to slow transmission of the virus, including cancellation of gatherings of people and social distancing in smaller gatherings.

State and local public health officials advise that the virus is circulating in the community and expect the number of cases to increase. The CDC reports that COVID-19 is most contagious when the individual is most symptomatic but may also spread before symptoms appear.

The number of COVID-19 cases continues to rise in Oregon. On March 8, 2020, at the time I declared an emergency, there were 14 presumptive or confirmed cases in Oregon. By March 12, 2020, there were 21. As of today, there are at least 161 cases and five deaths.

In a short time, COVID-19 has spread rapidly. Additionally, some Oregonians are not adhering to social distancing guidance provided by the Oregon Health Authority, as represented by crowds this last weekend at the Oregon Coast, Smith Rock State Park, the Columbia River Gorge, and other places around the state. To slow the spread of COVID-19 in Oregon, to protect the health and lives of Oregonians, particularly those at highest risk, and to help avoid overwhelming local and regional healthcare capacity, I find that immediate implementation of additional measures is necessary. The purpose of this Executive Order is to reduce person-to-person interaction with the goal of slowing transmission.

NOW THEREFORE, IT IS HEREBY DIRECTED AND ORDERED THAT:

Stay Home, Save Lives

1. It is essential to the health, safety, and welfare of the State of Oregon during the ongoing state of emergency that, to the maximum extent possible, individuals stay at home or at their place of residence, consistent with the directives set forth in my Executive Orders and guidance issued by the Oregon Health Authority. To that end, pursuant to ORS 433.441(3), ORS 401.168(1), ORS 401.175(3), and ORS 401.188(2) to (3), I am ordering the following:

    a. Non-essential social and recreational gatherings of individuals outside of a home or place of residence (e.g., parties, celebrations, or other similar gatherings and events) are prohibited immediately, regardless of size, if a distance of at least six feet between individuals cannot be maintained.

    b. Individuals are prohibited from patronizing businesses that are closed pursuant to paragraph 2 of this Executive Order, and from engaging in conduct prohibited by prior Executive Orders or inconsistent with guidance provided by the Oregon Health Authority.

    c. When individuals need to leave their homes or residences, they should at all times maintain social distancing of at least six feet from any person who is not a member of their immediate household, to the greatest extent possible, and comply with the other Social Distancing Requirements guidance issued by the Oregon Health Authority.

    d. Individuals may go outside for outside recreational activities (walking, hiking, etc.), but must limit those activities to non-contact, and are prohibited from engaging in outdoor activities where it is not possible to maintain appropriate social distancing (six feet or more between individuals).

    e. Failure to comply with any of the provisions of this Executive Order constitutes an imminent threat and creates an immediate danger to public health. Any person found to be in violation of this Executive Order is subject to the penalties described in ORS 401.990.

Closure of Certain Businesses

2. Pursuant to ORS 433.441(3)(a), (b), (d) and (f), ORS 401.168(1), and ORS 401.188(1) to (3), and effective 12:01 a.m. on March 24, 2020, I prohibit the operation of the following businesses, for which close personal contact is difficult or impossible to avoid:

    > Amusement parks; aquariums; arcades; art galleries (to the extent that they are open without appointment); barber shops and hair salons; bowling alleys; cosmetic stores; dance studios; esthetician practices; fraternal organization facilities; furniture stores; gyms and fitness studios (including climbing gyms); hookah bars; indoor and outdoor malls (i.e., all portions of a retail complex containing stores

and restaurants in a single area); indoor party places (including jumping gyms and laser tag); jewelry shops and boutiques (unless they provide goods exclusively through pick-up or delivery service); medical spas, facial spas, day spas, and non-medical massage therapy services; museums; nail and tanning salons; non-tribal card rooms; skating rinks; senior activity centers; ski resorts; social and private clubs; tattoo/piercing parlors; tennis clubs; theaters; yoga studios; and youth clubs.

3. Paragraph 2 of this Executive Order does not apply to restaurants, bars, taverns, brew pubs, wine bars, cafes, food courts, coffee shops, or other similar establishments that offer food or drink, which remain subject to Executive Order No. 20-07 (prohibiting on-premises consumption of food or drink, but allowing take-out or delivery service).

4. Indoor and outdoor malls, and other businesses subject to paragraph 2 of this Executive Order, are not prohibited from operating to provide food, grocery, health care, medical, pharmacy, or pet store services.

5. Subject to approval by the Governor, the Oregon Health Authority has the authority to determine if additional business closures are necessary to slow the spread of COVID-19 during the ongoing state of emergency.

Required Social Distancing for Other Retail Businesses

6. Pursuant to ORS 433.441(3)(a), (b), (d) and (f), ORS 401.168(1), and ORS 401.188(1) to (3), and effective 12:01 a.m. on March 24, 2020, I prohibit the operation of any other retail business not subject to paragraph 2 of this Executive Order, unless the business designates an employee or officer to establish, implement, and enforce social distancing policies, consistent with guidance from the Oregon Health Authority.

7. Retail businesses that fail to comply with paragraph 6 of this Executive Order will be closed until they demonstrate compliance.

8. Paragraphs 6 and 7 of this Executive Order do not apply to grocery, health care, medical, or pharmacy services, which also are encouraged to comply with social distancing guidelines.

Workspace Restrictions

9. Pursuant to ORS 433.441(3)(a), (b), (d) and (f), ORS 401.168(1), and ORS 401.188(1) to (3), and effective March 25, 2020, all businesses and non-profit entities with offices in Oregon shall facilitate telework and work-at-home by employees, to the maximum extent possible. Work in offices is prohibited whenever telework and work-at-home options are available, in light of position duties, availability of teleworking equipment, and network adequacy.

10. When telework and work-from-home options are not available, businesses and non-profits must designate an employee or officer to establish, implement, and enforce social distancing policies, consistent with guidance from the Oregon Health Authority. Such policies also must address how the business or non-profit will maintain social distancing protocols for business-critical visitors.

11. Businesses and non-profits that fail to comply with paragraphs 9 and 10 of this Executive Order will be closed until they demonstrate compliance.

Government Buildings

12. Pursuant to ORS 433.441(3)(a), (b), (d) and (f), ORS 401.168(1), and ORS 401.188(1) to (3), and effective March 25, 2020, all state executive branch offices and buildings, to the maximum extent possible, shall close to the public and provide public services by phone and online during regular business hours. To the extent that closure is not feasible, in-person interactions between staff and the public should be by appointment, whenever possible. When public services require in-person interactions, social distancing measures must be established, implemented, and enforced, to the maximum extent possible.

13. State executive branch offices and buildings shall facilitate telework and work-at-home by employees, to the maximum extent possible. When telework and work-from-home options are not possible, agencies must designate an employee or officer to establish, implement, and enforce social distancing policies, consistent with guidance from the Oregon Health Authority.

14. Paragraphs 12 and 13 of this Executive Order apply to all offices and buildings owned or occupied by the state executive branch. This Executive Order does not apply to offices and buildings owned or occupied by the state legislative and judicial branches, federal government, local governments, and tribal governments, but those governments are nonetheless strongly encouraged to adhere to the policies underlying these directives.

Childcare Facilities

15. Pursuant to ORS 433.441(3)(a) and (d), ORS 401.168(1), and ORS 401.188(2) and (3), it is ordered that any childcare facility licensed under ORS 329A.030 and ORS 329A.250 to ORS 329A.450 that does not meet the requirements of paragraph 16 of this Executive Order shall close from March 25, 2020, through April 28, 2020 ("effective period"), unless that period is extended or terminated earlier by the Governor.

16. Notwithstanding paragraph 15, childcare facilities are allowed to remain open during the effective period if they meet the following requirements:

    a. Childcare must be carried out in maximum stable groups of 10 or fewer children ("stable" means the same 10 or fewer children are in the same group each day), and in a classroom that cannot be accessed by children outside the stable group; and

    b. Facilities must prioritize the childcare needs of first responders, emergency workers, health care professionals, followed by critical operations staff and essential personnel, consistent with guidance provided by the Oregon Department of Education, Early Learning Division.

17. I delegate authority to the Oregon Department of Education, Early Learning Division, to set forth exceptions to the rules provided by paragraph 16 of this Executive Order, if it becomes necessary to do so.

Outdoor Recreation and Travel

18. Pursuant to the powers vested in me by ORS 433.441(3), ORS 401.168(1) and (3), and ORS 401.188(1) to (3), I hereby order all private and public campgrounds to be closed immediately. This order does not prohibit camp hosts or veterans from remaining in state campgrounds, nor does it extend to RV parks and other housing.

19. I authorize the Oregon Parks and Recreation Department to close any property or facility, when proper social distancing cannot be maintained.

20. I order the immediate closure of all pools, skate parks, outdoor sports courts, and playground equipment areas.

21. For public recreational areas that are permitted to remain open subject to this Executive Order, signs requiring social distancing must be posted at all entrances, exits, and in prominent areas. On-site restrooms must have trash cans, and soap and water or hand sanitizer available. Users of open public recreational areas must strictly adhere to social distancing guidelines.

22. Individuals are directed to minimize travel, other than essential travel to or from a home, residence, or workplace; for obtaining or providing food, shelter, essential consumer needs, education, health care, or emergency services; for essential business and government services; for the care of family members, household members, elderly persons, minors, dependents,

   persons with disabilities, or other vulnerable persons, pets or livestock; travel as directed by government officials, law enforcement, or courts; and other essential travel consistent with the directives of my Executive Orders and guidance from the Oregon Health Authority.

Enforcement

23. The directives in this Executive Order are effective statewide.

24. This Executive Order is a public health law, as defined in ORS 431A.005, and may be enforced as permitted under ORS 431A.010. Additionally, any person found to be in violation of this Executive Order is subject to the penalties described in ORS 401.990.

This Executive Order is issued under the authority conferred to the Governor by ORS 401.165 to 401.236. Pursuant to ORS 401.192(1), the directives set forth in this Executive Order have the full force and effect of law, and any law, ordinances, rules and orders shall be inoperative to the extent that they are inconsistent with this exercise of the Governor's emergency powers.

This Executive Order is effective immediately, and remains in effect until terminated by the Governor.

Done at Salem, Oregon this 23rd day of March, 2020.

Kate Brown

Kate Brown
GOVERNOR

ATTEST:

Bev Clarno
SECRETARY OF STATE

For more information or to get involved, visit:

PATRIOTBARBIE.COM

Made in the USA
Columbia, SC
13 March 2023

13660217R00178